Frederick Douglass and
the Atlantic World

Frederick Douglass and the Atlantic World

Fionnghuala Sweeney

LIVERPOOL UNIVERSITY PRESS

First published 2007 by
Liverpool University Press
4 Cambridge Street
Liverpool, L69 7ZU

British Library Cataloguing-in-Publication Data
A British Library CIP Record is available

ISBN 978-1-84631-078-2 cased

Typeset in Apollo by Koinonia, Bury
Printed and bound in the European Community
by Biddles Ltd, King's Lynn

Contents

Introduction

Frederick Douglass and
the Atlantic World

The Eagle Stirreth Her Nest', one of C.L. Franklin's[1] best-known sermons,
offers a critique of the United States, a nation predicated as much on
exploitation and oppression as on liberty and democracy. The eagle of
the title is not only the central image of the sermon, but emblem of the
American Republic, and metaphor of divine presence and protection.
The piece begins as exegesis, listing, then expounding the characteristics
shared by the eagle and the divine: strength, speed and vision. It subsequently slips into an apparently unrelated folk narrative of a captive eagle
being raised on a poultry farm. His difference from the rest of the birds
is soon evident, and the eagle is confined to a cage in order to prevent his
escape. As the eagle ages, he begins to outgrow his cage, as he does all
subsequent cages built for him, until finally, in pity, he is released by the
farmer. The correspondence with the initial biblical tale becomes clear
in a final analogy between the eagle's release and a Christian prophecy of
freedom and resurrection:

> My soul
>   Is an eagle
> In the cage that the Lord
>   Has made for me. ...
> My soul
>   Is caged in,
>   In this old body,
>   Yes it is,
> And one of these days
> The man who made the cage
> Will open the door
> An let my soul
>   Go.
> One of these days
> My soul will take wings
> My soul will take wings.[2]

1 1915–84. African American minister, civil rights leader and father of Aretha.
2 C.L. Franklin, 'The Eagle Stirreth Her Nest', in Nellie McKay and Henry Louis Gates

The eagle of the folk tale, of course, provides a metaphor for the captivity of the African American subject in the United States, a representation at odds with the eagle's official designation as divine protector and symbol of American democratic idealism. Confined, not merely by successive cages, as the story explains, but, less obviously perhaps, by the vernacular forms in which the story is inscribed, the captive eagle becomes symptom and symbol of its own failure as a trope of liberty and the ideals of the state. As such, the text, its performance, and the symbol itself are marked out as zones of contest, in which the meaning, stability and viability of icons of national identity come under scrutiny, and are ultimately found to be wanting.

Since the founding of the United States, those icons had been under pressure from internal inconsistencies within, and departures from, the national ideal; an ideal in which subjectivity, agency and identification with the state became inextricably entwined. The lived reality for many was very different. Slavery prohibited African Americans in bondage from identification with the nation, denied them common origin with the rest of the population, and severely curtailed political and personal agency. The racialist structures underpinning slavery, many of which continued into the postbellum era, also severely complicated the relationship between free African Americans and the country as a whole. It is no surprise then that the politics of identity – the search for the composite selfhood famously described by Du Bois – early became a central concern of African American letters.[3]

Implicit in that search was the need to challenge and rework the racialized tenets of the US cultural imaginary, the internalized image of the national ideal that underpinned political reality and representative norms. That challenge was mounted, not just from within the United States, but externally, from places where resistance was not only less perilous, but often encouraged. For slave narrators in particular the politics of resistance was early linked to the politics of location. In the nineteenth century, contact between African Americans and a range of radical, reforming, or colonial contexts across the Atlantic influenced the nature and terms of the debate around race and slavery. Arguably, those terms were both complex and international; dictated as much by British imperialism as US expansion; by Irish migration as well as Haitian independence; by the politics of labour as well as the symbolism of race.

Jr, eds, *The Norton Anthology of African American Literature* (New York and London: Norton, 1997), pp. 71–78 (77).

3 See W.E.B. DuBois, *The Souls of Black Folk* (Chicago: A.C. McClurg & Co., 1903), for an elaboration of the concept of the 'double consciousness' of the African American population.

Similarly, slavery and racial politics became key to Anglo-American ethical disputes, and were frequently used to mediate the competing claims of British and American nationalism. African Americans in the nineteenth century, seeking to challenge the shortcomings of US democracy, often mobilized discourses of British nationalism as a means of gaining representational agency and, conversely, positing themselves as US Americans. Of those that did so, Frederick Douglass remains the most significant. The most prolific African American writer of the nineteenth century, he embarked, after his escape from slavery in 1838, on a public career that would span the century and three continents. The narrative of his life in slavery remains a seminal work in the literary and historical canons of the United States, and has recently been included in the corpus of the American Renaissance.[4] This inclusion involves not just a reconsideration of the racial and political profile of American Renaissance writers, it de-segregates Douglass from the reformist margins by situating his work within the American aesthetic mainstream. It acknowledges the ways in which his work forms part of the larger context provided by the nineteenth-century American experience of national and literary evolution.

Much critical attention then has been accorded to Douglass's activities within the United States, his effect on socio-political reform, and relationship to an oppressed and marginalized community of African Americans. Yet much of his literary and political development occurred outside the United States. Arguably in fact, were it not for his early overseas sojourn, Douglass might never have attained the literary, economic, or political heights for which he is now justly famous. For Douglass's emergence as a major figure in American politics and letters owed as much to his international as to his national activities.[5]

Indeed, transnational encounters were key to Douglass's project of American self-fashioning, and it is his relationship with the world beyond the United States that is at the centre of this book. That relationship demonstrates that, far from engaging only with issues important within the United States, Douglass's career represents a tactical synthesis of national and transnational concerns, including slavery, citizenship, manhood, and broader debates concerning the relationship of the individual with the nation state.

4   See Walter B. Michaels and Donald E. Pease, eds, *The American Renaissance Reconsidered* (Baltimore and London: Johns Hopkins University Press, 1989), and Donald E. Pease, ed., *Visionary Compacts: The American Renaissance in Cultural Context* (Madison: University of Wisconsin Press, 1987).

5   Alan J. Rice and Martin Crawford, eds, *Liberating Sojourn: Frederick Douglass and Transatlantic Reform* (Athens, GA, and London: University of Georgia Press, 1999), is the seminal work in this field. An earlier pioneer of this scholarship was George Shepperson.

This book focuses specifically on Douglass's Atlantic encounters, literal and literary, against the backdrop of slavery, emancipation, and western colonial process. The emphasis is primarily upon the effects of Douglass's overseas experience on his political and literary profile. The key questions are the following: What effect does the introduction of the context of colonialism have on readings of Douglass's literary and political output? To what extent does a nineteenth-century, 'western' aesthetic of social justice inform his work? How is that aesthetic configured and what are its limits?

This discussion therefore centres on the expressive and political encounters occurring across class, cultural and ethnic boundaries during Douglass's lifetime, in an attempt to unpick the kind of representative selfhood they enabled him to construct.[6] Because of this, it is necessary to suspend at least some of the conclusions of Douglass historiography. This has inscribed him as at once both an entirely representative, yet utterly exceptional emblem of African American manhood in the nineteenth century. Douglass has been a key figure in the current of historical and literary revisionism in the United States that has, over the last forty years and in the face of considerable resistance, constructed an African American canon that is now unassailable. This process has also, understandably perhaps, resulted in the unequivocal lionization of individual figures – Douglass is a case in point – within the exclusive province of racial struggle in the United States. This has tended to conserve an African American exceptionalist position within an American cultural nationalist frame.

Given the moral complexity of the Atlantic space in which he was operating, such lionization oversimplifies Douglass's historical and literary legacy. Introduction of other historiographies, including that of colonialism, to discussions of Douglass's self-fashioning, however, opens wider debates in cultural history. In particular, it enables examination of transnational interfaces, involving the United States and its representative subjects, in which varying paradigms of privilege and representation, specifically those involving race, class and gender, apply.

Much of the analysis here deals with Douglass's relationship to Britain and Ireland, where the contemporary complexities of class, colonialism and subaltern activity provide the backdrop to any discussion of political mobilization and literary process.[7] Of particular interest

6 See Paul Gilroy, *The Black Atlantic: Modernity and Double Consciousness* (London and New York: Verso, 1993), pp. 112–13.
7 The methodology, domain and intentions of subaltern studies are limned out by Ranajit Guha, ed., in *Subaltern Studies: Writing on South Asian History and Society*, 5 vols (New Delhi: Oxford University Press, 1984). For the methodological complications of this approach see Gayatri Spivak, 'Can the Subaltern Speak?', in Cary

is the variety of interactions with popular and elite groups, interactions involving overlapping categories of class, race, gender and political culture within complex and particularized histories across the Atlantic and beyond. For Douglass's work was produced against a backdrop of concurrent historical processes, which include anti-slavery resistance, class agitation, colonial insurgency, the rise of the campaign for women's rights and women's increasing importance as a political constituency, and shifting domains of empire. Consideration of his work in these contexts and against the contemporaneous growth of western liberal capitalism and colonial expansion provides a broader perspective on his life, work and historiographical status as representative man.

In other words, it provides an opportunity to question his relationship to the premodern as well as the modern, and to examine the effect of these relationships on the politics of his work. For this reason, a postcolonial perspective is particularly useful, as it provides a gateway to a discussion of not only European colonialism, but to the colonial and orientalist activities of the United States during Douglass's lifetime. It equally enables analysis of overlapping struggles for political and representative agency across the Atlantic, outside of nationalist or cultural-nationalist historiography, struggles in which Douglass was a key actor.

Much of the extant scholarship on the nineteenth-century Atlantic emphasizes the 'embeddedness in the modern world' of peoples and cultures of African origin. This book takes Paul Gilroy at his word, however, when he writes that the Atlantic field is not restricted to the racialized (black) examples he uses.[8] For, while Douglass could be said to embody the relationship between the black American subject and the west, the 'double consciousness' to which DuBois refers, his work also illustrates the tension between the representative needs of the liberal self, and premodern or non-western subjectivity. This book examines Douglass's writing as it represents premodern and non-western groups on the fringes of the Atlantic – in Ireland, Haiti and Egypt – as well as his literary interactions with Garrisonian abolitionism and the British social elite.

Nelson and Larry Grossberg, eds, *Marxism and the Interpretation of Culture* (Urbana: University of Illinois Press, 1989), pp. 271–313, and Dipesh Chakrabarty, 'Minority Histories, Subaltern Pasts', *Perspectives*, 13 (November 1997), pp. 37–43. On Ireland, see Lee Jenkins, 'The Black O Connell: Frederick Douglass and Ireland', *Nineteenth Century Studies*, 13 (1999), pp. 23–46, and his 'Beyond the Pale: Frederick Douglass in Cork', *Irish Review*, 24 (1999), pp. 80–95 (89). For discussions of the broader context of the Black Atlantic, see articles by Alan Rice, Alasdair Pettinger, Henry Louis Gates, Vincent Carretta and Polly Rewt in Polly T. Rewt, ed., 'The African Diaspora and Its Origins', *Research in African Literatures*, special edition, 29.4 (winter 1998).

8 Gilroy, *Black Atlantic*, p. ix.

The diversity of these groups, however, and their differential relationship to structures of political and economic power, indicates any approach to Douglass's work needs to examine transnational debates in conjunction with the local realities that inform them. The existence of interlocking political realities suggests, for example, that debates surrounding race, class and empire in Britain are related to, and might profitably engage with, current discussions of whiteness and the formation of ethnic identity in the United States more generally. Similarly, Irish anti-colonial resistance, which was contemporaneous with mass migration to the United States and the emergence of Irish America as a white political constituency, meant that there were very different attitudes to slavery and servitude on different sides of the Atlantic. The rise of an Atlantic-wide ethical culture around anti-slavery occurred in part because of the discursive flexibility of the term 'slavery' itself, its amenability to causes and constituencies whose vocabulary might otherwise have quickly been excised from political dialogue.

These were among the many influences on Douglass throughout his writing career; therefore, although the relationship between his work and the literature and politics of the United States remains key, this book argues that the external influences on his work are often as seminal to its interpretation. Beyond this, it suggests that literary and historical criticism needs to address the sometimes uncomfortable politics of Douglass's overseas writing and the interpretative problems it raises. Douglass's representation of manhood, for example, can be considered in terms of his negotiation of both conservative Southern and bourgeois Northern models of masculine identity, and as an indicator of the representative authority he wielded over the Irish peasantry and urban working class during his first overseas visit to Britain and Ireland. The implications of this go beyond the national context of racial politics in the United States, requiring address to different kinds of difference embedded in his writing as a whole.

In this respect, Douglass's writing on Ireland provides a useful point of departure for any consideration of his negotiation of Atlantic politics. Unlike Britain and the United States, Ireland remained beyond the pale of modernizing forces at least until mid-century. Systematic overexploitation and underdevelopment had ensured that the majority remained poor, rural and marginalized from official structures of power and sources of change.[9] From the mid-nineteenth century, however, famine and post-famine migration brought about a qualitative shift in the Irish relationship to modernity, marking an alteration in internal social organization

---

9 For a complete historiography of this process see Thoedore Allen, *The Invention of the White Race*, vol. 1 (London: Verso, 1997).

as a result of the ongoing exit of large numbers of the population. Those who left emerged in new socio-economic structures with different historical trajectories.[10] Whereas previous migration had been minimal, that which occurred from the 1840s onwards fits into a broader pattern of population dispersal arising as a result of western capitalist expansion and the second industrial revolution.[11]

Most emigration was permanent and to the United States. It necessitated the development of a new national identity, one that defined the relationship of migrants and their descendants to the United States. Irish Americans, who so infamously 'became white', have become a test case of US racial identification. The structures that obtained in Ireland with respect to race, religion, language and economic and social power were of little consequence in the United States, where the combined forces of slavery, industrialization, democracy and expansion had established a very different set of internal hierarchies. As has been established by Theodore Allen, Noel Ignatiev and others, arrival in the United States saw concerted and successful Irish American attempts to differentiate themselves from the African American population, slave and free, often to the extent of participating in the pro-slavery lobby and involvement in violence against free blacks.[12] Americanization involved first and subsequent generations of Irish Americans in shedding the context and burden of colonial history. Becoming white and American was not just a strategy of survival, it was recognizable as a political and historical realignment that refused the moral perspective that the experience of sectarian oppression might otherwise have suggested. In short, governing hierarchies of race and class in the United States resulted in the creation of a new Irish American identity, one in which race (whiteness) and religion (Catholicism) were key signifiers.

Despite Irish American hostility to the African American population, slave and free in the United States, however, there was concurrent popular anti-slavery support in Ireland, where, in the context of ongoing anti-colonial and agrarian violence, the plight of American slaves was made

---

10 See Cormac Ó Gráda, *Ireland Before and After the Famine: Explorations in Economic History* (New York: Manchester University Press, 1993), and Robert James Scally, *The End of Hidden Ireland: Rebellion, Famine and Emigration* (New York: Oxford University Press, 1995).

11 Eighteenth-century emigration was largely of Ulster Scots (to become the Scots Irish in the United States), who tended to act as first-wave colonists in the southern frontier territories. See Patrick Griffin, *The People with No Name: Ireland's Ulster Scots, America's Scots Irish, and the Creation of a British Atlantic World, 1689–1784* (Princeton, NJ: Princeton University Press, 2001).

12 See Noel Ignatiev, *How the Irish Became White* (New York: Routledge, 1995), and Allen, *Invention of the White Race*, vol. 2.

analogous to that of the Irish peasantry. Like the many black speakers on the abolitionist circuit who crossed lines of race and class as well as national frontiers during the course of their transatlantic tours, contemporary Irish migrants engaged in a re-negotiation of the defining terms of political identity. The Irish American case illustrates, as do Douglass's own travels, the transformative power of geographic shifts on individual and group identity. Having left the United States in 1845, Douglass was able to return two years later a free man. The experience of slavery as an American reality, however, remained the political bedrock of the platform of racial inclusion he maintained throughout his life.

But the relationships between power, race and the popular imagination during the period, were complex, as were the moral and representative issues that ensued. Given the transnational dynamic of the politics of representation, Douglass's work can usefully be examined in terms of its engagement with several major historical questions, including those surrounding race and representation in the United States; the politics of race and class across the Atlantic; the British–Irish colonial relation and the rise of nationalism; and western imperialism more generally. This book investigates Douglass's literary and political career in the context of these questions, through emphasis on his representations of Ireland, Egypt and Haiti. The aim is three-fold. Firstly, the book investigates the impact of extra-territorial sites on Douglass's self-creation as a US American in class and cultural terms. Secondly, it examines the implications of this achievement on US and African American exceptionalism. Thirdly, through the lens of the postcolonial, it problematizes the relationship between the African American nation-subject and the external objects of its discursive structures.

In pursuit of this, Douglass's work is positioned within an Atlantic, rather than American interpretative framework. Because of the importance of Britain and Ireland to Douglass's realization of a subject position free of the restrictions he experienced in the United States, much of the book concentrates on the writing and speechmaking of his early overseas sojourn. Additionally, the different hierarchies of race and class in Britain, and the tension between anti-colonial resistance in Ireland and the impact of migrant communities on racial politics in the United States, made those countries an interesting testing ground for a selfhood claiming allegiance to an oppressed community and seeking to deconstruct racial hierarchies in North America.[13]

---

13 For a discussion of Ireland's involvement in transatlantic abolitionism, see Ninni Rodgers, 'Ireland and the Black Atlantic in the Eighteenth Century', *Irish Historical Studies*, 32 (2000), pp. 174–92; Richard S. Harrison, 'The Cork Anti-Slavery Society,

There were other sites of importance to Douglass across the Atlantic, however. In the nineteenth century, Egypt and Haiti emerged as important elements of the American and African American cultural imaginary. Like Ireland, each was a borderland space of racial, cultural or political alterity. In Douglass's writing, Egypt becomes a place of cultural spectacle, a borderland where internal US hierarchies of race can be questioned. Haiti, where Douglass achieved his highest national office, symbolized black achievement in the New World. It is presented in Douglass's writing as a black frontier, a site, like Egypt, open to appropriation by the US politico-cultural imaginary.

Douglass's visits to Ireland, Egypt and Haiti occurred at opposite ends of his career, in very different political and personal circumstances. The cultural politics of the United States changed considerably from mid to late century, with the postbellum period marked by shifting racial relationships and the emergence of the United States as a hemispheric power.[14] Douglass began his writing career, however, when there was little sign of an end to slavery and before the United States developed significant international interests. Chapters One and Two deal with the Irish editions of Douglass's first autobiography, *Narrative of the Life of Frederick Douglass, An American Slave, Written by Himself*, published in 1845 and 1846. They investigate the context in which these texts were produced and the extent to which they furthered Douglass's self-fashioning as US American. In this, Douglass's negotiation of gender identity, his representation of patriarchy and paternity as influences on personal and colonial relationships, is pivotal. These chapters argue that, in Douglass's hands, the slave narrative became a vehicle for a variety of politico-ethical battles across the Atlantic, enabling Douglass's upward social mobility and demonstrating complexities and continuities in his literary engagements with colonial history and the politics of gender.

Its Antecedents and Quaker Background', *Journal of the Cork Historical and Archaeological Society*, 97 (1992), pp. 69–79, and Ellen M. Oldham, 'Irish Support of the Abolitionist Movement', *Boston Public Library Quarterly*, 10 (1958), pp. 173–87. For an early discussion of the importance of the British–Irish trip to Douglass's public profile and political emergence, see Gerald Fulkerson, 'Exile as Emergence: Frederick Douglass in Great Britain, 1845–1847', *Quarterly Journal of Speech*, 60 (1974), pp. 68–82. For a more recent discussion of Frederick Douglass's international impact, see Paul Baggett, 'Transcending the Boundaries of Nation: Images and Imaginings of Frederick Douglass's, *In Process: A Journal of African American and African Diasporan Literature and Culture*, 2 (spring 2000), pp. 103–13.

14 For a discussion of the impact of the US Civil War on Douglass's life and thinking, and his contribution to the Union and emancipation causes, see David W. Blight, *Frederick Douglass's Civil War: Keeping Faith in Jubilee* (Baton Rouge and London: Louisiana State University Press, 1989).

Chapter Three investigates the degree to which the slave narrative genre blends the value systems of North and South, bourgeois and plantocracy. It considers the *Narrative*'s relationship to another body of writing produced by Douglass during this period, namely the open letters to Garrison that were subsequently published in the abolitionist newspaper, the *Liberator*. Chapter Four continues to explore the means by which Douglass's American selfhood was finally accomplished. It examines his relationship with his United States audience, and his role as an ambassador for Garrisonian abolitionism. The chapter subsequently looks at the use made by Douglass of representations of the Irish peasantry and urban working class as objects of difference in his early writing. His related appropriation of tropes of imperialism and morality in this writing is considered in terms of the importance of difference to the integrity of his identity as a United States subject abroad.

Chapter Five turns to the performative techniques adopted and developed by Douglass during the early stages of his public career. His debt to the African American vernacular and the burgeoning working-class form of blackface minstrelsy is examined in the context of nineteenth-century cross-cultural, transatlantic dynamics of representation and social control. The often overlooked importance of mimicry, minstrelsy and subversive speech acts to Douglass's early repertoire is investigated, and the degree and kind of his resistance to enlightened, often élite, western discursive forms weighed. The chapter concludes with a consideration of Douglass's use and manipulation of popular and populist forms during his early career, with emphasis on the subversive impact of the carnivalesque on the parameters of élite national identity.

Chapter Six takes Douglass's later writing and examines the extent to which it can be considered an indicator of a late alignment with the United States as empire. Recent considerations of the importance of empire to the US imaginary, including its role in constituting a nation uncomplicated by internal instabilities and contradictions, are used to anchor the discussion. These include Amy Kaplan's introduction to *Cultures of US Empire*,[15] and Molina Johar Schueller's related analysis of US literary Orientalisms.[16] For the symbolic importance of Orientalism for the United States in the late nineteenth century is evident in Douglass's late writing, complicating, as had the production of his Irish tour, the integrity of the African American nation-subject as an idealized revision of the

15 Amy Kaplan and Donald Pease, eds, *Cultures of United States Imperialism* (Durham, NC: Duke University Press, 1993).
16 Molina Johar Schueller, *US Orientalisms: Race, Nation and Gender in Literature 1790–1890* (Detroit: University of Michigan Press, 1998).

hegemonic, Anglo-American representative man. Douglass's representation of Egypt in particular demonstrates many of the dilemmas raised by his acquisition of representative authority and the ambiguities arising as a consequence of his self-portrayal as an idealized American. Particularly notable is his ongoing ambivalence towards the figure of the native. For the chapter shows that, even as Douglass dismantles internal ethno-racial hierarchies, he is implicated in the perpetuation of equally destructive, extra-national tropes in the US and African American imaginary.

Finally, Chapter Seven conducts a comparative analysis of Douglass's late representation of Ireland and Haiti and discusses his differing, racially and spatially based understanding of primitivism, progress and national status. It completes the analysis of Douglass's creation of a form of black Orientalism by describing his replacement of a founding trope of US national identity, the fast-disappearing frontier, with a new space of subjective enactment: the Atlantic. This space posits not just the possibility of further sites of conquest for the United States, but is rooted in and routed through black and white narratives, and counter-narratives, of US selfhood.

This book must of necessity exclude many texts in which racial representation and issues of national identity form core components. This is due to the focus on writing and speechmaking relating to countries outside the United States, and on the ongoing tensions created by representative disputes involving such matters as progress, imperialism and modernity. Much of the writing Douglass produced within the United States dealing with Irish immigrants, Chinese labour and internal African American migration needs to be read specifically in the context of internal class-racial dynamics, although, no doubt, the forms of external and internal representation he uses are implicitly related. An obvious complication to the internal-overseas model is, of course, Douglass's representation of the Native American population, as indeed is the relationship and alignment of the African American community with regard to the Native claim more generally. It is not within the scope of this work, however, to engage in an exhaustive examination of all of the sites or subjects represented in Douglass's work. Canada, for example, is excluded from this discussion, as is France. Rather the intention is to focus on the different discursive possibilities and uses made by Douglass of certain transnational resources, and to gauge their impact and consequences on his self-legitimation as a representative US American. Additionally, and more importantly, the complexity and importance of the Native–African American relationship is such that it merits separate discussion.

Each of Douglass's interactions with the Atlantic world, however, is in some way entangled in the identity politics of varied communities to which his texts and speeches were addressed. The interpretative context involves multiple audience constituencies, each with its own vested political interests. The subtleties of Douglass's writing and speechmaking are revealed in his capacity to address a range of constituencies across layers of power and resistance that cross lines of class, race, gender and political ambition. The transnational elements of that writing and speechmaking were central to his ability to fashion an identity that could occupy national, class and racial subject positions previously beyond the representative scope of African Americans.

Chapter 1

'The Republic of Letters': Frederick Douglass, Ireland and the Irish *Narratives*

Patriarchy and Patrimony

Frederick Douglass was one of the most notable visitors to Irish shores during the nineteenth century.[1] He had left the United States in 1845, following the publication of his autobiography, *Narrative of the Life of Frederick Douglass, An American Slave, Written by Himself*, in order to avoid recapture and re-enslavement, and generate support for the anti-slavery cause in Europe. His travels throughout the then United Kingdom in the two years from 1845 to 1847 had a lasting effect on his social and intellectual status. Alan Rice and Martin Crawford describe him arriving in 'Britain [and Ireland the] ... raw material of a great black figure; [and leaving] ... in April 1847 the finished independent man, cut from a whole cloth and able to make his own decisions about the strategies and ideologies of the abolitionist movement'.[2]

Douglass's personal and political transformation found correspondence in the shifting form of his literary work, which became enmeshed in those same strategies and ideologies. In Ireland, his autobiography was re-published by the Dublin Quaker printer, Richard Webb, shortly after Douglass's arrival in September 1845, and went to variant and second Irish editions in 1846.[3] Just as Douglass's personal and professional standing were deeply marked by the experience of being outside the United States, the reprinting of the *Narrative* in Ireland marks the beginning of a stage in Douglass's literary career that has an impact on contemporary readings of his life and work. Taken in conjunction with his other literary output at this time – the letters to Garrison from Britain and Ireland, which were

---

1 Biographical accounts of Douglass include William S. McFeely, *Frederick Douglass* (New York and London: Norton, 1991), and Benjamin Quarles, *Frederick Douglass* (1948; New York: n.p., 1964).

2 Alan J. Rice and Martin Crawford, 'Triumphant Exile: Frederick Douglass in Britain, 1845–1847', in Alan J. Rice and Martin Crawford, eds, *Liberating Sojourn: Frederick Douglass and Transatlantic Reform* (London and Athens, GA: University of Georgia Press, 1999) pp. 1–12 (3).

3 Both the first Irish and variant carry the date 1845, though the latter was not in fact published until 1846.

subsequently published in the abolitionist newspaper the *Liberator* –
the Irish *Narratives* mark a transitional phase in Douglass's emergence
as a modern subject and his mediation of nineteenth-century models
of identity, specifically those that emerged as part of the international
ethical culture of abolitionism.

For with the republication of the *Narrative* in Dublin came several
changes in the form of the work, involving the incorporation of various
prefacing devices and appendices that distinguish it from the US edition.
These include: preceding the body of the text, the incorporation of a
resolution of the Hibernian Anti-Slavery Society on the fly-leaf; varying
portraits of Douglass on the title spread; a verse by John Greenleaf
Whittier on the title page; and a 'Preface' to the editions written by
Douglass and inserted before the preface to the United States edition:
and, appended, the 'Address to the Friends of the Slave'; an 'Appendix'
introducing, reproducing and contesting A.C.C. Thompson's refutation of
Douglass's *Narrative* in the *Delaware Republican*; a selection of favourable
critical notices from American and British newspapers; and two testimonies from Protestant clergymen in Belfast.

Though the core narrative – the narrative of selfhood – remains the
same, then, the Irish editions of Douglass's work differ significantly in
form and geopolitical orientation from the US publication. The additions
they incorporate serve not only to develop the anti-slavery argument,
but they have implications for a work understood as inherently American
in its impact and execution. For they extend the boundaries of the text,
positing it and its central fiction, the slave subject, as cultural artefacts in
ongoing synthesis with their points of origin and the developing context
of Atlantic history.

In the nineteenth century, abolition and anti-slavery provide one of
the keys to any evaluation of transnational processes of identity formation. As an ethical culture of some prestige, linked to elements of the
Anglo-American establishment, abolitionism's effects greatly exceeded its
immediate focus, the United States, frequently affecting politico-cultural
spaces in which the issue of slavery per se did not arise. Equally, resistance
within the slave community, like the issue of slavery itself, resonated in a
range of international contexts.

Like many of the former slaves who had preceded him, Douglass's
association with abolitionism involved him in a transnational network,
one organized around the issue of American slavery, yet embedded in very
different political contexts. As this might suggest, Douglass's displacement
to Europe resulted in a radical shift in his social contacts, sphere of influence and political significance, a shift that likewise affected the *Narrative*.
The displacement therefore compels a re-evaluation of the *Narrative* in

the light of the issues arising in those discrete national contexts in which the work circulated, issues as class conflict, gender identity and colonial expansion. A text such as Douglass's *Narrative*, long since a cornerstone of the US American canon, needs to be read not merely as an American artefact emerging from the context of African American slavery in the United States, or indeed within the racially progressive agenda of Anglo-American abolitionism; both writer and text require consideration within a wider framework that addresses issues contemporaneous with the text's publication and allied to spheres of abolitionist and anti-slavery influence in their broadest terms.

Perhaps the greatest challenge to any reading of Douglass's text as an exclusively American artefact is the inclusion of a new introduction to the Irish editions. This 'Preface' usefully illustrates Douglass's strategic grasp of the social, economic and ideological realities of the Atlantic world, as well as his capacity to harness its representative opportunities. The preface first appears in the variant first Irish edition published in March 1846, and an extended version in the second Irish edition of May of the same year. Both editions were produced after Douglass had left Ireland for Britain and was lecturing on his famous 'Send back the Money' campaign against the Free Church of Scotland. The first introduction, therefore, was written in Ireland in 1845 and extended while Douglass was in Glasgow in 1846. As such its appearance and meaning can be seen as bearing directly on Douglass's Irish experience, an experience marked by economic success, social mobility and increasing ideological independence.

Before attending to the preface directly however, it is perhaps worth reviewing the relationship, historical and contemporary, that obtained between the United States, Britain and Ireland at the time. Most of Britain's North American colonies were lost to the United States in the American Revolution, though Britain retained the Canadian and Oregon territories. Britain had already made significant inroads into Asia, and European exploration and colonization of Africa had begun. African slaves had been introduced to North America by British colonists in order to provide labour for the new plantation economies, fuelling economic and industrial growth in Britain itself until the American Revolution. Britain's subsequent ending of the slave trade and imposition of an embargo on ships carrying African slaves led to further tensions between it and its former colony. Meanwhile, the United States was expanding westwards, fuelled by the desire for land and increasing immigration, largely from Europe. Ireland remained a British colony, despite significant anti-British agitation, while at the same time ever-increasing numbers of Irish people were leaving for the United States to avail themselves of the economic and other opportunities on offer.

These colonial and former colonial relationships significantly complicate the status, influence and effect of African Americans travelling abroad
on an abolitionist ticket. They also modify understandings of the ethical
cultures of abolitionism and anti-slavery operating across the Atlantic,
particularly the complicated power networks linking race, politics and
gender embedded within them.

It is against this background of mutually imbricated histories and
political ambition that the Irish editions of Douglass's *Narrative* operate.
The American edition of the *Narrative* can be read as a key text of
Garrisonian abolitionism, anchored firmly in the moral territory of the
United States. The Irish editions, with their additional 'Preface', expand
the text's frame of reference, and indicate Douglass's increasing awareness of the risks and opportunities of his new situation. Essentially, the
Irish *Narratives* provide an autobiographical and ideological commentary on Douglass's changing status within the transatlantic abolitionist
movement, an accumulation of evidence regarding his views, contacts
and developing political position. For while the US edition confined itself
to domestic matters – the exposure of slavery and an insistence on the
subjectivity of the slave – the Irish editions internationalize and rehis-
toricize the anti-slavery debate, linking it to wider discussions of liberal
masculine subjectivity. According to Douglass himself, the purpose of
the preface is to clarify what he calls the 'threefold object' of his visit to
Britain and Ireland. 'I wished,' he explains,

> to be out of the way during the excitement consequent on the publication of
> my book; lest the information I had there given as to my identity and place
> of abode, should induce my *owner* to make measures for my restoration to
> his 'patriarchal care!'
> My next inducement was a desire to increase my stock of information,
> and my opportunities for self-improvement, by a visit to the land of my
> *paternal* ancestors.
> My third and chief object was, by the public exposition of the contami-
> nating and degrading influences of Slavery upon the slaveholders and his
> abettors, as well as the slave ... as may tend to shame (her) [the United States]
> out of her adhesion so abhorrent to Christianity and to her republican insti-
> tutions.[4]

Clearly, Douglass attached significant personal as well as political meaning
to his overseas visit, designating it as a search for refuge, origins and
an opportunity to testify against the institution of slavery. The preface

---

4 Frederick Douglass, Preface to *Narrative of the Life of Frederick Douglass, An American
   Slave, Written by Himself*, variant first Irish edition and second Irish edition, vol. 3
   (Dublin: Webb & Chapman, 1845; 1846), emphasis original.

is primarily an explanatory note, detailing the reasons for Douglass's presence in the then United Kingdom, and acting as an autobiographical extension of the narrative. It therefore upsets any easy correlation between the slave-subject and American territory, opening up a series of questions concerning African American identity: historical, ethical and otherwise. The preface was written in Ireland, a site historically and culturally marginalized, yet politicized in both US and British terms by immigration and anti-colonial struggle respectively. Ireland's marginality complemented what might be described as Douglass's maroon status; it allowed him to engage with a range of discursive templates while constructing a distinctive transnational political constituency around himself.

Remarkably, for example, particularly given the audience at which the Irish editions were directed – the politically liberal middle and upper classes of the United Kingdom – the preface undermines the morally prestigious position held by Britain in US abolitionist circles after the abolition of slavery in the West Indies in 1833. Although certainly a place of safety from persecution, Britain, cast by Douglass as 'the land of my *paternal* ancestors', is less a paradigm of racial enlightenment than a cold reminder of personal dispossession. The remarks also ironize one of the key Southern myths regarding slavery – that it was a kindly, patriarchal institution – by echoing Douglass's contention in the body of the narrative that, though he is himself a slave, born of a slave mother, his father 'was a white man'. 'He was admitted to be such,' Douglass continues in his autobiography, 'by all I ever heard talk of my parentage. The opinion was also whispered that my master was my father; but of the correctness of this opinion, I know nothing.'[5]

In the preface, the loss of paternal genealogy appears to underpin a peculiar sense of cultural as well as individual disinheritance. Throughout his life, the absence of this unidentified father complicated Douglass's racial identity and indeed the masculine paradigm underpinning his project of self-fashioning. As Annette Niemtzow observes, '[in] choosing autobiography as a form, Douglass ... committed himself to ... its most salient requirement: that he legitimize himself by naming and claiming a father'.[6] In the preface, the trope of illegitimacy takes on an extra dimension, as Douglass extends its meaning to include his current alienation from his Anglo-American birthright. The moment of self-authentication that occurs in the preface, then, the naming and claiming of a paternal lineage

5   Frederick Douglass, *Autobiographies*, ed. Henry Louis Gates Jr (New York: Library of America, 1994), p. 15. Hereafter cited as Douglass, *Autobiographies*.

6   Annette Niemtzow, 'The Problem of Self in Autobiography: The Example of the Slave Narrative', in John Sekora and Darwin Turner, eds, *The Art of Slave Narrative* (Chicago: Western Illinois University Press, 1982), pp. 96–109 (98).

de-legitimated by slavery and obscured by colonial process, re-enacts on a cultural level the project of selfhood effected in the narrative proper.

These overdeterminations of the master–slave, ex-colonial relationships have significant implications for Douglass's racial and gender identity. They complicate the process of self-fashioning – the creation of a selfhood consistent with western models of masculinity or manhood – in which Douglass was engaged, on personal and cultural levels. Writing of transatlantic and colonial discourses, Jennifer Devere Brody describes the raced and gendered formulations of national identity in nineteenth-century British writing. 'Englishness', Brody argues, was constructed as white, masculine and pure, while 'Americanness' was cast as black, feminine and impure. British imperial identity was, she claims, irrevocably bound to figures of blackness, figures who frequently revealed the 'unseemly origins of [British] imperial power'.[7] By indicating his own hybrid origins, Douglass points to the unseemly outcomes – slavery and illegitimacy – of the British colonial presence in the Americas.

In doing so, he runs the gauntlet of two feminizing discourses: the colonial and the racial, something that he more typically tried to avoid. Some years earlier, for example, having arrived in the Northern states after his escape from Baltimore, Douglass changed his surname from Bailey to Douglass, a gesture that was standard practice for those fleeing slavery in the South. In doing so, however, as Henry Louis Gates remarks, Douglass 'self-consciously and ironically abandoned a strong matrilineal black heritage of five generations'; the name change, Gates observes, effectively 'silenced and effaced the mother's story'.[8]

But it also allowed Douglass to eschew the illegitimacy endemic in slavery as a result of the abuses and inconsistencies of the system itself. His self-naming after the protagonist of Walter Scott's poem, *Lady of the Lake*, and repeatedly stated admiration for the 'black Douglas' appearing in other works by Scott,[9] goes a step further than either anonymity or safety might require. Indeed, Frederick Bailey's adoption of the name

7 Jennifer Devere Brody, *Impossible Purities: Blackness, Femininity and Victorian Culture* (Durham, NC: Duke University Presss, 1998).
8 Henry Louis Gates Jr, *Figures in Black: Words, Signs and the Racial Self* (New York and Oxford: Oxford University Press, 1987), p. 114.
9 Black Douglass was a name reserved for Sir James Douglas and his descendants, who appear in *The Fair Maid of Perth* and *Castle Dangerous*. See Alasdair Pettinger, '"Send Back the Money": Douglass and the Free Church of Scotland', in Alan J. Rice and Martin Crawford, eds, *Liberating Sojourn: Frederick Douglass and Transatlantic Reform* (London and Athens, GA: University of Georgia Press, 1999), pp. 31–47. Scott's novels, which take the form of historical romance, provided literary consolidation to the British nation following the union between Scotland, and England and Wales.

Douglass, the origins of which he was often to comment upon, appears to embrace romanticized notions of heroic masculinity current in both European and Southern US literature of the period. It also plays to positive, even romanticized notions of 'blackness' already present in British and Anglo-American culture. In many ways then, Douglass's name change is double-edged: a negation of his matrilineal ties to slavery, but one that allows him to escape the emasculation of his former chattel status.[10] It represents a bid for a masculine identity that bypasses the need to establish individual paternal genealogy, confirming a transnational, hybrid identity that is the end result of colonial history.

Such naming and claiming of paternity as does occur in the *Narrative*, which takes the form of rumour rather than hard fact – it 'was whispered that my father was my master' – is, however, restated in the preface. This re-implicates the individual concerned – Douglass's father – in the abuses of sexual and social power that brought Douglass into existence.

But the repercussions exceed this personal history, for the preface underlines the colonial process through which the United States as an independent nation had emerged. Indeed, the illegitimacy vaunted in the 'Preface' echoes the theme of a speech given by Douglass in Limerick on 10 November 1845, when Douglass informed his audience: 'Americans, as a nation, were guilty of the foul crime of slavery, whatever might be their hypocritical vaunts of freedom. It was … not a true democracy, but a bastard republicanism that enslaved one-sixth of the population.'[11] The progenitor of that 'bastard republicanism' we might infer, is Britain, initiator of colonial process and of slavery in North America, a country now repositioned in the transatlantic as well as personal history from which slave-subject and slave text have emerged. By tracing and stating his paternal British ancestry, therefore, Douglass invents himself as consequence, and representative figure, of that early, transatlantic colonial alliance, placing the bounded, Southern slave subject firmly within the realm of its apparent antithesis, Atlantic cosmopolitanism.

One important effect of the preface, therefore, is its transhistorical as well as transatlantic effect, as past and present fuse in the physical and textual presence of the slave-subject. The later Irish editions of Douglass's

---

10 Free persons of colour were denied many of the civil and political liberties enjoyed by white males, including the right to vote, stand for public office, etc. The gendering of the black male subject was intrinsically linked to the black–white power differential, while the discourse of abolitionism, which became a political vehicle for élite women, is highly overdetermined by categories of gender.

11 John Blassingame, ed., *Frederick Douglass Papers*, Series One, *Speeches, Debates, and Interviews*, vol. 1 (New Haven, CT: Yale University Press, 1979), pp. 76–86. Hereafter referred to as *FDP*.

Narrative illustrate the unstable foundations of liberal western identity by bringing into question the problematic genealogy of the west's unacknowledged offspring, now emerging into representation through the slave narrative. Although grounded in autobiography, the paradigmatic formula used to establish US American identity, therefore, the *Narrative* resists closed readings of the text's central fiction – the author – within US American liberal nationalist paradigms. Additionally, the preface undermines polarized Enlightenment models of western subjectivity, such as those governing the social constituencies of slave or free, black or white, masculine or feminine. Douglass's genealogy subverts those established constituencies, as he constructs himself as the hybrid product of an historical union between master and slave, as an ironic emblem of the colonial past and the failures of the republican present.

Just as importantly, the preface illustrates that Douglass's European sojourn provided him with important literary opportunities that might otherwise have been unavailable. It allowed him the freedom to operate outside the immediate influence of the American abolitionist movement, to create for himself a masculine identity that exceeded, albeit through necessity, the strictures of patrimony and its literary consort, autobiography. The version of masculinity the abolitionist movement actually extolled, broadly that of the liberal, Northern self-made man, embodied in the figure of William Lloyd Garrison, was somewhat different from the Southern variety of aristocratic (plantation gentleman) masculinity to which Douglass had been exposed for most of his life. Douglass was not, however, averse to playing to the Northern prototype. For example, his apparently ironic remark that his departure from the United States was a demonstration of his intellectual liberty and an opportunity for 'self-improvement', not only had a strong basis in truth, it was ideologically consistent with Northern principles of self-advancement. As his sojourn in the United Kingdom demonstrates, Douglass was capable of successfully mixing both Northern and Southern models of masculine identity in order to avail himself fully of his new situation.

Regardless of the external opportunities available to him however, Douglass's status within the United States remained that of a fugitive. The preface shows him caught between the 'patriarchal' institution he is escaping and his intellectual affiliation to a cultural 'paternity' that, for all its liberal, abolitionist intentions, will never fully acknowledge him. Couched as it is in Garrisonian terms and echoing the central claims of the *Narrative*, the preface cannot be read as an unqualified expression of empowered black subjectivity, for it contains a bitter re-iteration of Douglass's indebtedness to white masculinity for both his literal and textual existence.

The preface can however be understood as marking a shift in Douglass's self-image, which moves towards transnational forms of historical representation. It complicates the ennobled image of white masculinity at the heart of British colonial ethos and its contradictory American offshoots: Southern aristocratic and liberal Northern culture. Although it undermines these western masculine paradigms, however, the preface indicates the degree to which Douglass remained both in thrall to, and alienated from, the cultural identity bestowed by his paternal heritage.

Formalizing Authority

The preface to the Irish editions of Douglass's *Narrative* raises important issues surrounding the issues of race and masculinity in the context provided by Atlantic abolitionism and the complications of the British–American colonial relation. It also contributes to the formal fragmentation of the text, providing yet another narrative frame to the central account of Douglass's life in slavery. Slave narratives generally carried a range of extraneous material in addition to the central narrative, from explanatory notes to personal testimony, to poetry, fable or argument. The primary function of such framing devices in US texts was to uphold the truth-claim of the work, while maintaining an important distance between the largely middle-to-upper-class audience and the 'I' of the narrative. Thus, the narrative structure allowed readers to empathize with the former slave, but fell short of implying their full identification, or moral equality, with him or her.

Douglass's preface – written in Ireland and addressed to a British audience – deviates from this formula by underlining the physical, racial and human proximity of slave narrator and implied reader, all presented as closely linked by history and genealogy. And the placement of the preface has further significance for any reading of the *Narrative* within this new, transatlantic context of production. It was standard practice in slave narratives to include framing testimonies from respected members of the Anti-Slavery Society as to the slave's personal integrity and the veracity of his or her account of life in slavery. Douglass's *Narrative* was no exception. 'I am confident,' runs William Lloyd Garrison's American preface, 'that [Douglass's account] is essentially true in all its statements; that nothing has been set down in malice, nothing exaggerated, nothing drawn from the imagination.'[12] The letter from Wendell Philips that follows confirms this, assuring readers that 'we have known [Douglass] long, and can put the most entire confidence in [his] truth, candor and sincerity'.[13]

12 Douglass, *Autobiographies*, p. 7.
13 Douglass, *Autobiographies*, p. 12.

In the American and first Irish editions of Douglass's *Narrative*, therefore, the text and the man are to be understood within the subjective and
political parameters of Garrisonian abolitionism. It is Garrison and Phillips,
rather than Douglass, who act as mediators of the American narrative; the
black message is apparently enclosed in the proverbial white envelope of
abolitionist control.[14]

Douglass's Irish *Narrative*, with its emphasis on colonial history and
the related issue of paternity, individual and cultural, exceeds contemporary discussions of slavery as a localized American problem. Additionally,
the Irish texts complicate the simple inside-outside relation implied in
Sekora's well-known trope of message/envelope. The number and function
of the testimonies in the Irish editions is a case in point. Given Douglass's
increasing acceptance and influence in upper class and abolitionist circles
in Ireland, it might be expected that framing testimonies would disappear
in the Irish editions. Certainly the need to establish credibility and moral
rectitude diminished as Douglass's range of consequential friends and
acquaintances in Britain and Ireland increased. Furthermore, the preface
points to an increasing confidence experienced by Douglass in Ireland,
presumably reducing the need for third-party interpretation of the text.[15]

But the Irish narratives retain the testimonials of prominent abolitionists, embedding the movement's value systems into the transatlantic
context. The placement of the preface to the Irish editions, however, where
it precedes that of the US production, provides an indication of the shift
in representative authority that occurred during this phase of Douglass's
career. Typically, the intermediary frames of the slave narrative define the
relationship between the black narrator and the white reader. Douglass's
preface, which frames Garrison's testimony, challenges the textual and
ideological authority of American abolitionism. In the light of his Irish
experience, Douglass clearly decided that he, rather than Garrison, was
the most appropriate mediator of the narrative of his life in slavery.

But it also suggests that the slave narrator–abolitionist relation cannot
be simply figured as a power struggle between black and white. Clearly,
from Douglass's point of view, Garrison's testimony had its virtues: the
retention of the American preface in the Irish editions suggests that,
though Douglass no longer felt the need for the abolitionist crutch, he
was willing to capitalize on the Garrisonian name, and reap its social and
economic rewards.

14 John Sekora, 'Black Message/White Envelope: Genre, Authenticity, and Authority in
    the Antebellum Slave Narrative', *Callaloo*, 10 (summer 1987), pp. 482–515.
15 For a discussion of Douglass's Irish contacts see Jenkins, 'Beyond the Pale', and
    Harrison, 'Cork Anti-Slavery Society'.

The existence of variant Irish editions of the *Narrative*, therefore, has an impact on the work's formal and thematic significance. In particular, the Irish editions compel a reading of the *Narrative* as a document addressing the historical complexities of Atlantic culture, rather than as an exclusively American text in which Northern liberal values collide headlong with Southern slaveholding reality. Douglass, whose American *Narrative* charts his progress from a state of bondage in the South to freedom in the North, with the qualified representational liberty bestowed on him by his association with the abolitionist movement, moves one stage further along the road to full representational authority in the Irish text. Paul Giles argues of the *Narrative* that it 'establishes an image of power as the central criterion and reference point within Douglass's world. Power becomes the one thing he can never forget, the commodity that will be negotiated, recirculated, and exchanged in all of his later works.'[16] If this is true, then the process of renegotiation begins not in the thematic structures or images of *My Bondage and My Freedom*, but in the rewritten *Narrative*, whose structure reflects shifts in actual power relations. The newly empowered persona of the Irish preface not only mediates the meaning of the central narrative, but establishes a hierarchy of interpretation in which the modernized slave-subject posits his own textual authority beyond the ideological framework of abolitionism.

The inclusion of the preface therefore requires the recategorization of the *Narrative* as a whole. In its Irish editions, the work takes one step further towards the *Bildungsroman* form it will assume in Douglass's later autobiographies, with concomitant implications for his subjective status and shifting relationship to Atlantic liberal culture.

Against this, the retention of the American preface indicates the ongoing importance, if declining authority, of the abolitionist movement as an international ideological and economic context for the work. The introductory frames of the Irish *Narratives* not only illustrate the tension between Douglass – the emerging black subject – and US abolitionism, but they affect the meaning and interpretation of the text in the wider transatlantic context in which it is inscribed.

Circles of Influence

The increasing ideological and literary independence that followed Douglass's departure from the United States suggests that there was a decreasing need for framing devices or authenticating testimony to be included in the *Narrative*. Paradoxically however, the number of

16 Paul Giles, 'Narrative Reversals and Power Exchanges: Frederick Douglass and British Culture', *American Literature*, 73.4 (2001), pp. 779–810 (785).

testimonials increases in the Irish *Narratives*. All of the Irish editions, for
example (first, variant first and second), include an additional frame to
that provided by the testimonies of Garrison and Phillips: the resolution
of the Hibernian Anti-Slavery Society adopted at a meeting in Dublin
in September 1845. This acknowledges Douglass's arrival in Ireland and
sees the Society 'recommending him to the good offices of all abolitionists
with whom he may meet'. Douglass, it states, 'has long been known to us
by reputation, and is now introduced to us by letters from some of the
most distinguished and faithful friends of the Anti Slavery cause in the
United States'.[17]

Clearly, the tendrils of the American Anti-Slavery Society had
extended their reach to Ireland, which formed part of the international
ethical context provided by anti-slavery and abolitionism. The resolution, like Garrison's preface, doubtless had merit in the marketing of the
work – an important consideration given Douglass's reliance on sales of
the *Narrative* for an independent income. This aside, however, the frame
had other, less material effects. Firstly, it officializes Douglass's status as a
noteworthy abolitionist 'just arrived from the United States on an Anti-
slavery mission to Great Britain and Ireland', locating Douglass firmly
within the Garrisonian camp. Paradoxically, however, Douglass's status
within the abolitionist movement in Ireland is achieved by confirmation
of the moral worth of his US sponsors – 'some of the most distinguished
and faithful friends of anti-slavery in the United States' – rather than that
of Douglass himself. Just who is vouching for whom, and why, becomes
increasingly difficult to determine as the geography of the *Narrative's*
circulation changes.

More remarkably, and like the preface to the variant and second Irish
editions, the resolution acts as a biographical extension of the core narrative. It confirms Douglass's de-territorialization in Ireland, as well as the
work's transatlantic scope. Though it emerges from US abolitionism, then,

17 The entire text, inserted on the fly-leaf, reads as follows:
    At a meeting of the Committee of the Hibernian Anti Slavery Society, held in
    Dublin, the 20th of September, 1845 it was RESOLVED – That as FREDERICK
    DOUGLASS (who is now present,) has just arrived from the United States on
    an Anti-Slavery mission to Great Britain and Ireland, we take the opportunity
    of recommending him to the good offices of all abolitionists with whom he may
    meet. He has long been known to us by reputation, and is now introduced to us
    by letters from some of the most distinguished and faithful friends of the Anti
    Slavery cause in the United States.

                                             James Haughton, Chairman
                                             Richard D. Webb, Secretary.
    (Frederick Douglass, *Narrative of the Life of an American Slave, Written by Himself*,
    first Irish edition [Dublin: Webb and Chapman, 1845], n.p.)

the text, in its Irish editions, begins to trace a route through peripheral sites of anti-slavery influence.

This voyage is reflected in Douglass's preface to the Irish editions, and the introduction from Webb. It is also particularly evident in the second Irish edition in the collection of 'Critical Notices' included at the end of the work. Taken from a variety of American and British newspapers, the reviews register the ever-increasing circle of influence in which the *Narrative* is active, with articles from Philadelphia, New York, London and Edinburgh included. Also incorporated are a number of personal notices by Protestant clergymen in Belfast, which provide the closing frame of the Irish editions. The Rev. Thomas Drew, DD, describes Douglass's writing as 'a metaphysical illustration of a mind bursting all bonds, and winning light and liberty for his own good and the good of millions'; while the Rev. Isaac Nelson claims that Douglass 'is indeed an extraordinary man – the type of a class – such an intellectual phenomenon as only appears at times in the republic of letters. … His name may yet be quoted both as an abolitionist and a literary man by those very States of America who now deny him a home.'

The acuity of these remarks with respect to Douglass's canonization aside, the notices provide an indication of the nature of Douglass's developing social circle in terms of its class, religious and cultural profile. That social circle was composed of the English-speaking upper and merchant classes; largely Protestant supporters of the British presence in Ireland, who shared much the same cultural profile as established Anglo-American populations in the United States, North and South. Douglass's social affiliations suggest the nature of the politico-literary mask he adopted during his Irish tour, which played to the ethical vanity of his hosts while downplaying the many internal tensions in the country. For Douglass and his hosts, Ireland became a space of social mobility that, unlike the United States, where merit was a function of skin colour, encouraged the full realization of his selfhood. Unlike their compatriots in the United States, the Anglo-Irish recognized Douglass's inherent worth: as a man, as a literary figure, as the social and intellectual equal of themselves and their class counterparts throughout Anglo-America.

Though located on the margins of contemporary political consciousness, then, Ireland provided the context of Douglass's political and literary evolution.[18] To underline this, he made constant public comparisons

18 For discussions of Irish marginality and the ongoing ambivalence of the relationship to Western modernity, see Seamus Deane, *Strange Country: Modernity and Nationhood in Irish Writing since 1790* (Oxford: Oxford University Press, 1997); Raymond Crotty, *Ireland in Crisis: A Study in Capitalist Colonial Underdevelopment* (Dingle: Brandon Books, 1986); David Lloyd, *Anomalous States: Irish Writing and the Post Colonial*

between his reception in Ireland and the treatment he had received in the United States. Many of his early speeches and letters deal with the absence of colour prejudice in Ireland, the warm welcome afforded him there, and otherwise creating a myth of social and literary success. Writing to Garrison from Cork, for example, Douglass remarked of a soirée given in his honour:

> It was decidedly the brightest and happiest company, I think, I ever saw, anywhere. ... Among them all, I saw no one that seemed to be shocked or disturbed by my dark presence. No one seemed to feel himself contaminated by contact with me. I think it would be difficult to get the same number of persons together in any of our New England cities, without some democratic nose growing deformed at my approach. *But then you know the white people in America are whiter, purer, and better than the people here. This accounts for it!*[19]

Just two months later Douglass was to write: 'I have spent some of the happiest moments of my life since landing in this country. I seem to have undergone a transformation. I live a new life.' His letter goes on to contrast his treatment in the United States with

> the warm and generous co-operation extended to me by the friends of my despised race – the prompt and liberal manner with which the press have flocked to hear the cruel wrongs, has rendered me its aid – the glorious enthusiasm with which thousands of my down-trodden and long-enslaved countrymen portrayed – the deep sympathy for the slave, and the strong abhorrence for the slaveholder, everywhere evinced – the cordiality with which ministers of various religious bodies, and varying shades of religious opinion have embraced me, the kind respects constantly proffered to me by persons of the highest rank in society.[20]

These remarks were contained in one of a series of open letters to Garrison written while Douglass was in Ireland and later published in the *Liberator*. The letters presented Ireland, or rather the upper- and middle-class Anglo-Irish reaction to Douglass, as a foil to the racialized, discriminatory and enslaving environment of the United States. 'Instead of a democratic government,' wrote Douglass from Belfast, 'I am under a monarchial [sic] government. Instead of the bright blue sky of America, I am covered with the soft grey fog of the Emerald Isle. I breathe, and lo!

Moment (Dublin: Lilliput Press, 1993); and David Lloyd, *Ireland after History* (Cork: Cork University Press 1999).

19 Douglass to William Lloyd Garrison, Cork, 28 October 1845, published in the *Liberator*, 28 November 1845; in Philip S. Foner, *Life and Writings of Frederick Douglass*, vol. 5 (New York: International Publishers, 1975), pp. 6–9 (7).

20 Douglass to Garrison, Victoria Hotel, Belfast, 1 January 1846, published in *Liberator*, 30 January 1846; in Foner, *Frederick Douglass*, 1, pp. 125–27 (126).

The chattel becomes a man.'[21]

Anyone reading might have been forgiven for believing Ireland to have been a liberal paradise on earth, where the sun might not always shine but where man was certainly not vile. The absence of any social commentary in the early letters is disconcerting to say the least. But the letters were part of Douglass's bid for an independent voice within abolitionism; part also of his consolidation of a class-cultural identity that allowed him to maintain at least one foot in the British and Anglo-American establishment throughout his life. In effect, they allowed him to become witness and spokesman for Irish society, its attitudes towards the slave, and its privileging of individual worth over racial profile.

Unlike the preface, which hinted at the implications of the British colonial presence in North America for Afro-American cultural identity, the letters omit any suggestion of the broader Irish social reality, or, given that social reality, the deeply contradictory moral position of many Irish abolitionists. But, though hardly accurate documentations of socio-political conditions, the letters did serve two important purposes: they provided public recognition of Irish enlightenment on the issues of slavery and race, and provided a distinctive discursive space for Douglass himself. Here was a man who, freed from the oppressive racial regimes of the United States, could blossom into his full potential; here was a country that, despite the absence of any republican pretensions, was happy to judge each man according to his merit.

This flattering picture certainly had a basis in truth. Typically, black abolitionist speakers were wholeheartedly embraced by the upper echelons of British and Irish society, often becoming an emblem of the enlightened principles of the visitors' surrogate country – a monarchy – in contrast to the oppressive reality of the American republic they represented. Audrey Fisch contends that the success of black speakers in nineteenth-century Britain was in part due to that country's need to discredit the United States' democracy and political institutions. In Britain, Fisch argues, blackness was lionized, as the 'spectacle' of the abolitionist movement (i.e. the black abolitionist) fused with a rising British nationalism aimed primarily at allaying the country's rising class conflict.[22]

21 Foner, *Frederick Douglass*, 1, p. 126.
22 '"Negrophilism" and British Nationalism: The Spectacle of the Black Abolitionist', *Victorian Review*, 19 (summer 1993), pp. 20–47 (25–37), subsequently published as chapter 4 of Fisch's *American Slaves in Victorian England: Abolitionist Politics in Popular Literature and Culture* (Cambridge: Cambridge University Press, 2000). For a general discussion of British racial attitudes during the period, see Douglas A. Lorimer, *Colour, Class and the Victorians: English Attitudes to the Negro in the Mid-Nineteenth Century* (Leicester: Leicester University Press, 1978).

In Ireland, the conspicuous tendency towards rebellion doubtless made anyone legitimating the political status quo an attractive proposition. With the exception of the activities of the Irish Friends, who had a long-standing record of attempted social reform, middle- and upper-class interest in human rights in Ireland was something of an aberration. As in Britain, however, abolitionism provided benefits that were not only ethical. The adoption of anti-slavery principles created a form of moral fraternity across the upper classes in Britain and Ireland, in a culture that often viewed the Anglo-Irish as the poor relations of their British counterparts. More importantly, class issues in Ireland were further complicated, even overridden, by the colonial hegemony that obtained throughout the nineteenth century. Certain class-related as well as moral benefits therefore accrued to British and Irish upper-class espousal of the anti-slavery cause, serving to displace arguments concerning human, civil and labour rights to a safe distance in the Americas.

In Britain, Douglass exploited that need for moral displacement by appealing to British nationalist sentiment. A speech given in Ayr, Scotland, provides just one illustration of the deliberate conflation of national and moral territory in his anti-slavery rhetoric. Predictably, the conceit involves the persecuted slave fleeing the spreading shadow of the republic in search of safety and succour in the bosom of the British nation. Speaking of the United States he claims:

> There is no spot on the vast domains over which waves the star-spangled banner where the slave is secure;- go east, go west, go north, go south, he is still exposed to the bloodhounds that may be let loose against him; there is no mountain so high – no valley so deep – no spot so sacred, but that the man-stealer may enter and tear his victim from his retreat. (Cheers.) [H]e rejoiced that he now found in the paw of the British Lion the safety which had been denied him under the widespread wings of the American Eagle.[23]

Similar rhetoric was used in Ireland, though the tone was less that of popular British nationalism than that of the civilizing mission of empire.[24]

---

23 *FDP* 1:1, pp. 200–01.
24 An exception to this occurred at a speech in Limerick on 10 November 1845, when, describing the *Cambria* incident, Douglass identifies Gough, an Irishman aboard ship, as one of the heroes of the piece. In the middle of recounting the story, Douglass called for 'three cheers for old Ireland' (*FDP* 1:1, p. 84). Other flirtations with Irish nationalist sentiment can be seen in Douglass's references to Daniel O Connell in the same speech, the mention of whose name was practically guaranteed to raise a cheer. Although Douglass referred to O Connell as the 'Liberator', he confined the application of that title to O Connell's stance on American slavery, thereby emphasising the enlightened credentials of the Irish upper classes while avoiding any possible conflict with his hosts over the issue of popular nationalism or Home Rule. Later, Douglass

In addition to the emphasis on the difference in British and American socio-racial stratification and *domestic* policy so evident in Douglass's British speeches, his rhetoric in Ireland shows a more general interest in the power of British *foreign* policy, notably that relating to US expansion and, of course, slavery. A speech given in Cork on 3 November on the annexation of Texas finds Douglass declaring, 'Americans should be considered a band of plunderers for the worst purposes ... The conduct of America in this particular has not been sufficiently dwelt upon by the British Press. England should not have stood by and seen a feeble people robbed without raising a note of remonstrance.'[25] That Britain was extending its own empire into Asia and Africa with equally regrettable consequences, and engaged in a long-running struggle to suppress Irish anti-colonial resistance, is conveniently overlooked. Indeed, Douglass's rhetoric in Ireland actively encourages the propagation of the ideology of progress that provided the ethical backbone of British colonial process, by casting the United States as an amoral space ripe for Christian conquest, displacing moral and political authority to Britain and reconstructing the United States as an unenlightened, pre-modern space.

Douglass's use of the analogy between moral suasion and colonial evangelization was progressive. In his first speech in Cork on 14 October 1845, he asked only that moral pressure be exerted on American slaveholders in order to force an end to slavery:

> We would not ask you to interfere with the politics of America, or invoke your military aid to put down American slavery. No, we only demand your moral and religious influence on the slave[holder] in question, and believe me the effects of that influence will be overwhelming. (Cheers.) ... We want to encircle America with a girdle of anti-slavery fire.[26]

Three days later, the object and objective of British influence had changed considerably. At a meeting held at Cork's Wesleyan Chapel, Douglass announced to an assembled company of 'highly intelligent and influential people', including numerous church leaders of various denominations:

> Three millions of these poor people [are] deprived of the light of the Gospel, and the common rights of human nature; [are] subjected to the grossest outrages ... the poor bondsman rattle[s] his chain, and clank[s] his fetters

---

was to recall that at the 1845 Repeal rally at which O Connell and Douglass met (and the only occasion on which they did so despite Douglass's ongoing self-identification with the Home Rule advocate), O Connell had 'called me "the Black O Connell of the United States"' (Douglass, *Autobiographies*, p. 682; see also Lee Jenkins, '"Black O Connell"', p. 28).

25 *FDP* 1:1, p. 74.

26 Cork, 14 October 1845. *FDP* 1:1, p. 42.

calling upon the Christianity of the world to relieve him. There [is] a wide field in America for missionary operations. (Hear, hear.)[27]

The link between the liberation of the slave and British moral expansion was restated in Douglass's farewell speech in Cork at the Independent Chapel, George's Street, when he pushed the analogy between missionary zeal, Christian enlightenment and freedom to include the acquisition of literacy, and, by inference, progress towards western subjectivity:

> To you who have a missionary spirit I say there is no better field than America. – the slave is on his knees asking for light; slaves who not only want the bible but some one to teach them to read its contents (hear, hear.) Their cries come across the Atlantic this evening appealing to you![28]

Clearly, Douglass was keen to harness the interest of the Irish upper and middle class in overseas reform and did so by representing the slave population of the United States as a worthy and eager recipient of evangelical zeal and the civilizing mission.

This is in stark contrast to the *Narrative,* in the body of which religion and ministers of religion are vilified. The American and first Irish editions contain an appendix explaining the negative light in which US religion is portrayed, and detailing Douglass's personal religious stance. 'I love,' he claims, 'the pure, peaceable, and impartial Christianity of Christ: I therefore hate the corrupt, slaveholding, women-whipping, cradle-plundering, partial and hypocritical Christianity of this land. Indeed I can see no reason, but the most deceitful one, for calling the religion of this land Christianity.' The appendix ends with the poem 'A Parody', described by Douglass as, 'a portrait of the religion of the south ... which I soberly affirm is "true to life", and without caricature or the slightest exaggeration'.[29]

This 'Parody' provides the closing frame of the US edition, which ends with Douglass 'subscribing myself anew to the sacred cause'.[30] Robert Stepto describes the American *Narrative* as fusing, 'in one brilliant stroke, the quest for freedom and literacy', and ending, according to its own logic, with Douglass stepping heroically forward into his public duties as an abolitionist advocate and anti-slavery speaker.[31] Those public duties, Douglass's Irish rhetoric seems to suggest, involved securing not just the emancipation of the slave, but his/her salvation.

27 Cork 17 October 1845. *FDP* 1:1, p.52.
28 Cork, 3 November 1845. *FDP* 1:1, p. 75.
29 Douglass, *Autobiographies*, pp. 97–102.
30 Douglass, *Autobiographies*, p. 102.
31 Robert B. Stepto, *From Behind the Veil: A Study of Afro-American Narrative* (Urbana, IL: University of Illinois Press, 1979), p. 26.

The tone of Douglass's speeches during his Irish visit therefore illustrates the complexity of his relationship with his Irish supporters and the public he addressed. Stressing for his Irish audience the enthusiasm of a pre-modern, (apparently) non-Christian population for enlightenment distracted from, and perhaps compensated for, a more intransigent population somewhat closer to home. Meanwhile, emphasis in his letters to Garrison on the allegedly unqualified support he received, and absence of racial discrimination, buoyed Irish abolitionist spirits and provided an unflattering comparison with the situation that obtained in the United States.

But the letters to Garrison were, like the rhetoric, above all an exercise in transatlantic self-fashioning. For while Douglass was widely feted in abolitionist circles in Ireland, the response to his stance on the abolition of slavery, the role of religion and even the consensus on the virtues of the *Narrative* was far from unanimously approving.

Considerable chagrin, for example, was expressed by some Irish abolitionists at the emphasis placed in Douglass's speeches on the links between churches in Ireland and those in the United States. In Cork, at a speech given in the city courthouse, Douglass had caused a stir by, it was alleged, unfairly singling out Methodists for attack in his denunciations of the American churches. The remarks that appear to have caused the offence were the following:

> It must also be stated that the American pulpit is on the side of slavery, and the Bible is blasphemously quoted in support of it. The Ministers of religion actually quoted scripture in support of the most cruel and bloody outrages against slaves. My own master was a Methodist class leader (Laughter, and 'Oh'), and he bared the neck of a young woman, in my presence, and he cut her with a cow skin. He then went away, and when he returned to complete the castigation, he quoted the passage, 'He that knoweth his master's will and doeth not, shall be beaten with many stripes.'

This speech was one of the very few given by Douglass in Ireland that was directed at a populist audience, and its tone differs significantly from much of Douglass's other rhetoric during this period. It relies more on vernacular forms, appealing to nationalist sentiment and popular understandings of class difference centring on denominational affiliation. At his next speech in Cork, with a very different audience, Douglass was taken to task for his remarks by the Methodist clergyman, Rev. Mr William Reily, who remarked that 'he could not but observe that an animus was evident in the language of Mr Douglas[s] not at all favourable to Methodists. Now it was well known that the Methodists did everything in their power, and never ceased until they banished slavery from the British

Colonies (hear, hear).' This was substantially true, and there were signifi-
cant black Methodist congregations among the black populations of the
US South and British Caribbean.[32] However, there was some justice to
Douglass's (and other abolitionist) claims that the Methodist churches
in the Southern United States were uncritical of the slave system and
did not discipline members, or even ministers, who were slaveholders.
But Douglass was courting controversy by somewhat unfairly singling
Methodists out for criticism. Although defended by William Martin,
Douglass was criticized for this by Rev. Mr Joseph Mackey, who

> felt offended at the language used by Mr Douglas[s], at the meeting in the
> Court-House, as it was calculated to cast opprobrium on Methodists in
> particular, whilst the Roman Catholic and other sects were passed by; and
> he need scarcely remark that the majority of the audience at that meeting
> was composed of persons who required but little incentive to induce them
> to cast opprobrium on their sect.

Douglass replied, somewhat disingenuously, that 'he was a fallible man;
and it would be requiring too much that he should know men's religion
by their faces'.[33] He did subsequently qualify his remarks, even going
so far as to state (falsely) that he was himself a Methodist.[34] The profes-
sion is interesting one, as Douglass habitually denied any sectarian affiliation, declaring on more than one occasion that 'as to religion, I belong to
none'. A letter to Webb from Belfast, detailing his experiences on a brief
visit to Birmingham made in December 1845, confirms this: 'I called on
the Rev. John Angel James DD to whom I had a letter of introduction. ...
He wished to know if I came recommended and if I ... was a member of
any Church – and if any to what Church. I told him I was not a member
of any Church.'[35] On the occasion of Douglass's speech in Cork, umbrage
was taken by the Methodists in the audience, who communicated their
displeasure to others of their persuasion. Writing to Webb from Belfast,
Douglass claimed, somewhat unjustly, that

32 See Sylvia Frey and Betty Wood, *Come Shouting to Zion: African American Protes-
    tantism in the American South and British Caribbean to 1830* (Chapel Hill, NC: North
    Carolina University Press, 1998).
33 *FDP* 1:1, pp. 43, 53–54.
34 The newspaper report reads: 'He was a Methodist himself; but he cautioned his fellow
    religionists how they defended their brethren in America, for in doing so they would
    be defending the men ... who scourged his ... female cousin until she was crimsoned
    with her own blood her head to the floor (hear, and oh, oh)' (*FDP* 1:1, p. 54).
35 Douglass to Webb, Victoria Hotel, Belfast, 20 December 1845. Boston Anti-Slavery
    Collection, Ms.A.1.2 v15, p. 89. Although unrecorded in Blassingame's 'Partial
    Speaking Itinerary', Douglass, according to the same letter, arrived in Liverpool on
    14 December, spoke in Birmingham's Town Hall on the 16th for '25 minutes amid
    cheers', and arrived back in Belfast on 19 December 1845.

the enemies of anti-slavery have been busy in creating prejudice against me, on the ground of my heterodoxy. From what I can learn, the Methodist minister in Cork as well as Dublin, have written here against me. So you see mine will be no bed of roses. These Revd Gentlemen are determined to identify themselves with their slaveholding brethren in America. They must take the consequences.[36]

These consequences were also to be felt by Douglass, who carried his own preconceptions concerning various religious denominations. Next day, he wrote to Webb informing him of his 'success in getting the Methodist meeting house, in the face of letters prejudicial to me both from Cork and Dublin', an indication that he had survived the unfavourable reaction of Methodists further south. The same letter describes Belfast as 'a field ripe for the harvest ... the very hotbed of presbyterianism and free churchism', concluding that 'a blow can be struck here more effectively than in any other part of Ireland'.

Free Church Presbyterians were certainly high on Douglass's list of desirable converts to the anti-slavery cause. The 'Send Back the Money' campaign, which formed the basis of Douglass's Scottish tour, targeted the Free Church of Scotland, which was in receipt of moneys from slaveholding co-religionists in the American South.[37] The Free Church had been established in 1843 and had immediately embarked on a fundraising drive in Britain, Ireland and the United States. By 1844 it was estimated that £9,000 had been donated by Presbyterians in the US South. Douglass's campaign urged churches to have 'no union with slaveholders', and specifically targeted the Free Church with the 'Send Back the Money' slogan.[38] The campaign against the executive of the Free Church actually began in Belfast, though the results, despite Douglass's declarations that he was everywhere met with approval, were not always happy. On one occasion on which the 'Send Back the Money' jingle backfired, Belfast was, during the night, placarded with the anti-Douglass slogan 'Send Back the Nigger'.

The incident was blamed on the presence of an American Methodist clergyman, the Rev. Smith, in the city, although presumably he was not

36 Douglass to Webb, Belfast, 5 December 1845. Boston Anti-Slavery Collection, Ms.A.1.2 v15, p. 85.

37 The campaign provides the only example of Douglass mobilizing popular support while in Britain and Ireland. For a history of the tensions between the free church and the anti-slavery movement, see George Shepperson, 'The Free Church and American Slavery', *Scottish Historical Review*, 30 (1951), pp. 126–42. For a more general history of Scottish anti-slavery, see C. Duncan Rice, *The Scots Abolitionists, 1833–1861* (Baton Rouge: Louisiana State University Press, 1981).

38 See Pettinger, '"Send Back the Money"', pp. 31–47.

acting alone. According to Webb, Smith also 'endeavoured to injure Douglass by calumnious reports against his morality & by imputing infidelity to him'.[39] No mention is made of the incident in the famous 'we don't allow niggers here' letter written to Garrison from Belfast on 1 January 1846, and later published in the *Liberator*, in which Douglass once again draws comparisons unfavourable to the United States between his treatment there and in Ireland. The letter, throughout which the phrase 'we don't allow niggers in here' appears nine times, details Douglass's experience in the United States, where he alleges he was repeatedly met with this remark and refused entry to churches, public buildings and eating houses. By contrast, in Ireland Douglass found

> no difficulty ... in gaining admission into any place of worship, instruction or amusement on equal terms with people as white as any I saw in the United States. I meet nothing to remind me of my complexion. I find myself regarded and treated at every turn with the kindness and deference paid to white people. When I go to church, I am met by no upturned nose and scornful lip to tell me 'We don't allow niggers in here'![40]

'The people here know nothing of the republican negro hate prevalent in our glorious land,' Douglass continued, '[t]hey measure and esteem men according to their moral and intellectual worth, and not according to the color of their skin.'[41] Ireland was presented to US abolitionists as a place of uniform and unqualified support for Douglass; no crack was to be allowed to be seen to have appeared in the myth of a stalwart anti-slavery wall, or related racial egalitarianism, in Ireland.[42]

The second Irish edition of the *Narrative* reflects the complex sectarian negotiations in which Douglass engaged, as well as marking the qualitative shift that occurred in his attitudes to religion during his Irish tour. Gone is the stinging 'parody' of Southern slaveholding Christianity, and, as noted, its place is taken by the 'personal notices' of two Irish Protestant clergymen, declarations included in defiance of Webb, Douglass's

---

39   Webb to Maria Weston Chapman, Dublin, 16 July 1846, Weston Papers Ms.A.9.2 v.22, No. 75.

40   Douglass to Garrison, Belfast, 1 January 1846, Anti-Slavery Collection, Boston Public Library, Ms.A.1.2 v16, p. 1.

41   Douglass to Garrison, Ms.A.1.2 v16, p. 1.

42   See Richard Blackett, *Building an Anti-Slavery Wall: Black Americans in the Atlantic Abolitionist Movement, 1830–1860* (Baton Rouge: Louisiana State University Press, 1983). For the wavering of the strength of the transatlantic alliance, see Richard Blackett, 'Cracks in the Anti-Slavery Wall: Frederick Douglass's Second Visit to England (1859–1860) and the Coming of the Civil War', in Alan J. Rice and Martin Crawford, eds, *Liberating Sojourn: Frederick Douglass and Transatlantic Reform* (Athens, GA, and London: University of Georgia Press, 1999), pp. 187–206.

staunchly anti-clerical publisher. In a letter to Maria Weston Chapman, Webb, himself a member of the Society of Friends, went so far as to describe 'Popery and Episcopalianism' as 'the curse of Ireland'.[43] Despite the objections of one of Ireland's leading abolitionists, Douglass insisted on the inclusion of the notices in the second Irish edition, informing Webb that he

> ought to have thought of [his] prejudice against priests sooner. If clergymen read my narrative and approve of it, prejudice against their office would be but a poor reason for rejecting benefit of such approval. The enclosed is from Mr Jackson, the Presbyterian Minister. I wish both it, and that of Dr Drew, to be inserted in the second edition.

'To leave them out because they are ministers,' he somewhat disingenuously continues, 'would be to show oneself as much and more sectarian than themselves.'[44]

In the event, the notices were included, underlining once again the extent to which Douglass had evolved as a political and literary agent during his time in Ireland. The notices give further evidence of Douglass's class affiliations in Ireland, where, according to his biographer William McFeely, Douglass's social leanings evolved 'upward rather than outward'.[45] These tendencies can be detected in the class and religious composition of his Irish audiences, which were predominantly upper class and Protestant, and much closer in outlook to the targets of anti-slavery rhetoric in the American South than either they or Douglass might have been willing to acknowledge.

The inclusion of the notices from members of that audience recalibrates the socio-political stance of the text, whose new alignment reflects Douglass's rising status in the moral politics of the Atlantic world by underscoring his power to reward enlightened attitudes with textual recognition. Free Presbyterianism and Anglicanism, through their acknowledgement of Douglass's moral and literary status, and their support of the abolitionist cause, are welcomed into the prestigious anti-slavery fold now represented by the *Narrative*, an inclusion that had the added advantage of leaving the myth of unfaltering support for Douglass in Ireland unscathed.

---

43 R.D. Webb to Maria Weston Chapman, Dublin, 16 July 1846, Weston Papers, Ms.A.9.2 v.22, No. 75. For an account of the quarrel that erupted between Webb and Douglass on this matter, see Richard S. Harrison, *Richard Davis Webb: Dublin Quaker Printer* (Cork: Redbarn, 1993).

44 Douglass to Webb, Glasgow, 16 April 1846, Anti-Slavery Collection, Boston Public Library, Ms.A.1.2 v16, p. 32.

45 McFeely, *Frederick Douglass*, p. 141.

Thus, Douglass's representation of the success of his Irish visit in his open letters to Garrison show him availing himself of the personal and literary opportunities provided in Ireland by a reforming upper class eager to establish its enlightened credentials, credentials finally established by the incorporation of letters from Irish clergymen as closing frames to the *Narrative*. In common with the preface to the variant and second Irish editions, these notices are testimony to Douglass's increasing literary and ideological independence. Ireland was central to the realization of that independence: not just as a refuge from re-enslavement and a safe platform from which to attack the United States' 'peculiar institution', but as an imaginary space which marked an important step in the development of his writing, *and* of a distinctive narrative persona which escaped the racial confines of the United States and the ideological control of the transatlantic abolitionist movement. Douglass's sojourn in Ireland enabled his emergence as a major cultural and intellectual force, an emergence that occurs in parallel with, indeed is bound to, his self-representation as arbiter, as well as author, of his own work. The *Narrative*, in its Irish editions, traces the complicated path of that subjective and literary emergence, formally marking Douglass's accession to the coveted 'republic of letters'.

Chapter 2

Friends and Allies:
The Economics of the Text

Shortly after Frederick Douglass arrived in Ireland in September 1845, his autobiography, *Narrative of the Life of Frederick Douglass, An American Slave*, was republished in Dublin by Webb and Chapman. The reasons for the republication were both dogmatic and economic. Aside from providing an opportunity for the dissemination of an anti-slavery argument of impact and importance, proceeds from the sale of the book provided Douglass with a degree of financial independence. While Douglass was in Europe, it was doubly important that he have an assured source of income with which to support himself and his family in the United States. Tours by US abolitionists in Europe were often used to promote and increase financial as well as moral support for the anti-slavery cause by encouraging contributions to anti-slavery bazaars and other fund-raising activities, but the out-of-pocket expenses of speakers on that circuit might not necessarily be met in full by anti-slavery organizations. In a letter to J.B. Estlin from London commenting on Douglass's UK tour, for example, W.L. Garrison observed, 'As to … [Douglass's] means of support, he is chiefly dependent on the sale of his Narrative, but I believe he is at this time receiving a small stipend from the Edinburgh friends, though they do not defray his travelling expenses.'[1] Sales of the *Narrative* in Ireland significantly augmented Douglass's overseas returns, providing him with a sizeable income above and beyond payment for his immediate expenses.

Lecture tours appear to have proved lucrative for black speakers in Ireland, who aroused considerable sympathy and support throughout the country. Writing in early 1842 shortly after Charles Lenox Remond's departure for the United States, Richard D. Webb claimed: 'Remond carried more money out of Ireland for himself than Collins got for the American Anti-Slavery Society. This was, first, because he was a coloured man; then because he was eloquent – then because he has good manners –

---

1 W.L. Garrison to J.B. Estlin, London, 8 September 1846 (Walter M. Merrill, ed., *The Letters of William Lloyd Garrison*, vol. 3 [Cambridge, MA: Harvard University Press, 1973], p. 400; see also Foner, *Frederick Douglass*, 5, p. 509 n16.

then because he is young, handsome and interesting.'[2] Frederick Douglass, younger, by all accounts extremely handsome, and doubtless even more interesting, could expect, and indeed received, substantial support from the abolitionist community and its satellites in Ireland.

Local abolitionists were quick to see the possible economic benefits accruing to Douglass's popularity and the sympathy he aroused. A letter to R.D. Webb from John Estlin, a Bristol abolitionist, in November 1845 asks:

> Is it possible that Douglass can pay his expenses in England by the sale of his book? I doubt not he has been well advised in not making his tour a money getting one; but I cannot see any good reason, why *after* any of his public lectures, when people's hearts are opened, a collection should not be made at the doors from those who would like to give something either for his private expenses, or for the cause?[3]

In fact, Douglass's expenses in Ireland were relatively few; he remained as the guest of abolitionists and their sympathizers throughout his stay, and his only necessary outlay was in travel costs.[4] These were more than offset by the proceeds from the sale of the *Narrative*, the first 2,000 of which had, according to Webb, 'brought him in certainly £150 nett' by the time they had all been sold in January 1846. 'If he go on as he has begun in Ireland, through Great Britain,' Webb continues, 'he will pocket 2500 dollars in twelve months time.'[5]

The success of the first edition prompted another run of 2,000 copies in early 1846 and the publication of a second Irish edition that April.

2   J.A. Collins was an anti-slavery speaker who visited Ireland in May 1841. R.D. Webb to Maria Weston Chapman, 'More jottings for Maria W Chapman', Dublin, 22nd of 2nd month (22 February) 1842. Boston Anti-Slavery Collection, Ms.A.1.2 v12 (2), No. 30.

3   John Estlin to R.D. Webb, Bristol, 5 November 1845, Weston Papers, Ms.A.9.2 v21, Nos. 87–88.

4   Douglass, according to his own account, had his passage from the United States paid by 'my warm and excellent friend JN Buffum ... [who] ... aware of my poverty stepped forward with his characteristic liberality and kindly offered to collect a sufficient sum to pay my passage to this land. He tried and succeeded in getting 68 dollars just two dollars short of my expenses in the steerage. I brought with me three hundred and fifty dollars, money which I had saved from the sale of my narrative – For means to sustain me while here I have relied – and still rely mainly upon the sale of my narration' (Douglass to Maria Weston Chapman, Kilmarnock, Scotland, 29 March 1846, Weston Papers, Ms.A.9.2 v22, No. 35).

5   R.D. Webb to Edmund Quincy, Dublin, 2 February 1846, Webb–Quincy Correspondence 1843–72, Boston Anti-Slavery Collection, Ms.960, p19. Webb charged Douglass £96 for the first print run of 2,000 copies. Douglass to Webb, Glasgow, 20 April 1846, Boston Anti-Slavery Collection, Ms.A.1.2 v16, p. 33.

Douglass's spirits appear to have risen in line with his unaccustomed monetary as well as popular success. Just two months after arriving in Ireland, he wrote from Belfast (with unusual naiveté given the recipient's irascible nature) to Richard Webb: 'I bought a watch yesterday, a right down good one, 7L 10 shillings. I swell but I think I shall not burst.'[6] One of Douglass's most scathing criticisms of slavery in the *Narrative* involves his description of life in Baltimore after completion of his caulking apprenticeship. In the period leading up to his escape, Douglass hired his time as a ship's caulker and handed his wages at the end of the week to his then master, Hugh Auld. 'I was now getting,' he writes,

> one dollar and fifty cents per day. I contracted for it; I earned it; it was paid to me; it was rightfully my own; yet, upon each returning Saturday night, I was compelled to deliver every cent of that money to Master Hugh. And why? Not because he earned it, – not because I owed it to him, – not because he possessed the slightest shadow of a right to it; but solely because he had the power to compel me to give it up. The right of the grim-visaged pirate on the high seas is exactly the same.[7]

Clearly, sales of the *Narrative* in Ireland were providing Douglass with a disposable income and the accoutrements of an economic success of which he could hitherto only have dreamed. The uses of slave narratives detailing the afflictions and injustices of slave life as a tool of abolitionism have long been clear. Yet as Douglass's work demonstrates (and those of Gustavas Vassa/Olaudah Equiano and Mary Prince before him), there were significant commercial and social, as well as moral gains to publication for the narrator him/herself.[8] Ironically perhaps, the *Narrative*, which detailed the violation and abuse of labour and economic as well as human rights under the system of slavery, projected Douglass out of the social category of skilled labourer, or ideological and financial dependent of abolitionism, and into a higher social and economic niche as a man of letters.

Douglass's economic success was not met with approval in all quarters and quickly became the cause of some friction between Douglass and the US wing of abolitionism. This centred on the growing dispute between the American Anti-Slavery Society and the British and Foreign Anti-Slavery Society as to how abolition might best be achieved. The organizational as well as ideological split was found on both sides of the Atlantic. William

---

6 Douglass to Webb, Belfast, 7 December 1845, Boston Anti-Slavery Collection, Ms.A.1.2 v15, p. 87.

7 Douglass, *Autobiographies*, p. 84.

8 It was arguably the commercial success of the slave narrative that facilitated its transformation into a fully fledged literary genre, existing independently.

Lloyd Garrison and his followers took over the American Society in 1834, leaving their opponents to form the American and Foreign Anti-Slavery Society, and pursued a new policy towards slavery in the Southern states. The organization eschewed the political route to abolition – lobbying of legislators, campaigning for legal change at state or national level – believing abolition would only come about when the pro-slavery lobby recognized the error of its ways. Their philosophy of moral suasion also meant that Garrisonians rejected the use of violence – within the slave community or otherwise – as a means to effect abolition.

Anti-slavery in Britain had a longer history, having emerged in the late eighteenth century in the context of British colonial slavery in the West Indies. Its emphasis was on the political route to change, a strategy which had proved successful, firstly, in ending the slave trade, and then in the abolition of colonial slavery itself. Political abolitionists were more equivocal about the use of violence, which they saw as a reasonable and potentially effective response to Southern slaveholding intransigence.

The British and Foreign Anti-Slavery Society, formed in 1839, had links to the American and Foreign, though some local anti-slavery societies (e.g. Dublin, Glasgow, Edinburgh) remained independent and aligned themselves with the Garrisonian American Anti-Slavery Society. Though sharing a common goal, each organization saw the other as ideological and economic competition. Douglass's success in Britain and Ireland provoked fears that his political position had begun to shift. In a letter to R.D. Webb from Boston, the grande dame of American anti-slavery, Maria Weston Chapman, expressed her reservations concerning the possible effects of his new-found fame and comparative wealth on Douglass, fearing that what she saw as his quest for economic independence augured a shift in his organizational loyalties. The letter, the contents of which were made known at a public reading of the letter from Chapman to a committee comprising James Haughton, the three Webb brothers and Richard Allen, as well as their guests, Douglass and James Buffum, concerns the growing rift between the American and British anti-slavery societies, and fears that Douglass would be 'bought up' by the London committee. 'I earnestly hope,' Chapman writes,

> he may not yield to temptation. When one work of concession, compro-
> mise or even a look marking a line of distinction drawn in *favour* of oneself
> between oneself and the American Society, will seem to promise so much of
> personal help and success, how hard not to say it.[9]

9 Quoted by Webb in letter to Chapman, Dublin, 16 May 1846, Boston Anti-Slavery Collection, Ms.A.1.2 v12 (2), No. 30.

Tensions already existed between Douglass and the Boston Anti-Slavery Society on two main issues: the organization's claim that the US Constitution was a pro-slavery document, and the exclusive use of moral suasion as a means of effecting abolition. William and Jane Pease argue that Douglass early rejected 'orthodox opposition to any action which might support a proslavery Constitution',[10] citing the remark of Edmund Quincy in a letter to Caroline Weston in 1844 – a year and a half before Douglass's departure – that 'we may yet see him fighting against us openly'.[11] There were also indications of dissent during Douglass's time in Ireland, apparently stemming from his belief that abolitionist agents should avoid involvement with other reform movements and concentrate exclusively on the issue of slavery. Douglass's position on this was long-standing and had already been the cause of some conflict in the United States. A very public dispute had erupted in 1843 in Syracuse when Douglass and Remond publicly denounced John Collins – who ended the anti-slavery convention a day early in order to facilitate his anti-property interests – as prostituting the anti-slavery movement for irrelevant ends.[12] In Ireland, a letter to Webb from Limerick dealing with a suggestion that he share a platform in Scotland with H.C. Wright, sees Douglass arguing:

> As to accompanying Friend Wright, I think it unwise to do so. I by no means agree with him as to the importance of his discussing in this country the disunion question, and I think our difference in this matter would prevent that harmony necessary to success. Beside our friend Wright has created against himself prejudices which I as an abolitionist do not feel myself called upon to withstand. ... [He] is identified with doctrines for which I do not wish to seem responsible. He is truly a reformer in general; I only claim to be a man of one idea.[13]

In the event, Douglass did tour Scotland with Wright and Buffum on the 'Send Back the Money' campaign. But a significant debate regarding the virtue of abolitionist engagement with other reform movements,

---

10 William H. Pease and Jane H. Pease, 'Boston Garrisonians and the Program of Frederick Douglass', *Canadian Journal of History*, 11 (September 1967), pp. 29–47 (38).

11 Quincy to Caroline Weston, 9 March 1844, Weston Papers, quoted in Pease and Pease, 'Boston Garrisonians', p. 40.

12 See Pease and Pease, 'Boston Garrisonians', p. 32. A notable exception to Douglass's stance on this issue was his attitude to temperance reform in Ireland. Though Douglass never lectured exclusively on the issue of temperance, he was willing to adopt the temperance platform and the rhetoric of drunkenness and sobriety to his own expressive ends (see Jenkins 'Beyond the Pale', pp. 85–90). The letters to Garrison also indicate that Douglass felt strongly about the temperance issue and its merits in Ireland.

13 Douglass to Webb, Limerick, 10 November 1845, Boston Anti-Slavery Collection, Ms.A.1.2 v15, p. 76.

Chartism in particular, was ongoing. Garrison, who undertook his own
tour of the United Kingdom in 1846, was inclined to cross-class associations, tendencies disapproved of and strongly resisted by British abolitionists. In a letter to Samuel May concerning Garrison's interest in social
reform, for example, J.B. Estlin expressed the following opinion:

> To one subject I cannot avert without some regret: it is Mr Garrison's course
> of action on this side of the Atlantic. ... He seems to consider it necessary
> ... to meddle with all sorts of questions that divide the population of this
> country – 'Universal suffrage,' 'the rights of primogeniture,' 'the observance
> of the Sabbath,' ... etc etc, are discussed in public and pronounced upon by
> him. ... Were the middle and lower classes of this country the parties likely
> to do much for the Am. Aboln. Cause, there might be some use in courting
> their favour, even at the risk of offending higher circles. ... But ... it is not
> kitchens and workshops that need anti-slavery agitation for America's sake,
> but our *drawing-rooms*, the salons of the wealthy, and the libraries of the
> learned.[14]

Taking the case up with Garrison himself, Estlin wrote: 'I think you
rather miscalculate the class of persons here who are most likely to benefit
your movement, and whom it was most desirable to enlighten. ... It is the
wealthy educated circles of this country whose desire to assist the abolitionists would do your cause most service.'[15]

Douglass's position on other social reform movements was clear.
Writing to Chapman of Douglass's wish to steer clear of anything other
than anti-slavery argument, Webb informed her that Douglass 'don't
incline to fraternise with HC Wright who is a far finer minded larger
hearted man than he is. It seems to me that Douglass's range is not large
and that he don't take half enough pains to extend its limits.'[16] A later
letter from Webb to Chapman addressing her concerns about the activities
of the London committee explains, 'I don't wonder at Douglass's having
met the British and Foreign as he has done. It must be difficult for him to
enter into your feelings on this matter, and he is not a man to enter into
what he don't comprehend.'[17]

Evidently Douglass neither appreciated the importance assumed
by the split in the transatlantic anti-slavery movement in abolitionist
circles, nor agreed with the radical wing of the movement as to the value
of popular and popularizing engagement with other reform movements.

14 Samuel May, Bristol, 1 October 1846, in Merrill, *Letters*, pp. 290–92.
15 J.B. Estlin to W.L. Garrison, Bristol, 17 October 1846, Boston Anti-Slavery Collection,
    Ms.A.1.2 v16, pp. 113–14.
16 Webb to Chapman, Dublin, 16 November 1845, Boston Anti-Slavery Collection,
    Ms.A.1.2.v15, pp. 78–79.
17 Webb to Chapman, Dublin, 16 July 1846, Weston Papers, Ms.A.9.2 v22, No. 75.

Understandably, he smarted under the suspicions expressed by Chapman – and, presumably, the very public manner in which they had been brought to his attention. In a rare moment of sensitivity, Webb admitted of Chapman's letter that he 'may not have been quite judicious in reading this to [Douglass]'. [18] On 29 March, Douglass wrote an outraged response to Chapman from Scotland, claiming that she 'betray[ed] a want of confidence in me as a man, and an abolitionist, utterly inconsistent with all the facts in the history of my connection with the Antislavery enterprise'. The letter continues:

> I can assure you dear Madam that you have mistaken me altogether if you suppose that either love of money – or the hate of poverty will drive me from the ranks of the old organized antislavery society. ... You have trusted me or seemed to do so, at home, why distrust me or seem to do so abroad. [19]

The difference of course was that Douglass, after initial introductions had been made, was not wholly dependent on the anti-slavery society for financial or, necessarily, organizational support, a position which differed from that obtained in the United States even after the publication of the *Narrative*. His popularity in Ireland, amongst women in particular, meant that he was never without accommodation, an audience or an income. Isabel Jennings, a member of the family with whom Douglass passed an extended stay in Cork, claimed that Douglass 'has gained friends wherever

18 Webb subsequently qualified this admission with the extenuation that 'he [Douglass] is a very much less sensible and magnanimous man, much less devoted to the cause and much more to himself than I took him to be. ... by my supposing that Douglass was a sensible man and that this advice or suggestion from one of his best friends would be taken in good part. F. Douglass was a very short time in my house, before I found him to be absurdly haughty, self-possessed, and prone to take offence. ... I do not mean to say or to insinuate anything to his prejudice as a public man. He has worked well and has not shown any disposition but what is straightforward and upright. In his money transactions he has been most honourable – and I have of late years been disposed to distrust any professions which are not accompanied by a strict sense of *meum & tuum*. But if his balance of mind, his good temper and his forbearance are not much lessened by his visit to Europe, I am greatly mistaken' (R.D. Webb to M. Weston Chapman, Dublin, 16 May 1846, Weston Papers, Ms.A.9.2 v22, No 51).

19 Douglass to Maria Weston Chapman, Kilmarnock, Scotland, 29 March 1846, Weston Papers, Ms.A.9.2 v22, No. 35. Chapman's letter obviously continued to rankle. It is mentioned in a letter from Buffum to Chapman date some months later includes a postscript: 'I meant to have stated before this that Frederick is not satisfied with a reference you made in one of your letters to R.D. Webb, *that he would* be likely to be influenced by the great temptations in this country and especially that of money – which he says he says that he has given you no reason to entertain – he is quite *sensitive* on that *point*' (Buffum to Chapman, Perth, 26 June 1846, Weston Papers, Ms.A.9.2 v22, No. 67).

he has been – he is indeed a wonderful man. ... He is the first intelligent *slave* who has ever visited Cork and it is only natural that he should excite more sympathy than any of the others.'[20] Somewhat perversely, race and enslavement, which had – until the publication of the *Narrative* at least[21] – undermined his intellectual and moral credibility in the United States and created a dependence on organizational support from abolitionists, became his greatest asset in Great Britain and Ireland. Douglass wrote to Francis Jackson:

> I am hardly black enough for British taste, but by keeping my hair as woolly as possible I make out to pass for at least half a Negro at any rate. My good friend Buffum finds the tables turned on him here completely – the people lavish nearly all of their attention on the Nigger.[22]

Sales of the *Narrative* indicate that that attention was translated into the commercial success that some in Boston found disquieting, and which underlined an increasing potential for ideological as well as economic independence.

So, the *Narrative*, as an economic as well as literary or ideological entity, became the cause of some friction between Douglass and Chapman. And it was the *Narrative* that went some way towards healing the rift. Douglass arranged with Webb to replace the closing frame of the original *Narrative* – the poem 'A Parody': 'a portrait,' Douglass claimed 'of the religion of the south ... which I soberly affirm is "true to life," and

---

20 Isabel Jennings to Maria Weston Chapman, n.d. 1844, Weston Papers, Ms.A.9.2 v20, No. 145.

21 See Henry Louis Gates Jr, 'From Douglass to Wheatley: The Politics of Displacement', in Eric J. Sundquist, ed., *Frederick Douglass: New Literary and Historical Essays* (Cambridge: Cambridge University Press, 1993), pp. 47–65.

22 Douglass to Jackson, Royal Hotel, Dundee, Scotland, 29 January 1846, Boston Anti-Slavery Collection, Ms.1.2 v16, p. 13. Isabel Jennings's letter to Maria Weston Chapman also opined, 'We think we have got contributions from persons belonging to the Church (of Ireland) who never could have been influenced except by a person who had himself suffered. ... they say "Mr Douglass said so and so – his authority is given – and who can no better than he"' (n.d. 1844, Weston Papers, Ms.A.9.2 v20, No. 145). From Belfast came a letter to Chapman, again attributing the success of the anti-slavery cause to Douglass: 'An intense interest has been excited by the oratory of Frederick Douglass during his late visit to this town and in consequence a female anti-slavery society is about being formed just at present. All who have listened to D— are warm in the cause of the slave, many are earnest and apologetic and if a fair development of these impulses were permitted I am convinced that there is scarcely a lady in Belfast who would not be anxious to join in any means calculated to promote the enfranchisement of the deeply injured Africans' (Mary Ireland to M.W. Chapman, R.A. Institution, Belfast, 24 January 1846, Weston Papers, Ms.9.2 v22, No. 14).

without caricature or the slightest exaggeration'[23] – with a new appeal, 'To the Friends of the Slave'.[24] This addition, a direct address to an imagined, liberal constituency created within the parameters of the slave narrative, details the activities of the American Anti-Slavery Society and advocates the support of the general public for the Society's work. The

23 Frederick Douglass, *Narrative of the Life of Frederick Douglass, An American Slave, Written by Himself* (Boston: Boston Anti-Slavery Society, 1845), p. 123.
24 The addition to the variant first and second Irish editions reads as follows:

TO THE FRIENDS OF THE SLAVE

Whoever may have been moved by the perusal of the foregoing pages, to *do* something for the abolition of Slavery in the United States, is informed that a society called the American Anti-Slavery Society is in active operation for this purpose. Its members have given their lives to the work, in full determination to spare no effort for the attainment of their object. Amongst the means which they employ are the following:

They publish a weekly newspaper in New York, called the North Anti-Slavery Standard, which is solely devoted to the advocacy of anti-slavery principles, and to the exposure of the religious, political and social evils of slavery.

They also circulate pamphlets and tracts, for the elucidation of such of their views as could not be suitably set forth in the ephemeral pages of a newspaper.

They send throughout the Free States, agents devoted to the cause, for the purpose of stirring up the public mind, and awakening the conscience of the people by lectures and public meetings. They rely more upon the promulgation of sound principles and a correct state of public sentiment, than upon any other instrumentality, for the over throw of American slavery. It is clear, from the popular character of the government of the United States, that every improvement in the institutions of that country must be preceded by a corresponding change in the minds of the people.

These means have been in operation for nearly fourteen years, and, in the face of violent opposition and appalling difficulties, have had a powerful influence in quickening the action of religious bodies and political parties, and in mitigating the shameful prejudice against colour.

The necessary funds have been obtained by extraordinary munificence on the part of a few, and at great personal sacrifice by the poorer friends of the cause.

The Boston Female Anti-Slavery Society (auxiliary to the national society, and one of its most effective coadjutors) hold an Annual Bazaar in Boston, which has for a few years past received some assistance from ladies in Great Britain and Ireland. It is now respectfully suggested that the extent of this cooperation should be greatly increased. Contributions from the British Islands have a double value; the hearts of those who labour in the cause of humanity are cheered by these tokens of sympathy from the 'Old Country,' whilst the proceeds sustain the efforts of the Society.

Contributions to the British Anti-Slavery Bazaar of any articles of use or ornament, which will bear to be packed without injury, ladies fancy work, or the products of manufactories, especially of such works of taste or art as are not manufactured in the United States; in fine, any products of British taste or industry, as well as donations of money, will be appropriated in an effectual manner for the promotion of the cause. (Frederick Douglass, *Narrative of the Life of Frederick Douglass, An American Slave, Written by Himself*, 2nd Irish edn [Dublin: Webb & Chapman, 1846], pp. 123–24)

text outlines and upholds the doctrine of moral suasion adopted by the Garrisonians, insisting that 'every improvement in the institutions of ... [the United States] must be preceded by a corresponding change in the minds of the people'. Thus amended, the text, and by extension Douglass himself, are publicly aligned with the American Anti-Slavery Society and its economic as well as political activities.

In addition to its clear statement of ideological affiliation, the appendix proposes that the links already extant between the 'friends of the slave' in Europe and the United States be considerably strengthened, in particular those connections which generated income for the cause, the annual anti-slavery bazaars organized by the Ladies' Societies. Douglass pointed to the changes in the *Narrative* as proof of his commitment and loyalty to the American Society. In the same letter in which he takes her to task for her 'want of confidence in me as a man, and an abolitionist', Douglass informs Chapman:

> I have inserted an appeal on behalf of the Bazaar in my narrative, so that wherever the narrative goes–there also goes an appeal on behalf of the old organized Anti-Slavery Bazaar. One of the first objects in my lectures has been to make that Bazaar prominent and increase its success by increasing its means. I have done so from no sordid motive, but because I believe it to be a powerful instrument in affording means to carry on our important antislavery machinery.[25]

The inclusion of the appeal stresses the economic connection between the slave narrative and the anti-slavery movement, foregrounding the narrative's capacity to disseminate information and opinion *and* garner financial as well as political support. And importantly from Chapman's point of view, the addition also recognized the central economic role played by the ladies' auxiliaries in the success and promotion of the anti-slavery cause. The bazaars were fund-raising events where items – handmade articles of clothing, bed linen, etc. produced and donated by women members – were sold in order to support the activities and salaries of full-time agents of the Society. The appeal for support of the bazaars publicly acknowledges, within the framework of what had quickly become anti-slavery's seminal text – Douglass's *Narrative* – the central role played by women in the movement's organizational and financial survival. Thus, Douglass's additional textual frame goes beyond support of the ideological parameters of American abolitionism to reflect and create the feminized profile of the organization's financial activities.

Moreover, the appeal for contributions lists those ladies – in alpha-

25 Douglass to Chapman, Kilmarnock, Scotland, 29 March 1846, Weston Papers, Ms.A.9.2 v22, No. 35.

betical order according to their address – in charge of collecting goods and other contributions towards the Annual Boston Bazaar, the most important single source of revenue for the movement. The list, including some thirty-one ladies in all, provides testimony to the individual and collective economic agency of middle- and upper-class abolitionist women in Britain and Ireland. By extending its geographical reach into Europe through the inclusion of the names and addresses of women activists, the text not only stakes a territorial claim in Europe for the American Society, it maps out another political space, that of feminine economic and organizational agency within abolitionism. The appendix thereby provides abolitionist women with a clearly defined, transatlantic identity, an identity based on economic activity and linked to the quest for human and civil rights for the slave. To some extent, then, the new appendix of the Irish editions, intended to assuage fears of defection to the British and Foreign Anti-Slavery Society, reconfigures Douglass's text as the site of an unacknowledged and often silent struggle *within* abolitionism for the promotion of female power in the public sphere.

The existence of this silent struggle may go some way towards explaining Douglass's overwhelming popularity among women in Britain and Ireland, when many men found him reserved and even difficult. His female following was often cynically attributed to what were considered his striking good looks and masculine charm, rather than to any tangible moral or political commitment on the part of the women concerned. But from the late eighteenth century onwards, anti-slavery had provided a vehicle for women in Britain and Ireland to enter into political debate and influence policy-making in a way that appeared not to threaten the domestic social order in terms of its gender or class structures.[26] By the time of Douglass's visit to Ireland, the Ladies' Associations existed as independent auxiliary bodies to the Hibernian Anti-Slavery Society, holding their own meetings, organizing fund-raisers, liaising with the female wing of the American society and perhaps most importantly producing their own texts.

26 For a discussion of anti-slavery text produced by élite women in Ireland in the late eighteenth and early nineteenth century, see Ninni Rodgers, 'Two Quakers and a Utilitarian: The Reaction of Three Irish Women Writers to the Problem of Slavery, 1789–1807', *Proceedings of the Royal Irish Academy*, 100C.4 (2000), pp. 137–57. The popular sentimental fiction of the day included Maria Edgeworth's 'The Grateful Negro', originally published in 1804 as part of the collection *Popular Tales*, and which vacillates between anti-slavery sentiment and affiliation to class hierarchies. See Maria Edgeworth, 'The Grateful Negro', in Anne K. Mellor and Richard E. Matlock, eds, *British Literature, 1780–1930* (Fort Worth: Harcourt Brace College Publishers, 1996), pp. 546–55.

The Dublin Ladies' Association, for example, had been producing anti-slavery tracts from as early as 1836. The publications of the Association address the 'Females of Ireland' as a discrete, active and numerous political constituency. The *Second Appeal from the Dublin Ladies' Association*,[27] to take one case, petitions its 'Beloved Countrywomen … ye who have already contributed your mite of influence by enrolling your names among the many thousands of our signatures, and on these speaking pages have entered your protest against oppression, pause not yet; another work remains for you to do.'[28] Though clearly embedded in the master discourse of slavery, this tract cannot be reduced to the conformist argument of racial struggle that regulates the production of textual meaning in official abolitionist doctrine. Its objective is not merely to promote the anti-slavery cause and to effect complete abolition by reproducing abolitionist ideas concerning slavery, but to establish an active political identity for a gendered feminine subject, who is seen to have, and exercise, real power. The text continues, in a reference to Victoria's recent ascent to the British throne, and linking the plight of American slaves with the bondage of the Israelites in Egypt:

> We rejoice to remind you that the time is near at hand when this subject will be submitted to the youthful and philanthropic Sovereign of these realms. 'That where her power is felt, / mankind may feel her mercy too.'… Let us use this one powerful engine, dear friends, until the sordid proprietor of the West, wearied out at length, and overcome by the many devices of benevolence, is driven to exclaim, perhaps in the bitterness of a royal Pharaoh, '*It is enough: let them go free.*'

Cynthia Hamilton argues that where victimization of male slaves occurs in the writing of white abolitionists, 'the male slave's emasculation prompts a corresponding aggrandisement of the abolitionist, whose active agency on behalf of the immobilised slave takes on heroic proportions'.[29] Much the same argument can be made of the work of élite Irish women. The racial struggle, which is repeatedly configured in terms of sexual/ gendered contest,[30] prompts an ennobled image of European femininity

27 *Second Appeal to the Dublin Ladies' Association to the Females of Ireland*, signed Catherine Elizabeth Alma, Corresponding Secretary, Blackrock, near Dublin, 26 October 1837 (George Ridings, Printer, 34 Patrick Street, Cork). Copy in the Goldsmith's Special Collection of Economic Literature, Senate House, London. Hereafter referred to as *Second Appeal*.

28 *Second Appeal*, p. 1.

29 Cynthia S. Hamilton, 'The Gender Politics of Reform', in Alan J. Rice and Martin Crawford, eds, *Liberating Sojourn: Frederick Douglass and Transatlantic Reform* (Athens, GA, and London: University of Georgia Press, 1999), pp. 73–92 (78).

30 This includes the feminization of slavery and the depiction of emasculated slaves:

striving on behalf of the disempowered slave. Interestingly, the *Appeal* also includes a cross-racial identification with women in bondage, at the mercy of predatory and immoral men, and whose fate rests on Britain's adherence to its somewhat marital obligations to its colonial subjects: '[W]oman is to plead with *woman* on behalf of her own sex, wretched, ruined and degraded, still held in bondage in our *Christian* colonies, and fearing with many fears that their bondage will be *lengthened if Britain be not faithful.*' In the *Appeal*, the fight for abolition is allegorically reproduced as a conflict between masculine and feminine values in the public sphere, each striving for political ascendency. Like the slave narrative, the standard propaganda text of anti-slavery, the *Appeal* relies on the representation of slavery as a chimeric violation of the Victorian cult of domesticity, typified by the brutality and violence inflicted on female slaves; but it also significantly modifies the gender code which everywhere overdetermines these narratives. Not only is the role of representative victim of slavery recast as male rather than female, ('He toils as a *Slave*, yet he feels as a man') the domestic institution is reconfigured as that of a jaded, political masculinity associated with western expansion, an atavistic reign incompatible with more enlightened feminine forms of power.

There is of course a degree of wishful thinking at work here. Although the rhetoric of the Ladies' Society plays on the nineteenth-century sentimental paradigm of the 'Empire of the Mother', it occurs, as does the broader abolitionist debate, in the context of the rising British Empire, suggesting that any reading of the conflict between Victoria and Pharaoh must address the issue of British imperial ambition. In this pamphlet, Britain replaces ancient Egypt, as Victoria replaces Pharaoh, as the major agent of western civilization, in realization of *translatio imperii*. This subtext of gender conflict, which persists throughout the writing of anti-slavery women, provides an ongoing, internal challenge to social hierarchies often unrelated to the issue of slavery. Textual emergence in the *Narrative* for those women part of an enlightened struggle for human rights acknowledges their comparable negotiation of the model of subjectivity to which the slave aspired; it is to their achievement in this regard that the *Narrative* testified.

Moreover, despite the undeniable tensions that emerged between Douglass and the American movement during his time in Ireland, his initial credibility did stem from his association with the Boston Society,

'Slavery ... may attire herself in the gay garb of a pretended freedom ... nevertheless, her heart, true to its nature, whispers that she is *Slavery* still. The iron of bitterest bondage still enters into the soul of her victim, and, though he lives, it is but to drag out a hated existence. He toils as a *Slave*, yet he feels as a man' (*Second Appeal*, p. 1, emphasis original).

and Garrison and Chapman in particular. Likewise, the many Ladies' Anti-Slavery Societies seem to have relied on Chapman's standing and respectability as a *raison d'être*, and as validation of the claims of visiting abolitionists such as Douglass. Writing in early 1846, Mary Ireland of the Belfast Ladies' Anti-Slavery Society, remarked to Chapman that

> even your *name* will do much. It was first whispered, but *dare not now be repeated*, that Frederick Douglass was an impostor – it has also been insinuated that C.L. Remond was a white man who had assumed the Ethiop tinge to suit a purpose, but every heart is filled with admiration of Mrs Chapman.[31]

To some extent then, the Irish editions of Douglass's *Narrative* formally reproduce a framework of dual, even mutually dependent emergence, that of the enslaved *and* feminine subject, into the economic matrix of western subjectivity.

While the formal changes to the *Narrative* in the Irish editions became a means of asserting the economic role and influence of the female anti-slavery societies, and balancing the hitherto exclusively masculine configuration of Douglass's work, the inclusion of another opening frame complicates any easy reading of those gestures as radicalizations of the central political argument to include the unequal socio-political position of women. Included on the title page is a verse by John Greenleaf Whittier, which runs as follows:

> What ho! – our countrymen in chains!
> The whip on *woman's* shrinking flesh!
> Our soil still reddening with the stains,
> Caught from her scourging, warm and fresh!
> What! Mothers from their children riven!
> What! God's own image bought and sold!
> Americans to market driven,
> And barter'd, as the brute, for gold![32]

It would be difficult to find a more representative instance of the canonical relationship between the theme of slavery and either the sentimental tradition in literature, or the cult of domesticity. Typically in this model, slavery is portrayed as the grossest violation of the domestic ideal, conjuring images of violence and the abuse of female bodies, the threat to modesty and perhaps even chastity, the sundering of the idealized relationship between mother and child, and the concomitant offences to God and natural religion. Hamilton has remarked on the tendency within

31 Mary Ireland to M. Weston Chapman, 24 January 1846, Weston Papers, Ms.A.9.2 v22, No. 14.
32 Douglass, *Narrative*, 2nd Irish edn, n.p. Whittier's anti-slavery poems were published as a collection the same year (1886) under the title *Voices of Freedom*.

the slave narrative to include 'episodes of extreme cruelty that have been witnessed rather than experienced … [in order to allow] the ex-slave to provide evidence of victimisation without compromising his masculine integrity'.[33] Here, the verse from Whittier echoes the two incidences of female victimization to which Douglass is youthful voyeur and witness: the beating of his aunt Henny and his cousin Hester; and Douglass's early separation from his mother and later his grandmother. Far from emasculating the author, however, the frame repositions Douglass within the creative paradigm previously the exclusive preserve of the white male abolitionist. The frame reinforces Douglass's standing as an agent of individual resistance to a feminized (and arguably feminizing) system of slavery by reproducing the organizing trope of abolitionism – slavery as an abhorrent transgression of an idealized domesticity – in an external parallel of empowered masculinity, that of the American male poet. Inclusion of this frame allows the narrative to take, albeit surreptitiously, one more step towards the achievement of Douglass's second autobiography, *My Bondage and my Freedom*, which sees his self-promotion to the status of representative man. By emphasizing the literary or artistic as well as political domains contextualizing the *Narrative*, the poetic frame allows the text to bridge the divide between literature and polemic. For though clearly affiliated to the anti-slavery cause, Whittier's work is, self-evidently, literature, as witnessed by the exalted poetic form and tone of the piece. Its inclusion unites moral intention and artistic process, connecting the slave narrative with a loftier poetic form; with a reciprocal doubling between the intimate autobiographical content of the narrative and the more distanced conceit of sentimental verse. What can be read in the American edition as Douglass's feminization by the domesticating forces of male abolitionist authority, exemplified in the framing testimonies and their anti-Promethean effects, emerges in the Irish editions as Douglass's aspiration to the status of artist, and latent suggestion of a more Promethean understanding of narrative voice.

Portrait of the Artist

Acting in support of this reading is the inclusion of Douglass's portrait on the fly-leaf of every edition produced, American and Irish. Juxtaposed with the title page and its extended chiastic trope of literacy, slavery and American identity, the portrait of Douglass, every inch the Victorian gentleman, confirms his textually evolving identity as artist, historical witness and man of letters. The portrait was of considerable importance

---

33 Hamilton, 'Gender Politics of Reform', p. 79.

to Douglass as it provided visual confirmation of the modernity, sophistication and enlightened reason of his narrative voice. Its inclusion in the *Narrative* produced a 'modern' image of the slave, associated with literacy and textuality, and at odds with concurrent vernacular, performative, and pictorial representations of the period. These portrayed slaves and African Americans in general either as an unsophisticated group living in a premodern Southern environment, or as parodaic examples of class aspirants unsuccessfully imitating their betters. An indication of the importance attributed by Douglass to his physical image can be seen in the correspondence with Webb concerning the production of the variant first and second Irish editions, when a new portrait was commissioned. Douglass was unhappy with the new portrait, which was included in the variant edition and dropped from the second, which reverted to a reproduction of the American lithograph.[34]

Aside from its function as a 'portrait of the artist', visually re-enforcing the textual aspirations of the narrative, however, the image also produces a particular *class* identity for Douglass, who is portrayed seated, immaculately attired in the costume of the gentleman scholar, a frown of concentration and sincerity creasing his brow. The portrayal is a far cry from contemporary American representations of 'Dandy Jim', the Broadway swell, who more commonly provided an unflattering image of African American social mobility and class aspiration, and, indeed, from the iconic representation of the bound and kneeling slave which had previously graced abolitionist texts, slave narratives and even society tea-services. Indeed, arguably the portrait reproduces Douglass in the image of the Southern gentleman, downplaying his association with liberal Northern US culture and suggesting his innate affiliation with Southern aristocratic codes of chivalry, honour and old money.

As already noted, Douglass's popularity among women was attributed, by men, to the handsome, well-dressed aspect he presented. Even Webb, never one to bandy compliments, described Douglass's physique as 'stately and majestic—with an air that makes Garrison a mere baby beside him'.[35] His association with women also drew remark. John Estlin wrote shortly after Douglass's arrival in Britain:

> You can hardly imagine how he is noticed – petted I may say by ladies. Some of them really a little exceed the bounds of propriety, or delicacy, as far as appearances are concerned. ... I doubt if he forms intimacies much with

---

34 See Douglass to Webb, Dundee, 10 February 1846; Glasgow, 16 April 1846, Boston Anti-Slavery Collection, Ms.A.1.2 v16, p. 16, and Ms.A.1.2 v16, p. 32.
35 Webb to Chapman, Dublin, 31 October 1846, Weston Papers, Ms.A.9.2 v22, No. 109.

gentlemen. ... My fear is that often associating so much with white women of education and refined taste and manners, he will feel a 'craving void' when he returns to his own family.[36]

This remark of course combines an incipient racism with well-developed class prejudice. It also indicates, however, that Douglass's social contact with women was considerable, and the interest between them reciprocal. And this interest paid mutual dividends: the ladies' attentions to Douglass facilitated their entry to political discourse and proved profitable in their eventual inclusion in the *Narrative*, whose shifting form embraced and acknowledged their anti-slavery efforts; Douglass, meanwhile, reaped the social benefits of his popularity and charm, becoming part of fashionable society in Britain and shedding, in public at least, the last relics of the class associations of his American roots. The support and interest of women provided Douglass with access to the upper echelons of power and privilege, strata for which a certain income and persona were necessary, but no guarantee of success. Mutual cultivation then produced mutual benefits, which included economic success, the consolidation of class and political status, and a degree of public recognition and empowerment across the spectrum of class, gender and race.

The *Narrative*, in its variant Irish editions, significantly augments the scope and consequence of the slave narrative in economic, gender and class terms. Douglass's Irish tour was more than just a moral crusade against slavery, it provided financial underpinning to his subsequent class rise and linked economic success to future ideological independence. This shift is reflected in the changing form of the narrative, as are several of the complex negotiations of gender-roles and articulations of female agency in abolitionist circles it incorporates. By courting Douglass, women gained access to a politicized clique, and earned textual recognition for their economic activity in a transatlantic arena. Douglass, in his turn, was able to avail of the social opportunities provided by his close associations with abolitionist women, who acted as mediators in upper-class social circles. This mutual assistance is, however, somewhat compromised by the gendered rhetoric of the Ladies' Associations, and by Douglass's interest in producing a masculine identity which was both figuratively liberating and promoted the artistic merits of his autobiographical narrative. Ultimately, these formal changes, which underline the literary and economic as well as moral power of the slave narrative, illustrate some of the competing claims and shifting loyalties arising as subtexts to the master narrative of the 'domestic institution'.

---

36 J.B. Estlin to Samuel May, Bristol, 12 January 1847, in Merrill, *Letters*, p. 310.

Chapter 3

An American Slave:
Representing the Creole Self

The overseas editions of Douglass's autobiography repositioned the *Narrative* as a forum in which transnational power relations and the struggle for agency were mediated. Such repositioning helps illustrate the opportunities provided to Douglass by the slave narrative genre, particularly in terms of its semantic engagement with pro- and anti-slavery discourse, and related negotiation of the domestic divide between North and South in the United States. For the transnational *Narrative* not only establishes the international impact of anti-slavery activity, it also enables new national readings. It is therefore useful to review the transatlantic *Narratives* against the literary and political context provided by the United States at mid-century.

The United States at this point reflected the changing circumstances of American self-definition. National identity was being refashioned amidst the competing pulls of North, South and West. None was immune to the problems of slavery. One of the major national debates of the period concerned western expansion, specifically the issue of slavery and its legality in the newly incorporated territories. Although discussions of western expansion in US culture have emphasized the primacy of the frontier experience – civilization's encounter with savagery leading to the metaphysical triumph of freedom within the American cultural imaginary – the frontier territories also involved more earthly considerations of liberty at an historical moment in the United States notable for its ideological divisions. Nebraska and Texas illustrate that locations beyond North and South were increasingly stages upon which the realities as well as the debates around freedom and bondage were played out.

Much of that debate took place in the Northeast, Douglass's home after his escape from Maryland in 1838. New England was also the home of the American Renaissance, and the transcendentalist vision underpinned by romantic ideals of nature and freedom that informed it. F.O. Matthiesson writes that the 'democratic core of North Eastern transcendentalism believed that an American historian must write in the interests of mankind, in the spirit of the nineteenth-century'.[1] At the heart of that 'democratic core' lay an ideal of freedom, an ideal increasingly confronted by the reality of slavery. Douglass's work, which combines personal history with social critique and an impulse towards reform, may be placed within the Renaissance camp. As Andrews argues, 'in an era charged with revolutionary romanticism ... the slave who endeavors to recover his freedom is associating with himself no small part of the romance of the time'.[2]

Transatlantic influence was at the heart of the romantic strain of American writing during a period in which slavery and freedom played an ever-increasing role in establishing literary identity in the United States. For black and white Americans alike, literary culture resonated with the influences and experiences of Atlantic transnationalism. Elisa Tamarkin even suggests that, for African Americans in particular, Britain became an imaginary domain in which blacks, as 'de facto cosmopolitans, [could] ... offer white Americans [a] ... vision ... of an idealized, civilized world in which the highest cultural accomplishment is a likeness to Britain'.[3]

Douglass's sojourn in the United Kingdom was marked by the Anglophilia Tamarkin notes, an Anglophilia expressed in many of the letters home to Garrison written during the period. At the same time, the *Narrative* came to bear the traces of Douglass's travels and contacts overseas. But the autobiographical narrative at the core of the text, which charts Douglass's struggle for a selfhood rising above the imaginative and social constraints of his early enslavement, is also structured around a number of metaphorical and actual journeys. Those journeys include Douglass's acquisition of literacy, his passage to manhood, and eventually his escape to freedom in the North.

Progress towards freedom therefore is expressed in terms of a move away from Southern structures of power and towards a Northern horizon. That horizon becomes, in literary and political terms, a rebirth. The move north meant Douglass could write and publish a work detailing his progress from a state of oppression to one of liberation; the *Narrative* represents the culmination of his journey from silence into articulation,

1 F.O. Matthiesson, *American Renaissance: Art and Expression in the Age of Emerson and Whitman* (London: Oxford University Press, 1968), p. 633. Matthiesson also discusses the influence of Coleridge (pp. 133–75); the links with German Romanticism (p. 629), and cites the importance of the Romantic vision of organic nature and society on US transcendentalists.
2 William Andrews, *To Tell a Free Story: The First Century of Afro-American Autobiography, 1760–1865* (Urbana, IL: University of Illinois Press, 1986), p. 98.
3 See Eliza Tamarkin, 'Black Anglophilia; or, the Sociability of Antislavery', *American Literary History*, 14.3 (2002), pp. 444–78 (473).

from plantocratic to democratic society. Douglass's intellectual worth is confirmed when he crosses the border, when he exceeds the intellectual and geographic parameters of slavery.

The *Narrative* therefore charts a cultural as well as political journey, a journey mirrored in the use of chiasmus or narrative crossing. In Douglass's case, that crossing was also literal, mirroring his passage from slavehood to subjectivity. The transition is formulated in the most famous instance of chiasmus in the *Narrative*, namely, 'You have seen how a man was made a slave; you shall see how a slave was made a man,'[4] which is followed by a description of Douglass's emerging consciousness and the actions taken to establish it. Material rather than metaphysical freedom, however, as the *Narrative* demonstrates, is only possible outside the slave South, and it is the political culture of the North that enables the full expression of Douglass's manhood. The embedded cross-border quality to this and many other slave narratives therefore suggests that the genre might usefully be understood as bridging Northern and Southern US value systems.

As such, the genre is a forum for the exploration of a range of national concerns, but particularly of the meaning, and means to, freedom. The cross-border, transformative quality of the chiastic structure is mirrored in the title of the *Narrative*, with the parallel tensions of the 'man/ slave' of the one echoed in the 'American/slave' of the other. Indeed, to describe the antithetical '*American Slave*' of Douglass's title as an early literary expression of the American 'house divided' is perhaps to state the obvious. But it also helps to emphasize that, in the antebellum period, slaves, individually and collectively, were key actors in the definition, synthesis and transformation of public opinion around slavery, the root of that division.

Narrative Models, North and South

A transformation of this kind was at the heart of Douglass's agenda. His work bridges the fault line between Southern aristocratic and Northern democratic culture, weaving elements of non-modern Southern culture into liberal democratic literary form. The *Narrative*, though published in the North and detailing the beginning of Douglass's public career, is largely an account of his Southern childhood and adolescence. It charts his formative years and the influences he was to carry with him to freedom on the North, illustrating that although Douglass could not be confined by his early Southern experience, that experience did to some extent define him.

4 Douglass, *Autobiographies*.

What then were the intellectual and other legacies of Douglass's Southern upbringing? Anne Goodwyn Jones suggests that Douglass's 'primary identification as a man was not as an idealized Northern bourgeois but as a white Southern master', pointing to the early gender identification that led Douglass to a determination 'to make himself into a gentleman'.[5] The details of the narrative certainly lend credence to this view. Douglass's childhood was split between the rural Eastern shore and Baltimore, during which time his duties were largely domestic. Until he was hired out on the Covey farm, that experience was also primarily urban.[6] Later, his apprenticeship and subsequent employment as a caulker in Baltimore introduced him to the world of wage labour, when he was permitted by his master, Hugh Auld, to keep at least some of the money he earned. This provided him with an albeit small disposable income, and therefore a degree of freedom within the confines of the city. The suggestion that Douglass was the son of his white master aside, his position of relative privilege in the Auld household indicates a sustained exposure to the family experience of the slaveowning class. His confidence, manners, and command of standard English indicate that Douglass's social formation, and perhaps his social expectations, differed from those of the majority of slaves, perhaps even those of many free blacks in the period. These factors lend credence to Jones's view that Douglass admired the gender profile of Southern slaveholding patriarchy, even as he despised the system it underpinned: for all its shortcomings, Douglass's relationship with Auld might be characterized as a kind of 'benign patriarchy'.

A useful contrast with this and other masculine relationships Douglass experienced in the South is provided in the description of his life with the slavebreaker Covey. The fight with Covey, unprecedented in the *Narrative* despite the many scenes of cruelty, more often than not against women, to which Douglass has been witness, has generally been read as a psychological rite of passage into manhood. The *Narrative* portrays Covey as not only cruel and brutish, but as unworthy, morally and socially, of the authority he wields. Covey's low class status – he is little more than a farm labourer himself – marks him out within the logic of the narrative as the appropriate target for Douglass's rage, one against whom he can rebel

---

5   Anne Goodwyn Jones, 'Engendered in the South: Blood and Irony in Douglass and Jacobs', in Alan J. Rice and Martin Crawford, eds, *Liberating Sojourn: Frederick Douglass and Transatlantic Reform* (Athens, GA, and London: University of Georgia Press, 1999), pp. 93–111 (104).

6   Franklin W. Knight points out that the experience of field and urban slaves differed substantially in three respects: firstly, the kind of labour engaged in, linked to an ability to engage in the cash economy; secondly, the social and sexual conduct typical of the two classes; and thirdly, the available legal resources.

on the grounds of racial equality, but in a contest in which patriarchy per se is never threatened. Arguably, the fight with Covey enacts a kind of displaced Oedipal struggle against the absent father/master Douglass will never fully know. The relationship with Covey also stands as a proxy for Douglass's relationship with Auld, an association that ends in flight rather than fight.

Thematically then, the *Narrative* explores the influence of Southern codes of manhood on Douglass's early self-fashioning. Narratively, on the other hand, Douglass's work problematizes the relationship between the slave narrative and another representative US literary form, autobiography.[7] Since Franklin, autobiography has been considered part of the exceptionalism of American writing, linked to the rise of capitalism and US forms of democracy.[8] It is quintessentially a Northern US form, the mainstay of the myth of the self-made man. It has also been instrumental in fixing a particular image of US subjectivity, reproducing the stable, autonomous self of the Enlightenment ideal, in an intellectual tradition that, according to Houston Baker, privileges '[e]gotism, self-consciousness, and a deep and abiding concern with the individual'.[9]

The slave narrative presents obvious complications to any tendency to privilege individuality and the developmental self – Northern values by no means hegemonic at the time at which Douglas was writing. The slave narrative also encounters practical obstacles to the achievement of autobiographical form in the Franklinian mode. One problem is the privilege given to the written word over the oral in autobiography, a complication compounded by the presence of amanuenses in many published narratives. This presents a subject distanced from itself by the layers of mediation through which that self is filtered before appearing finally in print. A related problem is the dependency on sponsorship, seen as shaping individual narratives in the interests of a particular political agenda, again casting doubt on the 'truth' of the final representation.

7 See Sekora, 'Black Message/White Envelope', pp. 482–515; and John Sekora, 'Is the Slave Narrative a Species of Autobiography?', in James Olney, ed., *Studies in Autobiography* (New York and Oxford: Oxford University Press, 1988), pp. 99–111.

8 Benjamin Franklin, *The Works of Dr Benjamin Franklin: Consisting of Essays, Humerous, Moral and Literary, with His Life, Written by Himself* (London: J. Limbird, 1824).

9 Houston A. Baker Jr, 'Autobiographical Acts and the Voice of the Southern Slave', in Charles T. Davis and Henry Louis Gates Jr, eds, *The Slave's Narrative* (Oxford and New York: Oxford University Press), pp. 242–61 (242). For a discussion of the exceptionalism of US autobiographic versions of the self in the nineteenth century, see Albert E. Stone, *Autobiographical Occasions and Original Acts: Versions of American Identity from Henry Adams to Nate Shaw* (Philadelphia: University of Pennsylvania Press, 1982).

The *Narrative* overcomes many of these obstacles, creating a literate, rational self and eventually demonstrating Douglass's independence as a literary agent. James Olney describes the work as operating 'both within and against the Franklinesque tradition',[10] while William Andrews argues that by the 1840s, 'there was widespread recognition and acceptance of black autobiography as a uniquely American literary form'.[11] But the competing pulls on national identity during the nineteenth century raise questions regarding the status of Franklinian autobiography. Whether or not that form's privileging of a self-conscious, masculine, liberal self can be considered anything more than a regional form feeding into a complex national matrix is open to debate. Baker argues that the slave narrative, as part of the American autobiographical project of representative subjectivity, 'entails questions directed not only at the black voice in the South, but also toward the larger context of the American experiment as a whole'.[12] Douglass's writing, which fuses social and economic realities: the newness of identity with the search for origins, the traditionalism of the South with the modernity of the North, the reality of slavery with the will to freedom, can perhaps be considered more indicative of the 'American experiment' to which Baker alludes. Indeed the slave narrative's position within literary history also suggests that it is more representative than Franklinian autobiography, for it presents a racially heterogenous United States, and bears closer relation to the jeremiad and conversion narratives that preceded it.

Overcoming Franklin

Many of the major questions that arise in discussions of the form, however, concern authenticity. The limitations placed on Douglass have been often and well established by critics of the genre. Wilson J. Moses argues that Frederick Douglass's development 'as an artist and intellectual was circumscribed by the time and place in which he was born',[13] while Andrews

---

10 James Olney, 'The Founding Fathers: Frederick Douglass and Booker T. Washington', in Deborah McDowell and Arnold Rampersad, eds, *Slavery and the Literary Imagination* (Baltimore: Johns Hopkins University Press, 1989), pp. 1–24 (3). For a discussion of Douglass as an alter-ego or 'specific shade' to Franklin's representative selfhood, see Rafia Zafar, 'Franklinian Douglass: The Afro-American as Representative Man', in Eric J. Sundquist, ed., *Frederick Douglass: New Literary and Historical Essays* (New York and Cambridge: Cambridge University Press, 1990), pp. 99–117.

11 Andrews, *To Tell a Free Story*, p. 99.

12 Baker, 'Autobiographical Acts', pp. 242–61 (242).

13 Wilson J. Moses, '"Writing Freely?" Frederick Douglass and the Constraints of Racialised Writing', in Eric J. Sundquist, ed., *Frederick Douglass: New Literary and Historical Essays* (New York and Cambridge: Cambridge University Press, 1990), pp.

points out that, as African Americans 'could not assume an equal relationship with the average white American reader, [they] ... set about writing life stories that would somehow prove that they qualified as the moral, spiritual, or intellectual peers of whites'.[14]

Though written after Douglass's escape to the North, the *Narrative*, in the early days of its publication at least, might reasonably have been considered to represent the black voice in the South, even if the life it described was not typical of black Southern experience. Yet the critical concern to disentangle an authentic, uncorrupted black subjectivity, embedded in the slave narrative, from the white influences that were instrumental in shaping the finished product, remains. This often overlooks the major opposition in Douglass's work, which is less a conflict between black or white literary or ideological expression than a tension between liberal Northern and conservative Southern values. This tension suggests that the text may be representative in more ways than one; that the slave narrative, far from representing a restrictive and rigidly policed form, demonstrates great flexibility in form, function and cultural referents.

Formal examination of the Irish editions, for example, illustrates the work's capacity to remake itself in new spaces and contexts. Generic examination of the *Narrative* also helps to clarify the literary politics with which it contends. Robert Stepto locates Douglass's text within the generic evolution of slave narratives as a 'Phase III "generic narrative"', in which 'the narrative and moral energies of the former slave's voice and tale so resolutely dominate the narrative's authenticating machinery ... that the narrative becomes, in thrust and purpose, far more metaphorical than rhetorical'.[15] Phase III narratives shares considerable generic overlap with history, fiction, and autobiography. Stepto argues elsewhere that only when all of the parts comprising the slave narrative are produced and mediated by the slave-author can the text be considered truly to have acquired generic integrity as, say, autobiography.[16]

Stepto's schema are useful indicators of changes in the status of both narrator and text. They also help illuminate the processes by which textual authority was mediated and understood in the greater abolitionist arena.

66–83 (66–67). For a discussion of the history and influences on black autobiography see Stephen Butterfield, *Black Autobiography in America* (Amherst, MA: University of Massachusetts Press, 1977).

14 Andrews, *To Tell a Free Story*, p. 2.

15 Robert Stepto, '"I Rose and Found My Voice": Narration, Authentication and Authorial Control in Four Slave Narratives', in Charles T. Davis and Henry Louis Gates Jr, eds, *The Slave's Narrative* (Oxford and New York: Oxford University Press, 1982), pp. 225–41 (226).

16 See Stepto, *From Behind the Veil*.

Douglass's Irish texts are a case in point. The 'Preface' posits Douglass as mediator of his own text, supporting Andrews' contention that '[t]he enlistment of the self, through the autobiographical act, in the antislavery movement required, subtly and simultaneously, literary acts of resistance to the anti-slavery movement in order to preserve the text as autobiography and the narrator as an independent entity, something more than a coopted organisation man'. The vocabulary of that preface, however, confirms that, at this stage in his literary career, 'Douglass, still in many ways Garrison's man, would not authorise himself at Garrison's expense'.[17]

The appendices to the Irish texts also point to the changing context of the *Narrative*'s existence, reception and transatlantic significance. However, despite the multiple changes in form undergone by the text once outside the United States, the Irish texts consistently bear the same title and have recognizable 'slave narrative' form. For economic and polemical reasons, it was important to maintain the distinctions that separated the slave-narrative from autobiography, or, more importantly, fiction. Lee Jenkins notes that Douglass's chiastic statement, which echoes the antithesis of the title, represents his 'triumphant transvaluation of values, [which] resists the telos of closure'.[18] All editions of the *Narrative* maintain distinguishing marks of the conflict around slavery – chiasmus, antithesis, polemic. These cast the work as a microcosm of a national debate around slavery and selfhood that, like the *Narrative* itself, continued to resist political closure.

The antithesis also underlines the existence of political dialectics, including black and white, North and South, slavery and citizenship. The consistency of the external frame, therefore, illustrates Douglass's success in manipulating narrative convention to particular discursive ends. By exceeding the normative perimeter of black–white power relations as defined by the US context, the *Narrative* moves ever closer to the autobiographical genre. By retaining the contradictions of the external frame, the work also operates as autobiography's antithesis – the narrative of otherness.

Andrews describes this tension in the slave narrative in ideological terms, as, 'the struggle ... between its role as the work of a movement, identified by its consistency with the ideology of that movement, and its role as the text of an other, identified by its inconsistency, its unresolved relationship within and without the movement'.[19] By defining self and

---

17 Andrews, *To Tell a Free Story*, p. 138.
18 Lee Jenkins, '"Black O Connell"', pp. 24–25. See also Houston A. Baker, *Blues, Ideology and African-American Literature: A Vernacular Theory* (Chicago: University of Chicago Press, 1988), p. 7.
19 Andrews, *To Tell a Free Story*, pp. 105–106.

other as overlapping categories confined within the same literary frame, Douglass collapses the boundary between the two. Blackness is inscribed into the text of Americanness, in much the same way that the somewhat British glamour of Southern patriarchy is inscribed into the Northern narrative of the masculine developmental self. Beneath a title expressing the dialectical contradictions of the 'American', then, the narrative, and the life itself, allow the adversarial context of their production to mimic, and indeed ironize, parallel processes in US autobiography. The title and ideological context of Douglass's work allow him, through manipulation of genre, to create a self equivalent to, but never the same as, the Franklinian model.

The Value of Difference

One of the generic strengths of the slave narrative then lies in its ability to sustain difference. That difference might be expected to prevent the self ever being untied from the anchor of anti-slavery polemic. It should have proved inadequate to the representative needs of a nation requiring a 'unique tale, uniquely told, of a unique life'.[20] But, despite its highly conventionalized structure (and Irish variations aside), the slave narrative, properly used, could provide an unparalleled opportunity for social criticism, and indeed heroic selfhood. After all, what other writer could hope to initiate and survive the kind of attacks made on institutions of church and state, and (relatively) powerful individual slaveholders launched by slave narrators without incurring severe legal and moral sanction? Aside from the danger of recapture, a danger offset in Douglass's case by his flight from the United States in 1845, sanctions against slave narrators were relatively limited; the narrator remained safe behind the moral and textual sandbags provided by abolitionism. The organization, as Andrews points out, 'applauded rebellion against authority ... as a demonstration of Negro nobility and [welcomed] his censure of the republic ... a sign of the Negro's powers of analysis and argument'.[21]

Such reckoning as might occur could easily be contained by the slave narrative itself. An early example of this is provided by another slave narrative, the *History of Mary Prince*. This narrative was pruned by Prince's editor, Thomas Pringle, from a transcript made by one of his friends, Susanna Strickland. As a result of Prince's complaints regarding her treatment and efforts to secure her right of return to the Caribbean

20 James Olney, '"I was born": Slave Narratives, Their Status as Autobiography and as Literature', in Charles T. Davis and Henry Louis Gates Jr, eds, *The Slave's Narrative* (Oxford and New York: Oxford University Press, 1982), pp. 148–74 (148).
21 Andrews, *To Tell a Free Story*, p. 101.

as a free person, a hearing of her case was held in the British parliament, with many counter-charges levelled against her by her former owners. In an appendix to the *History*, these charges are refuted. Although the author of the refutation is Pringle rather than Prince, Prince is the source of his information. The *History* provides a safe forum where the accusations can be refuted without granting textual space to the pro-slavery camp.[22]

Like Prince's *History*, Douglass's *Narrative* illustrates the range of national and transnational debates that could be integrated into an increasingly plastic textual form. An example of this is provided in the second Irish edition of Douglass's text, which engages, from Britain, with a public letter written by A.C.C. Thompson, published in the *Delaware Republican* and subsequently in the *Liberator*. The letter's republication in the *Liberator* illustrates the interdependence of pro- and anti-slavery rhetoric, and the vocabulary of their engagement. Thompson's letter is typical of pro-slavery rhetoric of the period, claiming, as a matter of public duty, to mediate between the *Narrative* and the public it finds itself 'measurably compelled to appear before'. Thompson denies Douglass's authorship of the *Narrative*, and the allegations of cruelty and abuse the *Narrative* makes against Southern slaveholders.

The second Irish edition of the *Narrative* incorporates Thompson's rejection of its contentions. Like Prince's *History*, however, it also includes a rebuttal of that argument. Thus the public voice of pro-slavery, Thompson's letter, is positioned against the authentic voice of the slave subject, Douglass's rebuttal. Both letter and rebuttal are placed within the controlled space of the text, included in an appendix before the selected reviews. The letter is prefaced by Douglass as a tract he has 'great pleasure in presenting to my readers', and followed by his 'final word' on the matter, the open 'Reply'.

Within the ethical framework of the slave narrative, then, the letter from Thompson strikes a note of discord, revealing the logic of pro-slavery as false, as well as of course morally unsound. The inclusion of the 'Falsehood Refuted' cuts Thompson's letter off from any further engagement with pro-slavery argument. Its incorporation into the *Narrative* denies the refutation any discursive parity in the world external to the text. Indeed, Thompson's argument becomes the means by which the slave narrative deconstructs the pro-slavery position on a critical as well as dialectical level. It allows Douglass to exert narrative authority over the dialects of pro- and anti-slavery rhetoric. Thus his control of the 'text's authenticating machinery' is, in the second Irish edition, extended to the

---

22   See *The History of Mary Prince, A West Indian Slave,* in Henry Louis Gates Jr, ed. *The Classic Slave Narratives* (London: Penguin, 1987), pp. 183–240.

point at which he can now police the entire discursive terrain on which the *Narrative* operates.

This position of discursive authority allows both pro- and anti-slavery rhetoric to be reproduced within the plastic structure of the *Narrative*. Thus the flexibility of the form, its generic range across literature, history and polemic, allows Thompson's challenge to Douglass's authority to be absorbed. That challenge is cast as a parasitical textual gesture, as Douglass's narrative of truth and reason draws in dissenting voices from peripheral sites of discursive engagement.

The text's heterogeneity, then, its resistance to generic identification, permits the inclusion of an apparently infinite variety of voices, allowing opposition from the textual periphery to be neutralized. Slave subjectivity is not merely the central referent of the work, it provides a template for its understanding and interpretation. What have traditionally been conceived of as weaknesses in the slave narrative form – the onus on the slave narrator to prove truthfulness, reliance on authenticating testimony, fear of moral and/or discursive embarrassment or reprisal – are disabled and reversed in the Irish editions of Douglass's work by a synchronic gesture which enforces and extends the generic jurisdiction of the central narrative voice. Indeed, the inclusion of Thompson's letter and Douglass's rebuttal posits an empowered, transnational version of African American narrative voice as always the only totalizing position in the discourse of the black US subject.

Another discursive sleight of hand exemplifies the interpretative agency being exerted by an increasingly confident Douglass. Thompson's letter sets out to dismiss Douglass's authorial claim, stating that he (Thompson) once 'knew this recreant slave by the name of Frederick Baily [*sic*] ... [as] ... an unlearned, and rather an ordinary negro, and am confident he is not capable of writing the Narrative alluded to'. The rest of the letter involves a defence of those vilified in Douglass's text, including Edward Lloyd, Aaron Anthony, Austin Gore, Thomas Lamdin, Giles Hicks, Thomas Auld and Edward Covey, 'most of [whom] ... I am intimately acquainted with, and shall give a brief sketch of their characters'. Far from undermining the Douglass contentions, however, we are informed that Thompson's arguments 'are valuable as a confirmation of the main facts of my Narrative', which, 'for the sake of the abolition cause, I was delighted to see'. The letter and its rebuttal finds stylistic echo in the chiasmus of Chapter Ten, when, having seen 'how a man became a slave', we are shown the process by which the 'slave became a man'. For just as the structure of the narrative mimics the thematic priority of fashioning a linear, developmental self, in line with the Northern liberal ideal, the form of the Irish editions of the work further extends the synchronic reach of the chiastic trope: it permits the continuing development of the public persona whose voice emerges in the closing lines of the narrative proper.

Douglass's interpretative authority is confirmed by his appropriation of Thompson's argument as a vindication and substantiation, rather than an injunction against, Douglass's own narrative position. Thompson's intervention is formally welcomed by Douglass as a confirmation rather than a refutation of his narrative truth-claim: 'The writer's admissions,' he insists, 'are valuable as a confirmation of the main facts of my Narrative, while the denials are only such as might be expected from an apologist of slavery.'[23] It is therefore Thompson, rather than Douglass, who falls victim to the master–slave dialectic from which Thompson, alleging himself an opponent of slavery (despite the obvious apologism of his remarks: 'I am positively opposed to slavery, for I know it is a great evil; but *the evil falls not upon the slave,* but on the owner'), is at pains to dissociate himself.

According to Douglass, 'the relation of master and slave is one of those monsters of darkness to whom the light of truth is death'. In this somewhat evangelical description, the polarity of the black–white, master–slave dialectic is displaced by Douglass's narrative voice, which interprets Thompson's text according to the representative template of the *Narrative*'s truth-claim. Douglass maintains that Thompson has 'come to my aid; you have removed all doubt and relieved me of embarrassment', casting them both as Southern gentlemen of honour anxious to save one another's blushes. Kenneth Greenberg suggests that the antebellum South was essentially 'a masquerade culture'[24] where honour, chivalry and other anachronistically European codes of behaviour provided a vocabulary for the public expression of cultural values, including class, masculinity and so on. At issue in Thompson's letter and Douglass's refutation are those very cultural values. Douglass is described as 'an unlearned and rather an ordinary negro', compared unfavourably in moral, educational and in class terms with his white betters, against whom, in the social and cultural stakes, he cannot hope to compete. By casting Thompson as an honourable Southern gentleman respectfully saving Douglass's 'embarrassment', Douglass parodies Thompson's class and racial position. And instead of refuting Douglass's claims, Thompson's words merely repeat them. This repetition with difference, the 'full, free, and unsolicited testimony in regard to my identity', illustrates the unassailability of Douglass's position within the moral framework of the *Narrative*.

That moral framework, like Douglass himself, is strengthened rather

---

23 2nd Irish edn, pp. cxxiii.
24 Kenneth Greenberg, *Honor and Slavery* (1996).

than undermined by the encounter with adversity. For just as Thompson repeats Douglass's argument with a difference, Douglass in turn has repeated and reproduced the attack made on himself through the inclusion of Thompson's letter. At issue then, is not the facts themselves, but control of the semantic field between meaning and representation. By arguing that Thompson's words are in fact verifying testimony, Douglass reads that text against the grain, demonstrating that argument can never hide truth. His discursive position collapses the variable, phenomenological relation between meaning and representation, as counter-discourses are consumed and subsumed by the slave narrative itself. For, regardless of the words used, the polemic employed, or the number of counter-arguments that emerge, the truth of Douglass's narrative is always already present. As such, the synchronic expansion of the work finds linguistic parallel in its embedded argument: all argument can be consumed by the text; all language acquires significance from the operation of the text's interpretative agent: Douglass; and all counter-claims confirm the rhetorical processes and positions they appear to critique. Formally then, the inclusion of the letter and its rebuttal produces greater unity and consistency of purpose for the work in terms of its autobiographical as well as polemical objectives. It translates the rhetorical to the metaphorical on a structural as well as thematic level, and synthesizes Northern and Southern codes of American masculinity, developmental and chivalric.

The Present Tense

The rebuttal, like much of Douglass's writing at this time, was initially produced as part of a series of open letters to Garrison subsequently published in the *Liberator*. The 'Dear Friend' to whom Douglass addressed his correspondence was the public face of American abolitionism and editor of the *Liberator*, as much as Douglass's friend and mentor. The letter to Thompson provides a clear example of the extent to which Douglass was able to adapt and manipulate the convention of the open letter.

The open letters to Garrison thematically mirror the *Narrative's* concern to represent Douglass's life to date. They also served specific polemical purpose in the comparison they drew between attitudes to Douglass and to slavery in Ireland and the United States. Their publication provided Douglass with ongoing opportunities for self-authentication: as a moral agent, social success, and an historical actor. The letters continue and expand the autobiographical performance of the *Narrative*. Indeed, Douglass's rebuttal of Thompson even contains specific commentary on the achievements of the autobiographical self that Thompson's attack denies. 'You remember,' Douglass writes,

> when I used to meet you on the road to St Michael's, or near Mr Covey's gate, I hardly dared to lift my head, and look up at you. If I should meet you now, ... I presume I might summon sufficient fortitude to look you full in the face; and were you to attempt to make a slave of me, it is possible you might find me almost as disagreeable a subject, as was the Douglass to whom I have just referred. Of one thing, I am certain – you would see a *great change* in me!

This 'great change' is marked by Douglass's development from the other, less admirable self of slavery, a development performed in the *Narrative*. Douglass's letter, in conjunction with his narrative, therefore limns out the process by which past history has led to this present state of being. Other variations of the Irish texts – the preface written in Scotland and the appendix detailing Douglass's range of British and Irish contacts – expose the ever-shortening gap between the writing and reading present. The inclusion of these letters in the second Irish edition allows the reader to encounter the stylized, heroic voice of the present. The immediacy of that voice confirms the metaphoric alliance of the present self with that romantic rebel, the 'ancient "black Douglass"' of old.

Olney contends that '[t]he metaphor making of the classic slave narrators of the 1840s and 50s participates in the movement toward organic, nonlogical literary discourse as espoused by the classic nineteenth-century Romantics'.[25] Douglass's invention of this ancestry bolsters the perception of heroic selfhood encoded in both the *Narrative* and the US national ideal, and dovetails with the literary ideals of Romanticism then providing inspiration to more mainstream American writers. Eric Sundquist argues for the inclusion of Douglass's work, in particular his second autobiography, *My Bondage and My Freedom*, in the American Renaissance canon, observing:

> Although it sacrifices some of the immediacy and visceral simplicity of the *Narrative* ... the expanded 1855 version, entitled *My Bondage and My Freedom* develops a philosophical frame and psychological depth for Douglass's moving autobiography and is a classic text of the American Renaissance – not least because of the literal rebirth into freedom it records and the rebirth, the reawakening, of revolutionary principles it advocates. Because it can carry Douglass's life forward to his alliance with Garrison and his break with him over the disunion issue, *My Bondage and My Freedom* is able to describe the new challenges of freedom faced by the escaped slave.[26]

The Irish editions of Douglass's *Narrative* sacrifice none of the immediacy to which Sundquist refers. In fact their structure relies on the continuous

25 Olney, 'Founding Fathers', p. 11.
26 Eric J. Sundquist, 'Slavery, Revolution and the American Renaissance', in Walter Benn Michaels and Donald E Pease, eds, *The American Renaissance Reconsidered* (Baltimore and London: Johns Hopkins University Press, 1985), pp. 1–33 (23).

present of his written and lived selfhood, and 'the dilemmas of freedom' which ensue, while the 'Preface' provides the work with the philosophical and psychological criteria Sundquist describes in the later work.

The public letters, then, reinforce the existence and rhetorical power of the autobiographical self in the reading present. The incorporation of the refutation and reply into the text of the *Narrative* extends the linear, developmental self, rooted in the chiasmus of the autobiographical tale, and continues to mediate between the historical, rhetorical and tropological elements of the discursive framework. Moreover, the letters allow Douglass to represent an empowered selfhood moving ever further from its genesis in slavery.

Regardless of their inclusion in narrative, however, and of course most were not, the letters represent Douglass's capacity to meld public media with private experience. The letters allow for an ongoing re-characterization of the autobiographical subject through episodic sketches of a self active in the discursive 'now' of the political context of slavery. This re-enforces the image of a cumulative self, unified across time. Taken together, the open letters, as literary convention, facilitated and augmented the temporal scope of the autobiographical *Narrative*.

Their dual existence inside and outside the *Narrative*, however, also points to the openness of the slave narrative form. The letters chart Douglass's progress through time, as well as shifts in his socio-political status as representative subject. Like the appendices that appear and multiply as Douglass circulates outside the United States, the letters represent a series of encounters with social and political contexts across the Atlantic that Douglass negotiates, then reproduces, in textual format as ongoing proof of his hard-won public voice. They can therefore be characterized as discrete episodes in a serial narrative Douglass is still in the process of creating, whose ultimate meaning will not become clear until the publication of his second autobiography, *My Bondage and My Freedom*.

In fact, the letters produce a parallel, external narrative more in line with the stylistic mores of the heroic quest than of autobiography. Even those letters incorporated into the narrative remain formally distinct, casting the Irish texts as generic hybrids of autobiographical and picaresque modes of self-creation.[27] As such, the letters, one of which is included in the *Narrative,* confirm the temporal scope of the text and the plasticity of its diachronic configuration.

---

27 For a discussion of the slave narrative as the journey of an African American trickster figure, see Alexis Brooks De Vita, 'Escaped Tricksters: Runaway Narratives as Trickster Tales', *Griot: Official Journal of the Southern Conference on Afro-American Studies*, 17.2 (fall 1998), pp. 1–10.

The open letters to Garrison therefore help knit together the text, the fashioned self and the various socio-political and temporal contexts of that self's enactment. They extend the temporal and spatial reach of the text and complicate any analysis of the slave narrative as generically homogenous in either its autobiographical or picaresque modes. Stuart Hall writes that '[a] theory of the subject must begin not from the subject but as an account of suturing effects, the effect of the joining of the subject in structures of meaning', insisting that suturing must be though of as 'an articulation which places identification firmly on the theoretical agenda'.[28] The suturing that occurs in Douglass's Irish texts recasts the polarities of the slavery debate, already displaced by the repositioning of Douglass's narrative voice as representative power, into a triangular frame in which the self is positioned both outside and inside the text and its generic conventions.

Perhaps it is therefore more useful to discuss the subjectivity expressed in this work, which bridges North and South, stretches across the Atlantic and back, as occupying, to borrow a term from linguistics, a creole continuum, along which a range of culturally variable yet equally legitimate US subject positions may be located. Thus the writing itself represents complex networks of culture and identity traced across ethno-racial and regional boundaries. The degree of that complexity, coupled with the multiple reference points and connections it includes, suggest that in both its American and Atlantic contexts, the slave narrative represents what might be called a 'networked text', one wired into a multiplicity of geographical, historical and cultural fields, American and Atlantic, rather than an oppositional framework generated exclusively by a dialectic of race.

28 Stuart Hall, 'Introduction: "Who Needs Identity?"', in Stuart Hall and Paul du Gay, eds, *Questions of Cultural Identity* (London and Thousand Oaks, CA: Sage Publications, 1996), pp. 1–17 (6).

Chapter 4

The Hidden Ireland:
Social Commentary and Public Witness

Douglass's *Narrative* operates within two fields: the United States and the Atlantic. The former demonstrates the degree to which the slave narrative as autobiography can be considered as representative in both form and content as the Franklinian template. Douglass's work incorporates elements of Northern and Southern literary convention, producing an American subjectivity that spans national and racial divides. In the Atlantic context, Douglass's travels and the overseas editions of his work link the issues of slavery and abolition into a transnational network of separate but interlocking agendas. These occupy, to a greater or lesser extent, the terrain of progressive liberal discourse, a terrain that includes the advancement of women's political agency, racial liberalism, British and American nationalism, evangelical mission, and hierarchies of religious affiliation.

Yet the interconnectedness of these agendas also illustrates the complexities of individual and group identity in the context of shifting, increasingly globalized networks of ethnicity, gender or political agency. The *Narrative* was progressively restructured by Douglass in the period following its initial publication, to the point where it became a key node in this diverse network. Other elements of his textual production during the period 1845–47, the letters to Garrison in particular, continued to build upon the project of self-fashioning initiated in the *Narrative*, specifically on the American element of that undertaking.

Douglass remained in constant contact with the United States whilst overseas, with bulletins crossing the Atlantic on an almost weekly basis. The letters were updates detailing Douglass's progress, reception and his impression of people and places encountered in the course of his travels. Their status as private correspondence was little more than a literary conceit, however. For the letters were destined not just for Garrison's eyes, but for the pages of the *Liberator*, a public forum instrumental in binding an imagined community of abolitionists in the United States and beyond.

Douglass's time in Ireland is remarkable for the absence of any appeal across class lines to the peasant population or the urban working class.

Particularly notable by its absence, despite the plethora of letters written by Douglass during his visit, is any commentary on the Great Famine of 1845–47, an event exactly contemporaneous with Douglass's time in Britain and Ireland. Given the scale of the disaster and Douglass's ongoing reportage of the people, customs and conditions he encountered overseas, the omission is striking.

Why then did Douglass not make any reference to the Great Famine in either his speeches or literary output at this time? The answer is inevitably complex. Part of that answer, however, may emerge from an exploration of the function of the letters themselves; firstly, as part of the power politics embedded in the network of Atlantic ethical culture; secondly, as negotiations of US political identity in a transnational context.

At first glance the letters to America may appear merely as marginalia to Douglass's literary work. In fact, they served several important functions. Firstly, on the most practical level, they maintained Douglass in the American public eye during what turned out to be an extended absence from the US abolitionist podium, the rhetorical front line of the anti-slavery movement. This enabled him to sustain and even expand his relationship with a US audience when he might otherwise have faded into obscurity.

Secondly, like the slave narrative, the medium through which the ex-slave represented his 'authentic self as a figure embodying the public virtues and values esteemed by his audience',[1] the letters provided an opportunity for self-fashioning in realms outside the immediate context of the abolitionist movement or United States slavery. In other words, the circles in which Douglass moved whilst overseas provided him with social opportunities that could be transferred to, and consolidated within the United States, through their narration in the letters.

Lastly, the letters allowed Douglass to characterize himself in ways impossible in the *Narrative*: as an American subject abroad, an ambassador representing the history, views and expectations of his liberal US audience. Arguably, then, the letters were key to the next phase of Douglass's self-fashioning. They confirmed him, ideologically and culturally, as a US American. In this role, he could provide that audience with an American eye-view of British and Irish society.[2]

---

1 Andrews, *To Tell a Free Story*, p. 252.
2 See Tamarkin, 'Black Anglophilia', pp. 444–78, for a discussion of the importance of British culture to the creation of African American subjectivity abroad.

Audience and Expectation

Douglass's audience and his relationship with it changed significantly while he was overseas. Broadly speaking, it included US abolitionists and their sympathizers, with whom Douglass's relationship was conducted exclusively through the written word, and British and Irish audiences, with whom he communicated through both the written and spoken word.

Just as the composition of individual societies in the transatlantic arena differed considerably, so too did the composition, needs and interests of audiences in those same spheres. The differences were twofold. First, US abolitionism was predominantly white (though many African Americans were involved in the movement) middle to upper class, and dissenting, while those involved in Britain and Ireland, although largely upper class, varied considerably in their membership of churches, were not in direct conflict with the institutional or political structures of their home country, and lived in societies in which social stratification and difference were determined by factors other than colour.[3]

Secondly, notable by its absence in the United States was any significant form of popular abolitionism, although middle-class philanthropy often extended beyond abolition into temperance, prison reform, anti-pauperism societies, and so on. Conversely, in Britain and Ireland, concern about slavery became at the very least a rhetorical element in the broader context provided by popular reform movements with political rather than social goals, including land redistribution, the organization of labour and campaigns for political rights. National differences, then, clearly existed in the socio-political bases of abolitionism, as well as in the cultural impact and understanding of the term as an indicator of the need for reform of one sort or another.

The circulation of the *Liberator* in British and Irish circles also meant that it was expedient for Douglass to provide a flattering picture of his most immediate social contacts. There was pressure too from those contacts and the wider social base they represented. In Ireland the feeling was that Douglass should extend his reform interests. Conversely, there was significant feeling among British abolitionists that only those of influence in society could or should be effectual in promoting an end to

3   This situation applied only to the British domestic sphere. Slavery in Britain's West
    Indian colonies had been predicated on purely racial distinctions. Additionally, as
    the British Empire grew and extended itself further into Africa and Asia, ideas of
    Britishness became increasingly dependent on racial difference, a situation mirrored
    in the internal colonization of Native and African Americans in the United States.
    For discussions of the class and religious profile of Irish abolitionism, see Rodgers,
    'Ireland and the Black Atlantic', pp. 174–92, and Harrison, 'Cork Anti-Slavery
    Society', pp. 69–79.

slavery. Those with the strongest links to Northern abolitionists therefore discouraged the popularization of anti-slavery, or the fostering of links with other reform movements. Even Garrison was not immune to criticism on this count. Writing to his wife from Britain, he remarked:

> I have been to Bristol, and held two public meetings, – one of them composed of the selectest sort, the mayor presiding – the other of a more popular cast, largely attended, and enthusiastically supported. ... Last evening, I addressed a large meeting of the moral suasion Chartists ... I wish you could have been present to see the enthusiasm that was excited. ... I did not appear before them in my official capacity ... but on my own responsibility ... fully identifying myself with all the unpopular reformatory movements in this country. This will probably alienate some 'good society folk' from me, but no matter. ... shall derive great assistance from the co-operation of William Lovett and Henry Vincent, the leaders of the moral suasion Chartists. ... They are true men, who will stand by us to the last . ... Such men I honor and revere.[4]

The alienation of the 'good society folk' was not long in being expressed. A letter from John B. Estlin to one of his correspondents finds him commenting on Garrison's approach:

> Another evil of a foreigner's intermeddling with English politics is the impossibility of his knowing the sort of persons with whom he must patronise. People here are much influenced by the maxim that 'A man is known by the *company* he keeps.' Now Mr Garrison's intimacy with and laudation of Henry Vincent ... would be sure to detract from his power of serving the AS cause in England. ... I know ... [Vincent] is only in favour with persons who have but little *power*; (even if they can be made to feel the inclination,) to aid in abolishing American Slavery.

Later, in a letter dated 17 October, Estlin wrote to Garrison:

> It cannot be otherwise that your visit to England must excite a great deal of new-born attention to American slavery. You know that my view was at first, (and observation and much communication with others has confirmed it,) that exclusively confining yourself to the issue of Anti-Slavery was the way to secure a willing attention from a most important and influential class of English Society, who would at once be repelled from an American Citizen who, *uncalled for*, made public statements of his political agitation in this country. ... American slavery is by no means yet sufficiently understood with us to qualify people to enter in to the minutia [sic] of what are called anti-slavery *principles*. ... And I think you rather miscalculate the class of persons here who are most likely to benefit your movement, and whom it was most

4 Garrison to Helen Garrison, London, 3 September 1846, Boston Anti-Slavery Collection, Ms.A.1.1 v4, p. 30.

desirable to enlighten. ... It is the wealthy educated circles of this country whose desire to assist the abolitionists would do your cause most service.[5]

Although demonstrating a broad interest in reform issues and in mobilizing working-class support, however, Garrison, like Douglass, drew strong distinctions between American slavery and the plight of the British working classes, denying that there was any direct analogy between the two cases.[6] Abolitionists were understandably wary of the metaphorical extension of 'slavery' to include wage slavery, insisting on the distinctive character of slavery – the question of ownership, not the material conditions of the slave – which meant that slaves were always worse off than even the most downtrodden of free labourers.

Unlike Garrison, however, Douglass increasingly identified with British and Irish elites. In Ireland, his addresses were largely confined to middle- and upper-class English-speakers, those in effect who enjoyed political and economic clout. His audience in both Britain and Ireland was interested in social and structural reform elsewhere, but, with some exceptions, resisted any attempt to effect corresponding changes in their own societies. Similarly, Douglass's US audience were exclusively interested in the issue of slavery, an interest that only extended itself to Britain and Ireland because of the rhetorical opportunities provided by Douglass's presence there for discursive counters to pro-slavery camps and the class-based racism of Irish Americans in the United States.

Audience expectation then, to some extent, explains the paucity of social commentary in Douglass's letters home, his exclusive focus on US slavery, and reluctance to demonstrate solidarity with the socially disadvantaged.[7] Even his alliances with women did not involve a significant challenge to the status quo of his host societies by raising difficult issues, such as poverty, dispossession, conditions in factories, etc. In Ireland, poverty and the limited literacy of the majority meant there was a limited market for the *Narrative*, which may also help explain the absence of any attempt by Douglass to mobilize popular support. Lastly, many of the letters addressed to Garrison fed into the abolitionist convention which allowed the monarchical system in the United Kingdom the moral status denied the United States and its republican institutions, making it politically inexpedient to launch any broader discussion on social reform.

5   J.B. Estlin to W.L. Garrison, Bristol, 17 October 1846, Boston Anti-Slavery Collection, Ms.A.1.2 v16, pp. 113–14.

6   See Blassingame, *FDP*, 1, p. 353.

7   Also remarkable by its absence, for example, is any commentary by Douglass on the West Indian emigration schemes then being operated by the British government to replace slave labour lost with emancipation and the cause of much controversy in Ireland and among British abolitionists.

The absence of social commentary and mention of the Great Famine in particular, then, may lie in part in Douglass's changing relationship with his audience. But, as a result of the success of the *Narrative,* Douglass's political voice was becoming ever stronger. One of the advantages of the slave narrative was that, once the truth-claim of the individual's testimony to slavery was established, it stood for all other observations as well.[8] Acceptance of the *Narrative* would therefore suggest that any opinion expressed by Douglass on social issues would have had significant credibility among his transatlantic audience. Indeed, commentary on the economic condition of the Irish at a time of famine might have been expected to augment rather than diminish Douglass's growing public image as spokesman for the suffering and voiceless.

The convention of the open letter should have provided Douglass with certain rhetorical advantages, allowing him significant moral authority across a range of issues. His decision to confine the subjects of his addresses to American slavery is therefore all the more remarkable. He was often to comment on the extent of his travels in Ireland, claiming he had 'travelled almost from the Hill of Howth to the Giant's Causeway, and from the Giant's Causeway to Cape Clear'.[9] Yet only one of the letters written during his visit deals with Irish social conditions. Lee Jenkins points out that, although Douglass's arrival in Ireland coincided with the failure of the potato crop in 1845, the full impact of that failure was not immediately realized in privileged and governing circles.[10] While the absence of any early commentary is perhaps explicable, his silence on the issue during his time in Britain, when Irish Famine conditions were extensively reported in the British press over the entire two-year period, is, however, nothing short of extraordinary.[11] Given Douglass's proven capacity to challenge vested interests, both institutional and individual, and his early and ongoing self-characterization as spokesman for the voiceless and oppressed, his silence on the issue of Irish social and political conditions can only be seen as a considered one. This is particularly true given the pressure exerted on Douglass by his most important contacts in Ireland to extend the scope of his remarks into the broader area of social reform.

8 Olney, '"I was born"', p. 149.
9 Douglass, *Autobiographies,* p. 373. Similar remarks are made in the original letter to Garrison, 26 February 1846, (Foner, *Frederick Douglass,* 1, p. 138) and in Frederick Douglass, 'Thoughts and Recollections of a Tour in Ireland', *AME Church Review,* 3 (1886), n.p.
10 Jenkins, '"Black O Connell"', pp. 22–46.
11 Indeed, no event of the time was so well reported internationally as the Great Famine. The *Times* and *Illustrated London News,* for example, regularly reported that the people were starving and dying all over Ireland.

Many critics view Douglass's attitudes to the Irish as entirely benign.[12] Writing of Douglass's attitude to Irish Americans in the 1850s, however, Richard Hardack argues that Douglass was by then in sympathy with nativist, anti-Catholic tendencies within US politics.[13] Hardack describes the 'casting out' of Irish Americans in Douglass's journalistic writing, remarking that '[t]hroughout the run of the *Douglass Monthly*, Irish Americans became the enemy within, former slaves now riddled with prejudice and corrupted by the church'.[14] Douglass also, Hardack contends, 'resorts to a rhetoric of nativism in trying to characterise blacks as native, as having precedence over foreigners',[15] demonstrating that Irish Americans remained the main antagonists in Douglass's subsequent American rhetoric. The seeds of the nativism Hardack identifies are apparent in some of Douglass's transatlantic correspondence, which form part of his reconfiguration as a representative American abroad.

Morality and Temperance

That Douglass witnessed the distress that obtained in Ireland during his visit is clear from the letter written to Garrison from Montrose, Scotland, almost two months after Douglass had left Ireland.[16] In an earlier letter, one of the first he was to write to Garrison, Douglass had made his position on the broader issues of socio-political reform clear, insisting that 'my mission to this land is purely an anti-slavery one, and although there are other good causes which need to be advocated, I think that my duty calls me strictly to the issue of slavery'.[17] Although presented with a very different socio-political context, Douglass's attention was not diverted from his American objective, and he retained slavery as his only direct political interest.

Douglass's moral involvement was, however, more general. He was particularly attracted to the temperance movement in Ireland, which, under the direction of Fr Theobald Mathew, aimed to curtail consumption

12 For example, Patricia Ferreira, '"All But a Black Skin and Woolly Hair": Frederick Douglass's Witness of the Irish Famine', *American Studies International*, 37.2 (1999), pp. 69–83 (72–73).
13 Richard Hardack, 'The Slavery of Romanism: The Casting out of the Irish in the Work of Frederick Douglass', in Alan J. Rice and Martin Crawford, eds, *Liberating Sojourn: Frederick Douglass and Transatlantic Reform* (Athens, GA, and London: University of Georgia Press, 1999), pp 115–40.
14 Hardack, 'Slavery of Romanism', p. 128.
15 Hardack, 'Slavery of Romanism', p. 130.
16 See Douglass to Garrison, 26 February 1846, in Foner, *Frederick Douglass*, 1, pp. 126–44.
17 Douglass to Garrison, 29 September 1845, in Foner, *Frederick Douglass*, 1, p. 120.

of alcohol, principally among the lower orders, as a means of improving their socio-economic and moral condition. Overindulgence in alcohol had, by the mid-nineteenth century, become one of the hallmarks of moral depravity in a transatlantic system of laissez faire that privileged forms of industrial morality as the socially – and economically – desirable norm for would-be industrial or modernizing populations. One of the stereo-typical representations of the lower classes involved their characterization as uncontrolled overconsumers of alcohol, a habit that bolstered their image as idle, irresponsible, morally degenerate and untrustworthy.

In the United States, Irish Americans, the largest immigrant group at mid-century, fell foul of the social codes underpinning these categories. Their position as unskilled labourers on the lowest rung of the US free labour ladder and the extremity of the behavioural and social shift required of them by emigration to the United States only exacerbated endemic cultural attitudes to alcohol consumption which often encouraged negative stereotypes. They were both reviled and exploited by US employers, who often paid their employees only in liquor.[18]

Irish Americans were not alone in being exploited in this way. Alcohol was also employed as a tool in the control of Native Americans and slaves. Douglass notes in his *Narrative* that slave holidays were often characterized by alcoholic indulgence. On the one hand, alcohol offered a means of relaxation and escape; on the other, it was made available in order to discourage slaves from thoughts other than work. 'From what I know of the effect of ... holidays on the slave,' Douglass claimed,

> I believe them to be among the most effective means ... in keeping down the spirit of insurrection. ... These holidays serve as conductors, or safety valves, to carry off the rebellious spirit of enslaved humanity. ... Their object seems to be, to disgust their slaves with freedom, by plunging them into the lowest depths of dissipation. For instance, the slaveholders not only like to see the slave drink of his own accord, but will adopt various plans to make him drunk. ... Thus, when the slave asks for virtuous freedom, the cunning slaveholder, knowing his ignorance, cheats him with a dose of vicious dissipation, artfully labelled with the name of liberty.[19]

Socially speaking, there were also two sides to the temperance coin. Overconsumption did lead to further state immiseration of the already

18 See David Roediger, *The Wages of Whiteness: Race and the Making of the American Working Class* (New York: Verso, 1986), and Ignatiev, *How the Irish Became White*.

19 Douglass, *Autobiographies*, pp. 66–67. For a discussion of Douglass's attitudes towards alcohol, see John W. Crowley, 'Slaves to the Bottle: Gough's Autobiography and Douglass's Narrative', in David S. Reynolds and Debra J. Rosenthal, eds, *The Serpent and the Cup: Temperance in American Literature* (Amherst, MA: University of Massachusetts Press, 1997), pp. 115–35.

exploited and was often implicated in domestic and other violence. The temperance movement therefore played an important role in instigating some degree of social improvement. On the other hand, temperance played into already extant attitudes to alcohol consumption, which frequently underpinned ethnic and class stereotypes.

By the time of Douglass's arrival in Ireland, these stereotypes had been established in Britain and the United States, and the temperance movement was well under way. US abolitionists had also been involved in a long-running if ineffectual campaign to enlist the support of Irish Americans – who were, to coin a phrase, in the process of becoming white – against the institution of slavery.

These factors, in conjunction with Douglass's class aspirations, clearly influenced his attitude to the Irish situation. A meeting with Theobald Mathew a month after Douglass's arrival, for example, provided the basis of a letter in which Douglass describes Mathew as 'the living savior of Ireland from the curse of intemperance'. As a result of Mathew's efforts, Douglass assures his US audience, 'the change already wrought in the condition of the whole people of Ireland is almost … miraculous'.[20] Douglass's impression of the nature and extent of that transformation can only have been arrived at through preconceptions derived from contact with or observation of Irish Americans in the United States.

On the occasion of his meeting with Mathew, Douglass requested the pledge, and also received, according to his own account, the badge of his virtue, a 'beautiful silver pledge'. While in Ireland, temperance was the only issue aside from slavery that Douglass addressed directly. Taking the pledge was a declaration of sorts, a demonstration of his moral fraternity with the forces for improvement in Irish society. And, as Jenkins notes, despite Douglass's jealous guardianship of the vocabulary of slavery, he was not averse to the use of the rhetoric of drunkenness and sobriety to drive home abolitionist points.[21] In the late 1840s, Douglass was to attack Mathew for his capitulation on the slavery question during a temperance tour of the United States, a position Mathew alleged that he adopted in the interests of maintaining the support of Irish Americans and not alienating powerful Southern slaveholders.[22] But during his Irish tour, Douglass

---

20 Douglass to Garrison, Cork, 28 October 1845; *Liberator*, 28 November 1845, in Foner, *Frederick Douglass*, 5, pp. 7–9.

21 Jenkins, '"Black O Connell"', p. 33.

22 Jenkins calls this Mathew's 'Atlantic double cross' ('"Black O· Connell"', p. 33). Douglass excoriated Mathew for his capitulation, describing him as 'chang[ing] his morality by chang[ing] his locality. … We are … grieved, humbled and mortified to know that HE too has fallen … and forsaken the cause of the oppressed, by pledging himself to the [o]ppressor that he will remain dumb on the subject of slavery during

clearly felt that temperance was one reform movement that would not impinge upon his anti-slavery duties. Matthew, meanwhile, was willing to express anti-slavery sentiments when there was effectively nothing at stake. Indeed temperance halls, along with Nonconformist churches and meeting houses provided the vast majority of anti-slavery venues,[23] with Douglass also acting as the abolitionist delegate at the World's Temperance Convention in London in 1846.

From the outset of his visit to Ireland, Douglass was, by his own account, heavily involved in temperance activities. In a letter to Garrison from Dublin dated 16 September 1845, Douglass remarked that he had 'attended several temperance meetings, and given several temperance addresses. ... I spoke today on temperance, in the very prison in which O Connell was put. I went out last Sunday to Booterstown, and saw Father Mathew administer the pledge to about one thousand. "The cause is rolling on."'[24] Evidently, the sobriety of the Irish – convict or free – was of some concern to US and UK wings of the abolitionist movement. But what of Douglass's own attitudes towards alcohol and the population at whom the energy of temperance reform was directed? Some inklings of Douglass's early impressions of Ireland filter through in the letters and refer specifically to the issue of alcohol consumption. 'I promised,' Douglass wrote to Garrison from Dublin,

> to keep you informed of my proceedings while I remained abroad. I sometimes fear I shall be compelled to break my promise, if by keeping it is meant writing letters to you fit for publication. ... I have work enough here ... were I to stay in this city a whole six months. The cause of temperance alone would offer work enough to occupy every inch of my time.[25]

Six weeks later, having apparently abandoned his stance on church attendance, and perhaps feeling he could be more flexible with his immediate social contacts, Douglass noted, 'I attended church today. Tis not a sin in itself. Everybody I meet with here seems full of religion, drinks wine, and prays.'[26]

---

his sojourn in this country' (Foner, *Frederick Douglass*, 5, pp. 147–49).

23 See Blassingame's 'Partial Speaking Itinerary', *FDP*, 1, pp. 1, lxxxvii–cii, xciv–cii.

24 Douglass to Garrison, Dublin, 16 September 1845; *Liberator*, 10 October 1845, Foner, *Frederick Douglass*, 1, p. 119.

25 Douglass to Garrison, Dublin, 29 September 1845; *Liberator*, 24 October 1845, in Foner, *Frederick Douglass*, 1, p. 122.

26 Douglass to Webb, Belfast, 7 December 1845, Boston Anti-Slavery Collection, Ms.A.1.2 v15, p. 87.

Irish Context, American Opportunity

Douglass was keen to portray Ireland as a non-racialized space in which his innate qualities were not hampered by irrational prejudice, a portrayal given credence by his acceptance in upper-class social circles. Ireland provided Douglass with a meritocracy in which his class rise could be effected. But, like abolitionism itself, Douglass did not threaten the moral or political security of his audience in the United Kingdom. His class rise occurred because of, rather than despite, his status as an American ex-slave.

Another opportunity of his expatriate status was the chance to consolidate his identity as a US American. In a country in which he 'met with much in the character and condition of the people to approve, and much to condemn',[27] Douglass was able to articulate his moral distance from the Irish peasantry and urban working class. His self-authentication, through difference, as an American, is the other singular achievement of the textual production of the UK tour.

For one of the challenges presented by autobiography to the ex-slave was the difficult position in which the narrator found himself. In US literature, Native or African Americans typically provided a foil to the symbolic moral as well as racial whiteness onto which selfhood was inscribed. In the *Narrative*, Douglass stages the much-celebrated crossover from slavery to selfhood through a recognition, then defence, of his own subject position. But while the use of chiasmus overcomes the problem of self-authentication, Douglass was still some way from any equality of access to the resource provided to the US writer by figures of difference. That said, much of Douglass's rhetoric from this period played on British attitudes to colonial process by casting the United States as a space ripe for moral conquest and the slave population as eager, even compliant colonial subjects. Some risks were attached to this strategy, however, which could not provide Douglass with an emblem of absolute difference, due to his own proximity to and ongoing relationship with that same population.

The Irish on the other hand presented no so such representative dilemmas. Not only were they readily understood and characterized by British and even nationalist élites as colonial subjects, their representative impact extended to the United States. There, the status and behaviour of Irish Americans – an unskilled, urban working class, often in competition with African Americans for the lowest-paid employment; clerical in their outlook and drunken in their habits; intractably opposed to the abolition of slavery in the South and often implicated in racist violence against African Americans in the North – allowed them to be understood,

27 Douglass to Garrison, Belfast, 1 January 1846, in Foner, *Frederick Douglass*, 1, p. 126.

according to abolitionist norms, as social and, more importantly, moral outcasts.

The Irish American slide in abolitionist estimation occurred in the early 1840s, after the general rejection of the 'Address from the People of Ireland', of which abolitionists had great hopes, by Irish Americans. Much to the dismay of leading anti-slavery advocates, in the 1840s, Irish Americans aligned themselves with the newly 'white' Democratic Party,[28] and adopted Repeal as their singular political interest, jettisoning the domestic human rights agenda in the process. In 1842, Garrison wrote:

> The Irish Address, I trust is to be the means of breaking up a stupendous conspiracy, which I believe is going on between Irish demagogues, the leading pseudo-democrats, and the Southern Slaveholders. Mark three things. First – the Irish population among us is nearly all Democratic. Secondly – the cry in favour of Irish Repeal is now raised extensively throughout the South, and sustained by the leading democratic journals. And why? To secure the aid of the Irish voters on the side of slavery, and to bring their united strength to bear against the anti-slavery enterprise![29]

For his part, Wendell Phillips, writing at around the same time, informed Richard Allen that

> between you and me ... the Irish are usually an illiterate mass in general and entirely and mostly under the control of those few among them who have education or those who act as their lawyers or the few who court office by begging their votes. ... The Repeal agitation in this country ... with those who conduct the movement ... is only a scheme intended to operate on this side of the water and secure offices for hungry demagogues.[30]

Repeal, an Irish domestic concern internationalized by emigration, became part of the process of racialization in the United States; increasingly part of Irish American ethnic identity, increasingly at odds with the principles of freedom that underpinned it.

The competing political claims of ethnic identity can be seen operating in much the same way in Douglass's attitudes to class, morality and politics in Ireland. That he was aware of the popular basis of Irish anti-British agitation is clear from his most significant letter to Garrison at this time. 'I had supposed,' he confessed, 'that much of what I heard from the American press ... [of the misery and wretchedness of the Irish people] ... was mere exaggeration, resorted to for the base purpose of impeaching

28 See Roediger, *Wages of Whiteness*, pp. 133–65.
29 Willaim Lloyd Garrison to George Benson, Boston, 2 March 1842, in Merrill, *Letters*, 3, pp. 171–72.
30 Wendell Phillips to Richard Allen, Boston, 30 March 1842, Boston Anti-Slavery Collection, Ms.A.1.2 v12 (2), p. 39.

the characters of British philanthropists, and throwing a mantle over the dark and infernal character of American slavery and slaveholders.' 'My opinion,' he concluded, 'has undergone no change in regard to the latter part of my supposition.'[31]

Despite his Irish visit, Douglass's concern regarding the propaganda effects of Repeal agitation in the United States remained. The success of his own determined focus on slavery in Ireland and Britain was, however, to some extent achieved at the expense of underprivileged sectors of British and Irish society, absolving the upper classes from any need for moral engagement with domestic issues. It also allowed Douglass, through the convention of the open letter, to construct a form of difference that was individually empowering and depended largely on the class (and indeed racial) associations of alcohol abuse. Attitudes to alcohol become, in Douglass's letters, important signifiers of the moral, and therefore class and racial identity, he was creating for himself: that of African American representative man.

For the letters take pains to suggest that, despite his reluctance to engage in political reform overseas, Douglass did consider himself part of a more general moral crusade, in which attitudes to slavery were the most important, but not the only, part. Temperance was, as noted, neither morally, class nor racially neutral, with the negative associations of alcohol borne in the main by those considered inferior in class or racial terms. Douglass's involvement in temperance, therefore, can be seen as part of a larger process of social identification which had been ongoing since his escape, but which accelerated and reached completion during his time abroad. It is marked by his increasing conformity to middle-class social values.

Although much critical work has been produced on the class–racial identifications of US immigrant groups, there has been little qualitative analysis of the profile of African Americans – a predominantly Protestant, native-born population – in the Northern states of the Union in the antebellum period, and extending into the postbellum era.[32] Presumably,

31 Douglass to Garrison, Montrose, 26 February 1846, in Foner, *Frederick Douglass*, 1, p. 138.
32 Foner's significant documentary history of the occupational patterns of African Americans in the North in the antebellum period does provide insight into the community's class profile. As he demonstrates, only a small minority belonged to the artisan class, with the majority 'confined to menial labor and the service industries' (Philip Foner and Ronald L. Lewis, eds, *The Black Worker: A Documentary History from Colonial Times to the Present*, vol. 1, *The Black Worker to 1869* [Philadelphia: Temple University Press], esp p. 116). See also David J. Hellwig, 'Patterns of Black Nativism, 1830–1930', *American Studies*, 23.1 (spring 1982), pp. 85–98.

many of the same criteria regulating class and national identity as operated in the broader US cultural context also obtained to some extent in African American circles. Attitudes to alcohol and temperance were one of a complex of socio-moral indicators operating across a range of ethnic groups.[33] Significant and understandable chagrin was also felt by the native-born African American population at the comparative ease with which immigrant groups attained voting and other rights of citizenship. Predominantly rurally based Southern slaves were deprived of education, income and social status, as well as the liberty that would have permitted any class rise. But largely urbanized African Americans in the North, despite an often hostile and discriminatory environment, did operate within specific frameworks of social identification. The emergence of the African Zionist Churches, the temperance movement and even the success of runaway slaves like Douglass, all contributed to the potential for the class rise of at least some members of the African American community.[34]

In many ways, these changes tended to align African Americans with nativist tendencies in US culture and distinguished them from immigrant groups, the Irish in particular, who, as an intemperate Catholic, rural peasantry, provoked considerable concern among right-thinking Americans more generally. Indeed one of Douglass's particular complaints regarding the discrimination suffered by African Americans in a country

33 Roediger comments on the central importance of African American festivals, such as Pinkster and Negro Election Day, to working-class culture in the North and South in the early decades of the nineteenth century, and which involved the usual festival entertainments, such as music, alcohol, dancing, etc. It would seem that early in the century, then, revelry and alcohol were associated with black and white, slave and working-class culture alike. With the increase in immigration and the industrialization of the North, however, these festivals were progressively banned in the rising tide of industrial morality and growing demonstrations of institutional racism in the non-slaveholding North, where mixed-race gatherings were often targeted by the authorities (Roediger, *Wages of Whiteness*, pp. 101–04).

34 Gregory Lampe notes Douglass's training as a minister of this church, and points to the important influence this training had on his rhetoric (*Frederick Douglass: Freedom's Voice, 1818–1845* [East Lansing, MI: Michigan State University Press, 1998]). For a discussion of a possible temperance trigger to the Philadelphia riots, see Roediger, *Wages of Whiteness*, p. 108. Additionally, although studies of whiteness stem from an understanding of white working-class, racial identity as a subaltern effect, i.e. stemming from the actions and intentions of those choosing to become white rather than the result of an imposed racial profile, such commentaries also tend to present a happy, folksy, premodern picture of African Americans, who are portrayed only as the victims of populist and official sanction and/or violence. A thorough investigation of the race–class identity interface must involve attention to the class and racial aspirations of all groups within this modern dynamic, including those formational elements internal to African American society. That society was itself a dynamic, determined, expanding and stratified social grouping.

that refused to recognize them as citizens involved the injustice of, 'Pat, fresh from the Emerald Isle, requiring two sober men to keep him on his legs, enter and deposit his vote for the Democratic candidate amid the loud hurrahs of his fellow citizens.'[35]

By contrast, African Americans, and Douglass as the representative figure of that group, projected an in many ways exemplary picture. And it was 'non-native,' moral characteristics, recognizable to his US audience, that Douglass identified in the Irish peasant population. As an immigrant population to the United States, acting in ways incommensurate with enlightened abolitionist ideals,[36] the Irish provided Douglass with a surrogate of social difference. The Irish could occupy the role usually reserved for the slave population without the accompanying racial dilemma.

The Hidden Ireland

Early in his tour, Douglass had cast that slave population as potential subjects of Christian abolitionist empire. In this stage of his self-fashioning, that slave population, through Douglass, is freed from the American dialectic of race by an external, but easily recognizable object of moral difference. Though initially absent from Douglass's observations, the Irish peasantry and urban working class become figures of a difference quantifiable in terms that are both class related and of domestic significance in the United States. Douglass becomes the arbiter of a moral constituency that relies for its existence on domestic forces immune to abolitionist influence.

Hints of a letter to come dealing with the Irish situation are contained in some of Douglass's earlier missives. Writing from Belfast, Douglass remarks that

> [in] the little more than four months [I have been in this country] ... I have given no direct expression of the views, feelings and opinions which I have formed, regarding the character and condition of the people in this land. I have refrained thus purposely. I wish to speak advisedly, and in order to do this, I have waited till I trust experience has brought my opinions to an intelligent maturity. I have been thus careful ... because whatever influence I may possess ... I wish to go in the right direction, and according to truth. I

35 Blassingame, *FDP*, 3, p. 579.
36 For a discussion of nativist reaction to Catholic immigrants, see Jenny Franchot, *Roads to Rome: The Antebellum Protestant Encounter with Catholicism* (Berkeley, CA: University of California Press, 1994); and Eric J. Sundquist, *To Wake the Nations: Race in the Making of American Literature* (Cambridge, MA: Harvard University Press, 1993). pp. 137–48.

hardly need say that, in speaking of Ireland, I shall be influenced by prejudice in favor of America.[37]

The reasoned caution of these remarks is a far cry from the exuberance of
Douglass's earlier letters. His intention is to provide his US audience with
rational, eye-witness accounts of the inseparable 'character and condition
of the people'. Despite his vilification of US attitudes towards slavery,
Douglass is still keen to maintain his national affiliations and bolster the
self-image of his audience. Understandably, Douglass was 'concerned
with depicting himself in ways that would appeal to liberal Christian
readers and valorize bourgeois social conventions'.[38] By foregrounding
the moral identification between himself and his US audience, Douglass
can act as both mediator and politico-moral representative of a distant, if
as yet imperfectly realized, republic. In so doing, his true identity, that of
an expatriate American rather than escaped slave, is brought into focus.

The subsequent letter to the *Liberator*, far from presenting an example
of cross-racial solidarity based on mutual experience of oppression, in fact
positions both Douglass, and the Irish peasantry and urban working class
within a nativist US interpretative mould. Written from Scotland on 26
February, the letter, in its address, adopts for Douglass, the *Liberator* and
its readership the heroic status of undaunted moral agents, in a missive of
self-congratulation published in full on 27 March 1846. 'It is the glory of
the *Liberator*,' Douglass rejoices,

> that in it the oppressed of every class, color and clime, may have their wrongs
> fully set forth, and their rights fully vindicated. ... So also, though I am
> more closely connected and identified with one class of outraged, oppressed
> and enslaved people, I cannot allow myself to be insensible to the wrongs
> and sufferings of any part of the great family of man.

Aside from the moral alignment occurring between Douglass and the
readers of the *Liberator*, the letter goes some way towards the adoption of the
role of 'liberator' for Douglass himself. Although he speaks of his association with the 'outraged, oppressed and enslaved', his self-characterization
avoids direct alignment with others of the 'family of man', pointing instead
to his ability to transcend his own political interests. His connection is less
with the downtrodden than with the humanist position of those striving
for greater justice. As such, the letter marks a shift in Douglass's political
position, as he recasts himself as representative not just of Southern slave
society, of which he is an exceptional example, but as black abolitionist
representative of US Northern liberal culture.

37 Douglass to Garrison, Victoria Hotel, Belfast, 1 January 1846, in Foner, *Frederick
  Douglass*, 1, p. 125.
38 Andrews, *To Tell a Free Story*, p. 69.

The description of Ireland that follows has much in common with nineteenth-century characterizations in the British media. In the absence of any visual marker of difference – a darker skin colour – the Irish were characterized by the 'barbarism' of their accents – the conflation of linguistic and racial 'corruption' – and particularly by their depiction against domestic backgrounds of filth and disorder. British racism, McClintock observes,

> drew deeply on the notion of the *domestic* barbarism of the Irish as a marker of racial difference. ... [T]he iconography of *domestic degeneracy* was widely used to mediate the manifold contradictions in imperial hierarchy – not only with respect to the Irish, but also to the other 'white negroes': Jews, prostitutes, the working-class, domestic workers and so on, where skin color as a marker of power was imprecise and inadequate.[39]

Douglass's use of the discourse and iconography of the Irish as domestic degenerates played a key role in his own racial reconfiguration. His descriptions of 'the Irish people' (rather than 'Irish friends, Irish abolitionists etc'), are, in his only concession to the political reality of his expatriate context, the letter describing Irish social and economic conditions, heavily overdetermined by a vocabulary of class and racial difference.

This finds expression in the descriptions of the misshapen humanity apparently teeming unchecked through the 'beautiful city of Dublin' of the earlier reports. 'I dreaded to go out of the house,' Douglass writes,

> for [t]he streets were almost literally alive with beggars ... some of them ... mere stumps of men, without feet, without legs, without hands, without arms – and others still more horribly deformed, with crooked limbs, down upon their hands and knees, their feet wrapped around each other, and laid upon their backs.[40]

Irish family structures are similarly distorted, with 'little children in the street at a late hour of the night, covered with filthy rags ... with none to care for them. If they have parents,' Douglass laments, 'they have become vicious, and have abandoned them. Poor creatures!'

Although skin colour is never mentioned, the grotesque, quasi-human figures, the parasitical images of those literally infesting the city streets, can be read as descriptions of racial difference and to play on a typology of contagion. Ferreira reads these, and other depictions of the Irish in Douglass's work[41] as examples of cross-racial empathy, citing

39 Anne McClintock, *Imperial Leather: Race, Gender and Sexuality in the Colonial Contest* (New York and London: Routledge, 1995), p. 53, emphasis original.
40 Douglass to Garrison, Montrose, 26 February 1846, in Foner, *Frederick Douglass*, 1, p. 138.
41 As for example his characterization of the Irish in one of his best-known speeches

his comparative treatment of such issues as alcohol abuse and economic deprivation in his discussions of the slave South. In the *Narrative*, the corrupting influence of the slave system tears families asunder, making orphans and widows a commonplace. But there is no acknowledgement of any political evil in Ireland, such as presented by the institution of slavery in the United States, which might explain Irish behavioural peculiarities.

Moreover, by the time of his Irish letters, Douglass's distance from the US slave population was well established, and, indeed, self-evident. His distance from the peasant Irish – with a concomitant class dividend in both Britain and America – is what is being confirmed in the Irish letter. Nothing could provide greater contrast to the polish of Douglass's own image, carefully cultivated in portrait and text, of the urbane, American gentleman of letters.

But his characterization of the Irish, which jars with Douglass's stated political interests and to some degree with his 'stylistic signature', served particular ends in his American self-fashioning. Firstly, the publication of the letter, complete with moral self-congratulation, relieved Douglass, and the *Liberator*, of any charges of partisanship that might have been levelled by pro-slavery factions in the United States. Secondly, the moral difference of the Irish afforded Douglass an opportunity to reconfigure, within a transatlantic context, the dialectical structure of British and US American technologies of the self.

Background images of the Irish as anatomically distorted and socially atavistic provided Douglass and his US audience with clearly identifiable objects of difference. That difference was uncomplicated by the standard, by abolitionist discursive norms unacceptable, distinctions of the colour code. Instead, the focus is on the instigators of British and American domestic disorder. The description of degraded living conditions of the Irish poor, whose 'rags … seemed to be held together by the very dirt and filth with which they were covered', reveals the corrupt state of Irish domestic conditions:

> of all the places to witness human misery, ignorance, degradation, filth and wretchedness, an Irish hut is pre-eminent. It seems to be constructed to promote the very reverse of every thing like domestic comfort. … Four mud walls about six feet high, occupying a space of ground about ten feet square, covered or thatched with straw – a mud chimney at one end, reaching about a foot above the roof – without apartments or divisions of any kind – without floor, without windows, and sometimes without a chimney – a piece of pine

and pamphlets, 'Claims of the Negro Ethnologically Considered'. Full text in Blassingame, *FDP*, 1.2, pp. 497–525.

board laid on top of a box or old chest – a pile of straw covered with dirty
garments, which it would puzzle anyone to determine the original part of
any one of them – a picture representing the crucifixion of Christ, pasted on
the most conspicuous place on the wall – a few broken dishes stuck up in a
corner – an iron pot, or the half of an iron pot, in one corner of the chimney
– a little peat in the fireplace, aggravating one occasionally with a glimpse of
fire, but sending up very little heat – a man and his wife and five children
and [of course] a pig. In front of the door-way, and within a step of it, is a
hole three or four feet deep, and ten or twelve feet in circumference; into this
hole all the filth and dirt of the hut are put, for careful preservation. This is
frequently covered with green scum, which at times stands in bubbles, as
decomposition goes on. Here you have an Irish hut or cabin, such as millions
of the people of Ireland live in. And some live in worse than these.

The organizing conceit of this description is that of factual reportage, with
Douglass positioned as agent and mediator. The tableau presented is a
gross perversion of any domestic norm, far from the idyll of the Victorian
household soon to be expounded in Stowe. In the Irish 'hut', humans and
animals occupying the same domestic space; a space without light, heat
or comfort; a paradigm of disorder with a pit of contagion at its centre.[42]

This domestic chimera casts the Irish as a transnational object of
difference against which liberal US subjectivity may be posited. The Irish
are located within US frameworks of racial and moral understanding,
with 'men and women, married and single, old and young, lie down
together, in much the same degradation as the American slaves'. But the
degraded conditions of the Irish, unlike those of American slaves, cannot
be structurally vindicated as impositions of the slave system. Although
Douglass goes on to remark, 'I see much here to remind me of my former
condition, and I confess I should be ashamed to lift up my voice against
American slavery, but that I know that the cause of humanity is the one
the world over,' nothing could be further from the cultivated self-image
constructed by Douglass during his Irish sojourn. And it is the Irish who
bring that image into focus for his US audience.

These comments also absolve Douglass from any allegation of partisanship by activating the moral code inscribing his stylistic signature. Far
from being selective in his attention to the cause of the American slave,
Douglass is in fact addressing the wider 'cause of humanity': 'He who
really and truly feels for the American slave cannot steel his heart to the
woes of others; and he who thinks himself an abolitionist, yet cannot enter
into the wrongs of others, has yet to find a true foundation for his anti-

42 Additionally, the picture of the crucifixion noted by Douglass provides a subtle
    hint of the Catholicism of these households, and is an easily recognizable signifier of
    difference for Douglass's Protestant audience.

slavery faith.' While Ferreira concludes that Douglass 'used the similarities as well as distinctions [between Irish and African Americans] as a means to give further legitimacy and power to their individual emancipatory interests',[43] the letter as a whole provides an interpretative dilemma for readings of Douglass which remain within the critical boundaries of his own self-fashioning. For rather than serving the emancipatory interests of the Irish (or indeed American slaves), the description of Irish people and living conditions acts as a means to power for Douglass himself, radically emphasizing his moral and social distance from the conditions witnessed and those elements of his past to which they bear relation.

'But,' as Douglass was himself to write, 'to the subject.' As noted, the social conditions observed by Douglass could not be explained by any structural or political evil such as that represented by slavery in the United States. Instead they are given a moral explanation. 'The immediate, and it may be the main cause of the extreme poverty and beggary in Ireland,' Douglass was to write, 'is intemperance. This may be seen,' he concludes, 'in the fact that most beggars drink whiskey.' He goes on to explain:

> The third day after landing in Dublin, I met a man in one of the most public of streets, with a white cloth on the upper part of his face. He was feeling his way with a cane in one hand, and the other hand was extended, soliciting aid. His feeble steps and singular appearance led me to inquire into his history. I was informed that he had been a very intemperate man, and that on one occasion he was drunk, and lying in the street. While in this state of insensibility, a hog with its fangs tore off his nose, and part of his face! I looked under the cloth, and saw the horrible spectacle of a living man with the face of a skeleton. The temperance cause has done much – is doing much – but there is much more to do, and, as yet, comparatively few to do it. A great part of the Roman Catholic clergy do nothing about it, while the Protestants may be said to hate the cause. I have been frequently advised to have nothing to do with it as it would only injure the anti-slavery cause. It was most consoling to me to find that those persons who were most interested in the anti-slavery cause in the US, were the same as distinguished themselves as the truest and warmest advocates of temperance ... at home.[44]

Douglass's enquiry into the causes of the man's disfigurement yields a story lacking nothing in horror or dramatic effect. The account casts Douglass as an amanuensis, a position from which he can speak for,

---

43 Ferreira, '"All But a Black Skin"', p. 77.
44 Douglass to Garrison (Foner, *Frederick Douglass*, 1, p. 141). That Douglass claims to have witnessed such a scene on the third day after his arrival in Dublin is an indication that he had, from the outset of his visit, the opportunity to witness such scenes of deprivation, though he was not, with the exception of this occasion, ever to write of them.

then interpret, the significance of the man and his story. That story clearly illustrates the case for temperance. Consumption of alcohol is an indicator of moral inferiority, producing effects as reprehensible as those occasioned by slavery. In common with the creatures described elsewhere in the letter, the man Douglass encounters on the streets of Dublin is only marginally human, a 'living man with the face of a skeleton'.[45] There is no redemptive explanation for this, however, for, according to Douglass, '[An Irishman] is still master of his own body.'[46]

Mastery of the self is a key concern in the *Narrative*, where the master's power over the slave body is seen as the negation of selfhood.[47] The achievement of that selfhood involves a moral contest, played out in the physical struggle between Douglass and Covey, in which Douglass exceeds, then discards the role of slave. In the letter to Garrison, the Irish have surrendered their selfhood to the vice of intemperance. The story told does not involve racial contest, but the self-inflicted effects of moral degeneracy, sufficiently horrifying as to provide a parallel with the more shocking scenes of the *Narrative*, are not of a kind. Framed by the context of domestic corruption, the story reinforces the moral distance between Douglass, the situation he describes, and the population he encounters. What initially appears to be a sympathetic comparison between two disadvantaged groups settles into an image of difference, in which the Irish, rather than reflecting the oppressed image of plantation slaves, embody the abuse of the freedom for which they, the Irish, are unfit.

Two of Douglass's biographers have noted in this letter Douglass's discursive proximity to British stereotypes of the Irish, which laid all distress at the door of intemperance.[48] Given the letter's intended audience,

45 The analogy between the Irish and living skeletons was frequently made by other travel writers in Ireland at this time, though the emaciation witnessed derived from starvation rather than alcohol (see, e.g., William M. Thackeray, *The Irish Sketchbook* [1843, Dublin: Gill & Macmillan, 1990]). The comparison appeared frequently in the press. In May 1848, for example, a reporter from the *Cork Examiner* on a trip to Cléire described being 'met by moving skeletons with swollen legs and distorted features'. Of the people he visited he described 'one man dead in his hovel. His mother had died a few days before and another woman in the next house was dying' (*Cork Examiner*, 5 May 1848). These accounts are more or less typical of the scenes described throughout the country at the time.

46 Blassingame, *FDP*, 1.1, p. 422.

47 For a discussion of the interrelation of manhood and power in Douglass's work, especially in the contemporary context of the construction of manhood in American writing, see David Leverenz, *Manhood and the American Renaissance* (London: Cornell University Press, 1989), chap. 4.

48 Benjamin Quarles states that Douglass ignored 'the potato famine which then gripped the country, [and] attributed all of Ireland woes to the dram shop' (*Frederick Douglass*, p. 41), while McFeely, according to Jenkins, describes Douglass as resorting

this account might also be said to reproduce the class–colonial relation within a US discursive framework, where it is reinforced by both nativist and abolitionist moral norms. The alcoholic excess of the Irish at home rebuts the black–white configuration of US moral hierarchies by helping to popularize the stereotype of Irish Americans as wastrels and drunkards among American readers. The intemperance of Irish Americans, added to their support of slavery, can acquire, through the lens provided by Douglass's letter, a specifically racial focus by activating a nativist dialectic. Through the process of creating an object of difference to US selfhood, who, like the African, has representative effect both within and exceeding national borders, Douglass introduces a new paradigm that censures forms of moral degeneracy rather than shades of skin tone.

The letter, then, does not merely reproduce British imperial stereotypes, it replicates US moral expectation in an overseas arena, establishing beyond doubt Douglass's American credentials by activating principles of conduct and class, easily identifiable and understood by his US audience. It also posits the struggle with Irish American attitudes so familiar to US political liberals at home, within a transnational context of virtue or the lack thereof. Abolition and temperance, twinned in the closing lines of the extract, are seen as complementary modes of social and moral improvement, a position confirmed by their adoption by an international moral elite. Escape from the racial dichotomies of US society finds Douglass reconstructing his identity around other sets of oppositions, notably those related to class and morality, whose support of the myth of America he might as readily have questioned.[49] In this letter, as part of his ongoing self-fashioning, Douglass the American ex-slave becomes Douglass the expatriate American, voice of US civilization, morality and modernity, and policing the discursive perimeter of nativist standards.

Reform and the Self

In the *Narrative*, Douglass moves from slavery to manhood, in a work now established as 'the great authenticating text of the first century of African American autobiography'.[50] David S. Reynolds writes:

to 'the familiar dodge' of blaming Irish distress on drunkenness (McFeeley, *Frederick Douglass*, p. 126; Jenkins, '"Black O Connell"', p. 31).

49 A similar point is made by Andrews concerning Douglass's presentation of the United States (as a colonial construct) through an adapted form of the jeremiad, noting that the nation and nation-subject could be understood only in terms of 'alternatives generated by the symbol itself', and arguing that though he tried in some sense to liberate himself from the symbol of America, he 'maintained that symbol within a field of meaning of its own making' (*To Tell a Free Story*, p. 131).

50 Andrews, *To Tell a Free Story*, p. 138.

the major writers [of the American Renaissance] were distinguished among their contemporaries by the breadth of their awareness of the various popular reform movements and by their success in rechannelling the reform impulse imaginatively in their own works. All of them recognised the immense cultural influence of reform movements and, as part of their efforts to create culturally representative texts, they repeatedly used reform images.[51]

In Ireland, Douglass, through engagement with the transnational politics of temperance reform as well as abolition, seized the reform agenda, becoming an arbiter of moral direction, and exponent and critic of the myth of America. Jenkins observes that 'according to contemporary postcolonialist theory, Douglass represents himself in terms of hybridity', citing his use of chiasmus as the appropriate form of racial expression for 'a mulatto, site of racial crossings, ... chiasmus personified'.[52] That hybridity, Douglass's reform work seems to suggest, involves the union of 'native' strains of morality, and the corresponding expulsion of 'non-native' socio-cultural elements. His Irish transformation is achieved by extension of the vector of chiasmus through careful creation of a metonymic relationship with his US audience. In this relationship, Douglass becomes representative of US liberal opinion as a whole. It is his position in Ireland that allows this to happen, positing the existence of productive, even transformative spaces on the geographic, discursive and ethnic racial margins of the modern. There, the hybrid American nation-subject can summon itself fully into existence by activating a new technology of the self. Douglass becomes part of a larger process of nativist identification, one that seeks to circumvent the racial paradigms underpinning slavery by replacing them with specific moral or behavioural standards.

The Irish letters provide nativist America and Douglass with an emblem of difference that supersedes (rhetorically, if not in fact) the racial difference occasioned by slavery. The Irish peasantry and urban working class allow Douglass to move a step further towards representative Americanness. The Irish letters become the means by which Douglass is transformed, in American eyes, from exoticism to authenticity, fully exploiting the representative potential of his hybrid racial, if determinedly nativist, US identity.

If chiasmus is the appropriate mode for the expression of a hybrid self that will become representative of a hybrid nation – the United States – how much more representative of that hybridity then are the

---

51 David S. Reynolds, *Beneath the American Renaissance: The Subversive Imaginary in the Age of Emerson and Melville* (New York: Knopf; Random House, 1988), p. 92.

52 Jenkins, '"Black O Connell"', p. 35; see also Houston A. Baker Jr, *Long Black Song: Essays in Black American Literature and Culture* (Charlottesville, VA, and London: University Press of Virginia, 1972), p. 76.

Irish editions, which formally posit multiple origins for both subject and text? Moreover, the representative status of the *Narrative* is, in Ireland, increased by its capacity continually to project itself into the present context of a symbolic selfhood. The open letters may be read as episodic extensions of a core history of American subjective emergence.

Nineteenth-century US ethnic autobiography is normally character-ized as a work of assimilation, as the ethnic self is absorbed to the greater cultural whole. Douglass's escape from slavery was followed by his entry into the political and racial turbulence of the North. There, the dynamics of identity formation centred on the adoption of national codes, social and moral, and a nativist prerogative necessitating the creation of a self differentiated from all that the nation was not. Stephen Raitton remarks of the literary milieu of the American Renaissance that '[s]ocial freedom for Douglass and his fellow blacks [in the US] was ultimately dependent on the place they could occupy in the consciousness of the larger white culture',[53] while Andrews observes that 'black autobiography tried to move its white reader in one direction, from an alien to a consubstantial relationship with the text and the black self presumably represented by the text'.[54] The Irish letters formally identify Douglass as representing those standards crucial to understandings of the liberal-democratic, masculine persona of the contemporary United States, and the enlight-ened moral codes of abolitionists.

Douglass's visit to Ireland and Britain and the texts he produced there were the proving ground of his Americanness. His writing confirmed his affiliation to Northern liberal humanism, while simultaneously exploiting the Southern plantocratic values of his upbringing.[55] By demarcating the moral, rather than racial barrier with difference, Douglass's reveals both the imaginary impact and problematic nature of the US experiment as a whole.

---

53 Stephen Raitton, *Authorship and Audience: Literary Performance in the American Renaissance* (Princeton, NJ: Princeton University Press, 1991), p. 198. David van Leer comments on 'the many white discourses Douglass must appropriate if he is to have any audience in the North', but concludes that 'audience expectations cannot account for all the irregularities of Douglass's mode of presentation' ('Reading Slavery: The Anxiety of Ethnicity in Douglass's *Narrative*', in Eric J. Sundquist, ed., *Frederick Douglass: New Literary and Historical Essays* (Cambridge: Cambridge University Press, 1993), pp. 118–40 (119–20).

54 Andrews, *To Tell a Free Story*, p. 137.

55 Andrews describes the slave narrative as 'building a bridge of sympathetic identification' between the black Southern fugitive and white Northern audience. The letters provide an extension and solidification of this process (*To Tell a Free Story*, p. 137).

Chapter 5

'Mask in Motion':
Dialect Spaces and Class Representation

Douglass's writings, his autobiographies in particular, have long been cornerstones of the literary and historiographical scholarship generated around his life and work. Other major sources have included Douglass's private correspondence and editorial writing, with the letters in particular casting light on a range of relationships, public and private, throughout his career. The publication of Series One of the *Douglass Papers: Speeches, Debates and Interviews* by John Blassingame from 1979 to 1986 greatly expanded the body of material readily available to Douglass scholarship, compiling newspaper and other reports of his speechmaking from a wealth of sources, across a fifty-year period from the earliest days of his career. The papers help to round out the public figure Douglass presented, framing him within contemporary institutional politics in the United States. An important corollary of this is that Blassingame's collection allows for a directional change in Douglass scholarship. With their focus on the very public realm of rhetoric and performance, the three volumes in the collection facilitate critical approaches less concerned with genre, textuality or formal, one-to-one relationships than with the contingencies of group interaction in the public sphere. In short, Blassingame's collection suggests that attention to the nature and form of the performative self and its interaction with wider culture is both possible and necessary.

The first formal study of Douglass's training in public speaking and rhetorical inheritance, Gregory Lampe's *Frederick Douglass: Freedom's Voice, 1818–1840*, appeared in 1998, initiating a directed debate around the issues of voice and rhetorical structure.[1] Lampe's work suggests, amongst other things, a more formalized apprenticeship to the protocols of church and state rhetoric than Douglass's self-fashioning might have allowed. Clearly, Douglass's rhetorical persona was as important to his public and political success as was his writing. Stepto has argued that Douglass's *Narrative* sees the creation of a public personage who can step confidently forward into the rhetorical world of abolitionist politics. Yet

---

1 Lampe, *Frederick Douglass.*

that rhetorical engagement also precedes the production of the narrative, emphasizing the degree to which the public domain of abolitionist politics was an important arena of public debate and self-fashioning.

Although the overlap between Douglass's written and rhetorical personae has been noted, then, little attention has to date been accorded related issues of performative self-fashioning or indeed audience constituency with regard to Douglass's career. Not only were the early years of that career as an abolitionist speaker key to Douglass's subsequent public profile, they are of interest for Douglass scholarship and historiographies of African American performative culture more generally. In particular, they cast light upon the dynamics of reform and other political movements playing out in national and transnational arenas.

The range of social fora in which Douglass appeared in the course of a career that spanned a greater part of the nineteenth century are an indication of the breadth of his influence and appeal. They also help illuminate the performative processes of identity formation that form part of the larger project of imagining the US national character during this period of ethnic and economic flux. In fact, though normally seen as the preserve of white ethnic groups transforming economic and social marginality into racial prerogative at the expense of the black population of the United States, the performative spaces of US nineteenth-century popular political or ethical culture, which included minstrelsy and burlesque as well abolitionism and political stump speaking, also provided an environment in which Douglass and other black Americans could engage in dialogue with, perhaps even help to shape, the codes of popular political discourse during the period. The class–race dynamic current in the United States during the period, deriving from attitudes to labour, issues of modernization and naturalization, and resulting in the creation of racial categories, specifically whiteness, linked to class, is crucial to understanding Douglass's representation of slavery and his relationship with the US nation-state.

But it is still but one side of the Atlantic political coin. Taken in conjunction with dialogues simultaneously occurring across a range of national and international spaces, this discursive interaction provides a useful tool for historicizing the influence of rhetorical, performative elements of major political debates in informal arenas during the nineteenth century. As with Douglass's written work, whose meaning is derived substantially from the regions in which the texts were produced, it is necessary to contextualize Douglass's public speaking within the specific national contexts in which it occurred. Doing so has implications for historiography on two major fronts. Firstly, it clarifies the importance of Douglass's international experiences in his self-fashioning as an

American, and the criteria which enabled it. Secondly, it allows an examination of concurrent forms of popular radicalism at play within discrete domains of the local; that is to say, it permits both analysis and problematization of the intersection between degrees, kinds and contexts for resistance across a range of social or national spaces.

Modes of key importance here include mimicry, masking and metonymy. These raise the possibility of examining the operation of informal political culture in the popular sphere, within the realm of what Bakhtin describes as 'carnival', an informal arena in which the dynamic of the marketplace crowd moves beyond the strictly rational in order to create meaning outside the parameters of official culture. Deriving from the different but not unrelated domains of class, colonialism, migration and nationalism, these local meanings overdetermine the carnival dynamic at play across the spaces of popular negotiation in the nineteenth-century Atlantic. Indeed the performative character of Douglass's early public career requires consideration of these structural hinterlands, which underpin the evolution of cultural standards within the Atlantic framework, yet frequently remain unacknowledged by it. For the contexts in which Douglass spoke and performed, within the United States and beyond, are distinctive historical spaces that, although demonstrably permeable, are not necessarily comparable either in terms of their historical development or national ambitions. The range of sites, though confined to the Atlantic, nevertheless includes areas of considerable political diversity, with Ireland in particular complicating the cultural paradigms of race and class as they obtained in Britain and the United States.

Particular difficulties of course attach to reimagining and interpreting the performative rather than written self. Performance produces public meaning in the moment and context of its enactment in a way that texts, even when approached through the lens of reader-response theory, as individual events of private engagement cannot. A range of elements, including voice, appearance, gesture, audience composition and participation, form part of the specifics of context of any performance. The debate regarding performance incorporating a racial or ethnic element has, in the United States, also become fraught by broader issues of sectarian oppression in which it has historically been implicated. As Eric Lott and others have shown, US racial and ethnic performance at mid-century was highly problematic to say the least.[2] W.T. Lhamon's work, however, suggests that

---

2 Eric Lott, *Love and Theft: Blackface Minstrelsy and the American Working Class* (New York and Oxford: Oxford University Press, 1993); Roediger, *Wages of Whiteness*.

blackface performance could be both flexible and politically radical.[3] This discussion requires that the elements of carnival, within what are now seen as politically dubious performative modes, be acknowledged. This chapter examines public stagings of political issues through ethnically overdetermined performance outside the United States during Douglass's early overseas sojourn, exploring the pursuit of political agency through performances constrained by audience expectation, organizational control and individual ambition.

The debate regarding ethnic performance is therefore set at one remove from the context of the genre's initiation, the industrializing North, and from the object of its representations, the slave South. The emphasis is not on whether such performance is morally good, but on its function as an object and expression of popular political engagement. Such emphasis enables a more nuanced evaluation of the different national dynamics of political subjectivity in the public spaces of popular democratization and the overlapping domains of popular and polite culture of the period. Key to this is an understanding of an Atlantic context in which masking, mimicry and minstrelsy operate as interrelated forms of tactical behaviour often linked to group identities or sites in transition to modernity, yet retaining an affiliation to residual forms of premodern practice. Firstly, the chapter discusses the level of overdetermination between the abolitionist platform and other populist forms of public discourse and performance during the period. Secondly, it casts blackface performance within a wider context of subaltern activity that sought to undermine élite structures of power and discourse, and which set up interlocking forms of protest that crossed national borders. Thirdly, it discusses the nature of Douglass's use of mimicry and expression of his Anglophilic tendencies, challenged the parameters of abolitionist discourse, and operated within a particular class idiom. Lastly, the chapter looks at the specifically African American modes incorporated into Douglass's early performative rhetoric, with particular attention to the figure of the trickster. It examines the degree to which Douglass appropriated the tropes of minstrelsy, its stock characters and use of dialect spaces, to engage in a sustained, ironic and populist critique of the slave system and the racial structures that underpinned it.

3 W. T. Lhamon, *Raising Cain: Blackface Performance from Jim Crow to Hip Hop* (Cambridge, MA: Harvard University Press, 1998).

Minstrelsy: Entertainment or Protest?

The Atlantic interface on which Douglass operated in his early days as an abolitionist speaker was both complex and nuanced. The interface itself was also occupied by populist forms of racialized entertainment and political protest, whose presence Douglass was forced, directly or indirectly, to acknowledge. The most important and controversial form of performative racialization in the United States was blackface minstrelsy, a form that emerged in the 1830s and quickly became a major player in the cultural politics of the period. From the time of its inception, blackface minstrelsy had massive popular appeal, becoming, according to Richard Toll, 'an instant rage and a national institution virtually overnight'.[4]

It also provided a forum in which difficult issues of acculturation could be played out by immigrant groups. Studies of the genre have demonstrated that early minstrelsy involved the performance of a class identity bound to the notion of free labour, with race acquiring new significance as a visible label of labour difference. Speaking of the minstrel show's relationship with mass urban culture, Alexander Sexton notes that, 'what made the first minstrel show a "glad" surprise was that it provided a window into the complex culture developing in the new cities'.[5]

Immigrant groups to the United Sates were, more often than not, moving from premodern rural societies to a modern urban industrial setting. The stereotypical figures of the slave South represented in minstrelsy were, it is argued, a displacement of the loss of community, natural order and premodern patterns of life, labour and so on. The minstrel stage, then, was not merely an arena of entertainment, it was a highly politicized space. As Eric Lott puts it in his discussion of minstrelsy in the United States, '[i]t was in rowdy theatrical spaces that an emergent racial politics was both registered and created, and that the racial feeling underlying and shaping but many times eluding the official narratives of race ... began to appear'.[6]

Without wishing to romanticize a form that was clearly complicit, firstly, in the appropriation and exploitation of black plantation culture by whites, and secondly, in modes of class reconfiguration which incorporated a strongly racist ideology, it is useful also to see minstrelsy, as Lott suggests, as the 'public emergence of slave culture ... or pointed political

4   Richard C. Toll, *Blacking Up: The Minstrel Show in Nineteenth Century America* (London, Oxford, New York: Oxford University Press, 1974), p. 21.
5   Alexander Sexton, *The Rise and Fall of the White Republic: Politics and Mass Culture in Nineteenth Century America* (London: Verso, 1990), p. 166.
6   Lott, *Love and Theft*, p. 63.

protest'.[7] Understanding minstrelsy as incorporating and publicly staging a link between the idea of slavery or slave culture and the politics of protest can help illuminate wider contexts of resistance both within the United States and beyond.

In the United States this 'protest' involved the representation of slavery as labour bondage as a means of criticizing the exploitation of wage labourers, corresponding rather too neatly with aspects of the pro-slavery position, which often exploited this same analogy. Simultaneously, the idea of the slave as a non-citizen was used to speed the acceptance and assimilation of immigrant groups. Notoriously, blackface minstrelsy often targeted the slave population it purported to represent, depicting southern slaves as lazy, stupid yet wily, prone to a life of the emotions, generally happy with their lot and liable to burst into song or dance at any moment. Although slaves themselves were often negatively depicted, however, their musical culture was the key attraction of minstrelsy itself. Indeed, minstrelsy marks the beginning of the (albeit interracial representation) of black popular or *folk* culture on the American stage. Minstrelsy introduced African American dialect, music and dance to an extended public on the American stage half a century after the textual representation of African American culture had surfaced in the poetry of Phillis Wheatley, and is contemporaneous with the emergence the African American slave narrative.

In his chapter entitled 'Blackface Minstrelsy', Sexton observes that the themes of minstrelsy were more concerned with the wish-fulfilment of white immigrant groups than with black Southern reality; that that form, 'reinforced the image of the South as symbol of the collective rural past and of individual childhood'.[8] Such representations did, however, also help embed ideas about Southern slave experience in Northern minds. Contemporary abolitionist accounts of the plantation South were keen to dispel the popular minstrel image of the African American slave population. According to M.D. Conway, for example,

> The impression has gone around the world with ubiquitous sable minstrels that the slaves are a merry, singing, dancing population, far removed from the cares that gnaw the hearts of more civilised classes. In all the twenty three years of my life in the land of slavery, I never saw a Negro dance ... The slaves in the Border States are almost invariably members of the Baptist and Methodist societies, which are particularly rigid in denying them such amusements. On the large plantations of the far South, dances are encouraged, and formerly were frequent; but of late years they have become

7 Lott, *Love and Theft*, p. 17.
8 Sexton, *White Republic*, p. 176.

infrequent, through the all-absorbing tendencies of the Negroes toward religious meetings ... I have rarely known their enthusiasm enlisted in any thing except prayer-and-experience meetings and funerals.[9]

Polemical intent aside, these remarks point to the undeniable gap between Northern perceptions of the South and the Southern reality itself. Yet authentic or not, blackface minstrelsy incorporated elements of African American culture – banjos, dialect expression, storytelling – reinventing and representing them to a Northern audience. The point here is not that minstrelsy was a legitimate or genuine representation of slave culture – clearly it was not – but that its efficacy did not rely on the representational integrity of its purported subject. Rather, by presenting slavery on the American and Atlantic stage, and establishing 'blackness' as a form of political subversion, the stage itself was set for the appropriation of the tropes of minstrelsy as vehicles of popular resistance. As a non-literary form, performance was, unlike polemical genres, such as the slave narrative, sentimental novel or political pamphlet, accessible to a non-literate as well as reading public, thereby widening the audience base and the number of political constituencies the form could address.

Perhaps predictably, Douglass expressed strong opposition to blackface minstrelsy. On the surface at least, he was keen to discredit the form. Writing in 1848, one year after his return from Britain, he described blackface imitators as 'the filthy scum of white society, who have stolen from us a complexion denied to them by nature, in which to make money, and pander to the corrupt tastes of their white fellow citizens'.[10]

Given the negative light in which blacks were usually portrayed in blackface entertainment, Douglass's reaction to the minstrel show is understandable. He had good personal reasons to feel the affront of this contradictory form of racial politics. One of the stock characters of the minstrel stage, Zip Coon, whose other manifestations included Dandy Jim and Count Julius Caesar Mars Napolean Sinclair Brown, portrayed a black urban dandy whose 'vanity, stupidity and sheer ludicrousness' neatly reinforced what whites wanted to believe about Northern blacks, and promoted a unifying sense of working class identity by producing a discreditable representation of upper and aspiring classes.[11] Apprenticed as a ships' caulker during his teens, Douglass had been forced off dockyards by white Northern workers after his escape from slavery and

---

9   M.D. Conway, A Native of Virginia, *Testimonies Concerning Slavery*, 2nd edn (London: Chapman & Hall, 1865), p. 113.

10 *North Star*, 27 October 1848, in Philip Foner, *Frederick Douglass*, 1, p. 547.

11 Toll, *Blacking Up*, pp. 68–69.

could only earn a living doing menial work. Despite these relatively humble origins however, Douglass had, by the time he died, amassed considerable personal wealth and served as US Marshall to Washington, DC and US Ambassador to Haiti. In short, for a man who was literate, articulate and enjoyed a significant degree of social mobility even at this early stage of his career, such portrayals must have cut rather close to the bone.[12]

As an anti-slavery speaker Douglass had suffered the prejudice against any aspiration to cross class boundaries endemic to these Zip Coon representations, as well as occasional fear of African American intellectualism.[13] For example, exhorted by abolitionists in the early days of his public speaking to '[g]ive us the facts ... we will take care of the philosophy'; it was even suggested that Douglass adopt the plantation dialect of the Southern 'darkie' in order to present a more authentic portrayal of black identity and to add the gloss of truth to his description of bondage. 'People won't believe you ever was a slave, Frederick,' advised Friend George Foster, while John A. Collins remarked that Douglass had '[b]etter have a *little* of the plantation manner of speech than not; 'tis not best that you seem too learned', he concluded.[14]

Though in his autobiography Douglass intimated that Collins's intention was racist, Collins may have been as concerned with the continuing credibility of the abolitionist movement as with keeping Douglass in his place. A controversy surrounding the authenticity of black abolitionists claiming to be escaped slaves had arisen in 1841, when James Williams, who alleged himself a runaway, dictated a slave narrative that was then published by the abolitionist movement. Williams's story was subsequently revealed to be a fabrication and the anti-slavery society was discredited.[15]

---

12 Foner's biographical account of Douglass sees him, as Henry Louis Gates Jr notes, 'simultaneously accept[ing] a racial and class identity', reading Douglass (somewhat wishfully) as leading 'a racially defined class struggle for freedom'. Douglass's own class profile and association give the lie to this reading however (Foner, *Frederick Douglass*, pp. 1–5). For a different reading of Douglass' class-racial profile, see McFeely, *Frederick Douglass*. Additionally, Wilson Jeremiah Moses points to Douglass's relatively privileged upbringing in his '"Writing Freely?"', pp. 66–83 (67).

13 At one point in the *Narrative*, Douglass appears to rationalize his enslaved status through an unwanton interpretation of his current class status as a necessary and indeed typical phase in an artisan's career: 'Besides,' Douglass wrote, 'I am but a boy, and all boys are bound to some one.' Though read by van Leer as Douglass's philosophizing of the apparently inescapable, the remark actually had a basis in truth: apprentices were indeed 'bound' to their masters, enjoying little freedom and few rights (Douglass, *Autobiographies*, p. 67; Van Leer, 'Reading Slavery', pp. 118–40).

14 Douglass, *Autobiographies*, p. 367.

15 See Gates, 'From Wheatley to Douglass', pp. 49–50.

As a result of this embarrassment, the credentials of those claiming to be former slaves were more open to question. Northern abolitionism therefore required signifiers of authenticity from the ex-slaves they saw themselves as sponsoring. Dialect, which indicated class, as well as colour, which indicated race, was considered an important element of this authentication, suggesting perhaps the degree to which what was legitimate and credible in the rendition of the slave experience was being influenced by the more general cultural climate of blackface representation.

The degree of overdetermination with regard to class, race, culture and authenticity is also evident in Douglass's own remarks concerning minstrelsy. He was loath to grant any legitimacy to those who had 'stolen [the] complexion' of African Americans, parodied and debased their identity in the interests of material gain. Evidently the issue of authenticity and ownership was even then a thorny one. But, as George Rehin points out, one of the paradoxes of minstrelsy was that it allowed for cultural interchange in both directions across the colour line in the United States. Commenting on the mutability of the form, Rehin goes on to remark that 'minstrelsy also contributed to the development of a distinctive Afro-American style as well [as blackfaced white], when many professional entertainers among the caricatured race embraced the form after the Civil War'.[16]

Douglass's remarks indicate that he considered minstrelsy a debased white form of cultural expression, an ill-gotten gain of slavery and racial oppression. The association Douglass makes between corruption, blacking up and whiteness provides an inkling of his class views, with minstrelsy linked to the morally 'filthy' whose depravity was illustrated by the 'corrupt tastes' of their white public. Indeed, as elsewhere in his rhetoric, Douglass appears to making a case for class as a moral and sometimes racial, rather than strictly economic category. His denunciation of the 'filthy scum' (black, he insinuates, due to lack of soap and water) parodies Victorian conventions of moral colour coding which during the nineteenth century became the representative trope of class identity. According to McClintock, this coding drew on the British domestic cults of cleanliness and contagion, internalizing the racial tropes of imperialism by associating blackness with occupational dirt as a means of racializing many in the working class, including housemaids, chars, sweeps and miners.[17] In a curious manipulation of the class/race model, this remark sees Douglass squarely denouncing minstrelsy as symptom and symbol

16 George F. Rehin, 'Harlequin Jim Crow: Continuity and Convergence in Blackface Clowning', *Journal of Popular Culture*, 9.3 (1975), pp. 682–701 (686).
17 McClintock, *Imperial Leather*.

of the moral corruption of lower-class whites, who are, to coin a phrase, neither clean nor godly.

While this class–race overdetermination typified British class structures during the period, Douglass's class attitudes may also have an American basis. Wilson Jeremiah Moses has commented on Douglass's relatively privileged upbringing; even as a slave Douglass was a member of the artisan class. In the Southern United States in the antebellum period, issues of class were by no means clear-cut, with poor whites often perceived as occupying a lower class status than slaves. Conway notes the ambivalence in class attitudes between black slaves and free whites in the South and describes the destructive effects of race prejudice that prevented cross-racial solidarity amongst the most deprived. He describes poor whites as 'blindly fighting against their own interests', claiming:

> They are worse off than the Negroes, being not so well dressed or fed; hence there is a violent animosity between them, the Negro counting himself far superior to 'the poor white trash,' which is his name for them, and which is the most offensive term which one Negro can cast at another.

In an interesting reversal of the tendency to portray slaves as occupying the lowest rung of the social ladder, Conway concludes that '[t]he two classes correspond to the labouring and the pauper classes elsewhere'.[18] Given his own background, then, Douglass's characterization of minstrelsy as a debased form of white popular culture gestures towards another paradigm in which the positions of high and low culture are complicated by a form of racial overdetermination not necessarily conforming to typical configurations of the white–black polarity. That framework may have its roots in class attitudes current in the United States as well as Britain.

Another staple of the minstrel show was the stump speech, a distinctive feature of the olio, the second or variety section of the show's programme.[19] In the antebellum period, 'bubolitionists' were by far the favourite target of minstrel stump speeches, though such issues as temperance and women's rights also came under attack.[20] Overblown, blackface parodies of abolitionist rhetoric, ridiculing not just African Americans but their claims for political and social justice must have taken on an added irony for Douglass, one of the few black anti-slavery speakers on an abolitionist circuit dominated by the white middle class.

---

18 Conway, *Testimonies Concerning Slavery*, p. 115.§
19 Toll, *Blacking Up*, p. 55; Lott, *Love and Theft*, p. 5.
20 Toll, *Blacking Up*, p. 56.

For Douglass, like the blackface parodists of the minstrel shows, was in the business of representing race, and did so far beyond the borders of the United States. His 1845–47 tour saw him vigorously campaigning against the United States' 'peculiar institution'. By the time he arrived in Britain and Ireland, minstrelsy had already crossed the Atlantic and was fast becoming a music hall staple.[21] His visit coincided with that of the US minstrel troupe the Ethiopian Serenaders to Britain, a coincidence which Sarah Meer argues provided Douglass with a 'competing representation' of African American cultural authenticity.[22] In other words the ideological content of the minstrel show in Britain, which depicted slavery as a virtual peasant utopia, detracted to some degree from anti-slavery arguments based on physical abuse, material deprivation and so on.

Authenticity was very much to the fore in the scramble for representational control of class and racial identifications, with many minstrel shows claiming to be 'original' or 'true Ethiopians'. This claim to authenticity provided entertainers with the kudos on which their attractions depended. Politically it was also important: the authority of the representation depended on the credibility of those performing. Criticizing white performers in blackface on the grounds of authenticity, then, was for Douglass a means of undermining the credibility of the caricatures and set of social relations they depicted.

Yet even when the minstrels behind the blackface were African Americans, Douglass still saw fit to protest. In a review of Gavitt's Original Ethiopian Serenaders, one of the few all-black troupes operating in the 1840s, Douglass claimed that '[t]heir singing was but a poor imitation of white performers, and not even a tolerable representation of the character of colored people'. He went on to urge the troupe to

> represent the colored man as he is, than as Ethiopian Minstrels usually represent him to be ... [to] rely more on the refinement of the public, than its vulgarity, let them strive to conform to it rather than to cater to the lower elements of the baser sort, and they may do much to elevate themselves and their race in popular estimation.[23]

21 For a discussion of the popularity of blackface in Britain, its 'native' predecessors in blackamoor pageantry and links with carnival and clowning, see Rehin 'Harlequin Jim Crow', and George Rehin, 'Blackface Street Minstrels in Victorian London and Its Resorts: Popular Culture and Its Racial Connotations as Revealed in Polite Opinion', *Journal of Popular Culture*, 15 (summer 1981), pp. 19–38.

22 Sarah Meer, 'Competing Representations: The Serenaders and Ethnic Exhibition', in Alan J. Rice and Martin Crawford, eds, *Liberating Sojourn: Frederick Douglass and Transatlantic Reform* (Athens, GA, and London: University of Georgia Press, 1999), pp. 141–65.

23 Foner, *Frederick Douglass*, 5, pp. 141–42.

This assessment reflects the centrality of class and authenticity in the evaluation of a performance which cannot hope to achieve representational legitimacy. The Serenaders imitate white cultural practice rather than relying on their knowledge of blackness which exceeds that of their blackface competitors. For Douglass, even authentic blackness can be sullied by its association with working-class white culture, with African Americans in blackface seen as masked, debased and implicated in white distortions of black cultural practice.

And, like his earlier adaptation of moral colour-coding to indicate the class status of minstrel performers, these remarks suggest a tendency to see the class configuration of the minstrel audience as playing a key role in the truth and refinement of the representation. Douglass's attitude to the performance seems to be mediated as much by his concern with the quality of the audience as that of the characterization. In this instance, just who and what constituted a 'tolerable representation' of African American folk culture seems to be very much bound up with the class perceptions, affiliations and ambitions of both white *and* black spectators.

Douglass was acutely aware of his own role in staging race on the anti-slavery platform. Commenting on his life's work at the end of the Civil War, he recalled that 'I felt I had reached the end of the noblest and best part of my life. ... The anti-slavery platform had performed its work and my voice was no longer needed. "Othello's occupation was gone."'[24] John Earnest concludes that 'there is a certain cultural inevitability in Douglass identification with Othello',[25] an identification that characterizes him as a lone, black actor striving for representational authority on the historical and racial stage. It also indicates the degree to which Douglass felt the need to counteract the populist American image of the platform with the nobler, increasingly Anglo associations of mainstream theatre.

The identification with Othello suggests an analogy with Douglass's contemporary, the African American tragedian Ira Aldridge. Known as the 'African Roscius', Aldridge enjoyed considerable popularity throughout the then United Kingdom, particularly in Ireland, where he performed frequently in the years from 1829 onwards. Aldridge first visited Belfast

---

24 Douglass, *Autobiographies*, p. 811.
25 John Earnest, *Resistance and Reformation in Nineteenth Century African American Literature* (Jackson: University of Mississippi Press, 1995), p. 170. For a discussion of Ira Aldridge's portrayal of Othello and the general context of the representation of blackness on the nineteenth-century stage see Joyce Green MacDonald, 'Acting Black: Othello, Othello Burlesques, and the Performance of Blackness', *Theatre Journal*, 46.2 (May 1994), pp. 231–49.

in 1829 and Dublin in 1831.[26] Although famed for his representations of Othello, Aldridge's stage performances also incorporated more politicized sketches, such as 'Liberty and Equality, or the American Slave Market' *and* minstrel songs, such as 'Jump Jim Crow', 'Lucy Long' and the popular favourite, 'Opossum up a Gum Tree'.[27] The diversity of Aldridge's performances illustrates the degree of cross-fertilization that occurred between established and popular stage forms of the period, in which both black and white were seminally involved. Additionally, although Paul Robeson, an actor later famed for his portrayals of Othello, was to say of minstrelsy that '[i]n a popular form, Negro music, launched by white men – not Negros – has swept the world!'[28] in Aldridge's case, minstrelsy only added to his appeal and 'race' to his performative glamour. As an African American he could capitalize on the popular appeal of minstrel songs and may even, George Rehin suggests, have set the British (and Irish) stage for minstrelsy, though this connection was not made at the time.[29] Indeed, although Riach sees indications that Aldridge 'had to overcome considerable hostility [in élite circles] when he came to Ireland',[30] a comparison between the social mobility enjoyed by Douglass and Aldridge there is possible. In 1838, Aldridge was made a Brother Mason of the Grand Lodge of Ireland, an appointment that doubtless improved his social as

---

26 Anon., 'The Theatre Royal in Dublin, from 1830–1831', *Dublin University Magazine*, 72 (1870), pp. 454–71 (460).

27 Herbert Marshall and Mildred Stock, *Ira Aldridge, the Negro Tragedian* (New York: Rockliff, 1958), pp. 150–51. According to the author of 'The Theatre Royal in Dublin', 'Possum up a Gum Tree' 'elicted more applause' than did Aldridge's portrayals of Othello ('Theatre Royal', p. 460). Rehin also points to the eclecticism of Aldridge's performances ('Harlequin Jim Crow, p. 687).

28 Anon., *Paul Robeson Speaks* (London: Quartet Books, 1978), p. 92.

29 Rehin, 'Harlequin Jim Crow', p. 647.

30 Apparently the manager of the Theatre Royal in Dublin, John W. Calcraft, had reservations about employing an African American actor, while 'one American was furious at the prospect of his wife appearing on the same Dublin stage as Aldridge'. (Note: Riach's discussion of black and blackface performers in Ireland is not complicated by class/colonial distinctions. (See Douglas C. Riach, 'Blacks and Blackface on the Irish Stage, 1830–60', *Journal of American Studies*, 7.3 (December 1973, pp. 231–41 [239]; see also Anon., 'Theatre Royal', p. 560.) Aldridge's fame in the African American community later generated a black minstrel troupe, known as the Ira Aldridge Troupe, in Philadelphia in the 1860s, which specialized in Irish burlesque. Speaking of a piece entitled 'The Irishman and the Stranger', Jack Shalom remarks that '[p]erhaps the Aldridge Troupe's audience got its biggest satisfaction … from the role reversal inherent in the piece … Since the beginning of minstrelsy, minstrels of Irish heritage … had been caricaturing Black men – now it was the turn of Black men to caricature the Irish' ('The Ira Aldridge Troupe: Early Black Minstrelsy in Philadelphia', *Journal of Popular Culture*, 28.4 [1994], pp. 653–58 [656]).

well as professional opportunities. Blackness could be as much an aid as a hindrance to class rise outside the United States.

Given the overlap in popular and polite form, then, and the necessity for broad popular appeal, it is unsurprising that there were many similarities in the staging of minstrel shows and abolitionist meetings. The latter often included music, songs, mimicry and other crowd-pleasers, with audiences frequently drawn as much by the promise of an interesting spectacle as by any moral conviction. As Audrey Fisch points out, 'the British penchant for the "genuine" black extended beyond the street and music hall to "respectable" anti-slavery gatherings'. The 'attraction of rubbing shoulders with the black American abolitionists made black speakers "essential" at British antislavery gatherings'.[31] Richard Blackett makes the further point that, through their role on the anti-slavery platform, visiting African American abolitionists might even have played an 'unwitting role in perpetuating American minstrelsy's depiction of the Negro',[32] a depiction decried by Douglass as a 'contemptuous sneer ... originating in the spirit of slavery'.[33] Be that as it may, slaves and African Americans more generally were by no means unique in being parodied on the Victorian stage, with several other groups suffering the brunt of popular humour as a means of social control. Unflattering depictions of the working class, colonial subjects and female sexuality were also current in this period, fast becoming icons in the increasingly politicized sphere of popular entertainment.

Minstrel shows also travelled to Ireland with some fifteen minstrel shows appearing in Dublin before the American Civil War.[34] A programme from the Virginia Minstrels show in Dublin in 1844, one year before Douglass's visit, promises the audience views of the 'sports and pastimes of the Virginia Colored Race, through medium of Songs, Refrains, and Ditties as sung by Southern slaves'.[35] The form even generated some early native imitators. At a speech given in Limerick on 10 November 1845, Douglass publicly rebuked a local actor named Bateman who performed 'Jim Crow ... apes of the negro' in city playhouses.[36] Writing of the infamous reaction of Irish immigrants to American slavery, Riach argues

31 Audrey A. Fisch, '"Negrophilism" and British Nationalism: The Spectacle of the Black Abolitionist', *Victorian Review*, 19 (summer 1993), pp. 20–47 (21).
32 Blackett, 'Cracks in the Anti-Slavery Wall', pp. 187–206.
33 Blassingame, *FDP*, 3, pp. 335–36.
34 Riach, 'Blacks and Blackface', p. 231. For an account of visiting troupes see also Harry Reynolds, *Minstrel Memories: The Story of Burnt Cork Minstrelsy in Great Britain from 1836–1927* (London: Alston Rivers, 1928).
35 Virginia Minstrels, Dublin, Ireland, 1844, programme, Harvard Theater Collection. Quoted in Toll, *Blacking Up*, p. 34.
36 Blassingame, *FDP*, 1, p. 77.

that 'the cause of the Negro in America suffered from the failure of the abolitionists in Ireland to condemn as wholly inaccurate the image of the Negro most often presented on the Irish stage, and carried to America in the minds of countless Irish emigrants'.[37] The number of Irish people who would have seen such performances is questionable, and the effect of the minstrel stage in forming racial attitudes amongst Irish emigrants to the United States may not be as significant as Riach suggests. But Douglass's intervention indicates the outrage he felt at what might at best be described as the political naivety of actor and audience.

His was not the only view, however. The editor of a local newspaper, the *Limerick Reporter*, defended Bateman, considering him a 'clever actor whose representation of a particular negro character, debased by his white despot is no more to be considered as a description of negros generally than the representation of ... any of the Irish buffoons represented by LEONARD or Miss Heron be viewed as types of Irish character'.[38] This report suggests that Bateman's portrayal reproduced the highly dubious racial burlesque of its American predecessors, as well as pointing to the proliferation of forms of ethnic and sexual parody in the popular stereotypes of the period. But it also indicates that, whether the editorial view be considered either excessively naive or unusually enlightened, the understanding of the minstrel, tavern or music hall audience was not as uniformly unsympathetic to the subjects of these representations as is sometimes suggested. This was particularly true outside the United States where there was no social or political need for a derogatory minstrel image of African Americans. In fact in Britain the contrary was the case; far from being despised, authentic blackness was lionized as the 'spectacle' of the abolitionist movement – the former slave – fused with a rising British nationalism, serving to discredit US democracy and political institutions, thereby allaying class conflicts in Britain.[39]

Nor were the boundaries of the spheres of politics and popular entertainment clearly defined. In Irish nationalist politics for example, minstrelsy had the potential to manipulate the high profile of American slavery in Britain by parodying the moral prestige enjoyed by abolitionism among the middle and upper classes. An illustration of this is provided by a bizarre incident that occurred on 2 October 1843 at a meeting of the Loyal National Repeal Association in Dublin. According to the Repeal press, after the meeting had adjourned, a 'Negro' stepped onto the Speaker's platform and made the following little speech:

37 Riach, 'Blacks and Blackface', p. 241.
38 *Limerick Reporter*, 11 November 1845.
39 Rehin, 'Harlequin Jim Crow', p. 689; Fisch, '"Negrophilism"', pp. 25–37.

I am vera glad to see Massa Dan O Connell, for he save the life of black people (cheers and laughter). I hear of him when no bigger than that (placing hand within a foot of the surface of the table), and though I was brought up a Protestant, I am now a Catholic, and will die in that religion for the sake of Massa Dan O Connell (loud laughter in which the Liberator heartily joined followed this burst of eloquence.)[40]

O Connell was noted for his espousal of the rights of the slave and had made anti-slavery headlines in 1842 when he sent back money collected in the United States in support of the Repeal movement because it came with the proviso that he abandon his anti-slavery stance. He was in fact being duplicitous, using the issue to provide himself with moral credibility without paying the economic price of his anti-slavery stance.[41] This aside, it is clear that in Ireland the subversive potential of blackface as a tactic of class censure was retained. Apart from the dubious taste of this performance, the irony of presenting O Connell – a large landowner with political ambitions – as the dominant partner in an evoked slave–master relation is dangerously close to criticism of the emerging class of Loyal Nationalists in Ireland. For this instance of racial masking is used to facilitate the contravention of another ethnic signifier: the religious divide that had formed the legal basis of British discriminatory practices in Ireland, and was the defining component of British (anti-Catholic) and Irish bourgeois (later Catholic) nationalism. The 'Negro' who 'converts' from Protestantism to Catholicism in gratitude to 'Massa Dan O Connell' suggests, in this relatively minor performance, an ambivalence in the relationship between the Repeal movement and its populist power base.[42] This ambivalence finds expression in the portrayal of the subaltern population as subject to continuing servitude in a reformed colonial,

---

40 *Pilot*, 4 October 1843.

41 As Lee Jenkins points out: 'That O Connell, despite Douglass' protestations to the contrary, was receiving money for his Repeal cause from Southern slaveholders at the time of Douglass' Irish tour is evident from a letter addressed to O Connell, from Dublin abolitionist James Haughton in the Irish press' ('"Black O Connell"', p. 40 n14).

42 This incident occurred when the British government was considering prosecuting O Connell for seditious libel. Before a decision had been taken, the Loyal National Repeal Association announced the monster meeting at Clontarf in terms strongly suggestive of a planned insurrection. O Connell decided to obey its subsequent banning by the British government and cancelled the meeting. The incident remains contentious, one view being that O Connell obeyed the ban in order to save lives (the government had threatened to send in troops), and the other that he had never intended to support populist revolt but had overplayed his hand in the hope that the British government would back down.

that is to say nationalist, context; the inference being that a nationalist bourgeoisie would duplicate the colonial élite in all but name. In other words, blackface allows the performance of subversion, in this case a critique of O Connell's political ambitions, perhaps even of his apparently enlightened anti-slavery stance.

Significantly, this incident occurred in a country with neither an Africanist population nor the modern industrial base that gave minstrelsy in the United States its particular class–racial dynamic. Ireland was, however, experiencing considerable unrest as the activities of the imperial power and nationalist movement came face to face with the non-modern populations of the rural base whose political interests were very different from those of their social betters.[43] Adopting and *articulating* blackface in this context therefore has a rather different import to that of the minstrel show in the United States. Used in this way blackface imitation effects a bond between non-modern social formations: black (slave) folk are linked to the Irish peasantry through a metonymic alliance which allows the subjection of the slave to reverberate beyond the immediate context of the discourse of nationalism.

There were further radicalizations of African American impersonation in Ireland at this time that pointed to the mutual experience of oppression. These disturbances of cultural, racial and historical difference can be read as an attempt to counter what Bhabha has called 'the narcissistic demands of colonial authority',[44] by displacing, or at least complicating, the prestigious image of elite abolitionism. Popular pairings of the plight of the American slave and that of the Irish poor were commonplace, as Irish peasants seeking land reform and political rights drew direct comparisons between themselves and those enslaved in the Americas, exploiting the symbolic and increasingly political potential of the slavery issue in Britain.[45]

And in the early 1840s, controversy raged in Ireland regarding the forced emigration of some of the Irish poor to the West Indies (specifically Jamaica) to replace slave labour lost to planters with emancipation in

---

43 David Lloyd remarks of the emergence of the Irish state that 'it is a paradox of nation-
    alism that though it may often summon into being a "people" which is to form and
    subtend the nation-state, it is always confronted with that people as a potentially
    disruptive *excess* over the nation and its state' (*Ireland after History*, p. 33).
44 Homi Bhabha, 'Of Mimicry and Man', in *The Location of Culture* (London and New
    York: Routledge, 1994), p. 88.
45 Speaking of Marxism and feminism, Lloyd remarks on the 'continuing dynamic by
    which nationalism is formed in articulation or conjuncture with other social movements',
    a position which could usefully be expanded in this context to include transnational
    movements such as anti-slavery, and vice-versa (*Ireland after History*, p. 23).

1833. Fears of enslavement on arrival in Jamaica had the effect of raising the ideological stakes and further enforcing the analogy with slavery in the popular imagination. A letter in the *Limerick Reporter* of 12 January 1841 states that 'passengers' on a vessel bound for the West Indies had been 'forcibly detained', going on to declare that '[t]his forced detention is an undoubted violation of the liberty of the subject, and is virtually an early announcement of the system of slavery that is likely to await the unfortunate emigrants'.[46]

While slavery in the West Indies had by then been abolished, the system of indentured labour that replaced it bore great similarity to the previous institution. This was exacerbated by the fact that few would live to complete their contracts and repay their debt of passage. There was also a precedent for Irish enslavement in the West Indies in the Cromwellian deportations to Monserrat, Virginia and Barbados in the mid-seventeenth century,[47] linked in the popular imagination, like later forced indenture, with British colonial policy in Ireland. The tone of the debate regarding the 'Jamaica Emigration Scheme' shows that there was certainly popular belief in the British intention to enslave those participating, and indeed the evidence is that most who sailed did not do so willingly.

These plays on the similarities of colonial and slave bondage point to concurrent, un-racialized conceptions of the various economies of oppression at play across the Atlantic during the period. This is not to equate slavery with colonial oppression, but rather to suggest the existence of an interface between marginalized groups, often resisting modernization, in the emergent west. That interface is formed through associative patterns, and through interactive and imitative strategies of resistance and reform. Such associations, based on metonymic alliances across marginal or subaltern groups, permitted the use of the *idea* of slavery as an expression of radical resistance. This strategy therefore did not, unlike minstrelsy – perhaps the dominant mode of the interface in the international arena – rely on the minstrel mask as a signifier of difference, maintaining instead the political potential of international associations that blackface imitations of slave culture in the United States often worked to undermine.

There was also both context and precedent for masking in Ireland, where, from the early nineteenth century, it played an important role

46 Many of the ships carrying these indentured servants sailed from the West Clare ports of Kilrush and Kilkee. For competing contemporary accounts of this emigration, see *The Limerick Chronicle* (an establishment broadsheet) and *Limerick Reporter* (Whiggish newspaper broadly aligned with Repeal), 1840–43.
47 See Seán O Callaghan, *To Hell or Barbados: The Ethnic Cleansing of Ireland* (Dingle: Brandon Books, 2001).

in subaltern insurgency, although it was commonly associated with whiteface. Radical subaltern groups known as the 'whiteboys' disguised themselves by painting their faces with ash before engaging in nocturnal raids involving the killing or punishment of recalcitrant landlords, agents or rent collectors, the theft of food supplies, arson, the killing and maiming of farm animals, and the ploughing of pastureland for conacre.[48] Other forms of masking were also employed. For example, the activities of the notorious 'Captain Rock' were similar to those of the whiteboys. Although individuated by name, Captain Rock was never one particular person, but rather an identity assumed by whosoever was playing the part for the night, week, etc.; as such, the name signified not a person but a form of violent resistance. Irish agrarian activism re-emerged in the United States, though its radicalism did not survive the Atlantic passage. It acquired a distinctly racial cast in the industrial cities of the East, where black rather than whiteface was adopted and what Roediger calls 'blackface on black' violence became a convenient means of venting class frustrations, with African Americans often the victim of working-class (and/or) Irish American mobs.[49]

Blackface masking, however, also retained a subversive political appeal for Irish Americans. In the 1870s and 80s the 'Molly Maguires', a group of Irish American Pennsylvania coal-miners, adopting masks and women's clothing, killed sixteen mine bosses during the labour agitation of the period.[50] The 'Mollies' provide a useful example of the use of masking as transgression; crossing lines of gender and race was in some way an appropriate contravention of the modern, industrial, capital–labour relation. Of course, the relationship between the minstrel stage and the consolidation of structural and class-based racism in the United States is not undermined by these subaltern effects. Metonymic alliances did not survive the Atlantic passage, which involved the Irish in a shift from the position of colonial subjects to that of imperial agents, with predictable consequences for their new relationship to internally colonized populations. But, at a time when African Americans were called 'smoked Irish', Irish Americans were dubbed 'white niggers'[51] and workers in both Britain and

---

48 For a discussion of whiteboy violence and its context see Michael Beames, *Peasants and Power: The Whiteboy Movements and Their Control in Pre-Famine Ireland* (Sussex: Harvester Press, 1983).

49 Roediger, *Wages of Whiteness*, p. 106.

50 Twenty men were afterwards hanged for these killings. For an extended discussion of the Molly Maguires and their relationship to whiteboy violence, see Kevin Kenny, *Making Sense of the Molly Maguires* (Oxford: Oxford University Press, 1998).

51 For a discussion of contemporary uses of the comparison between Irish and African Americans in Irish political discourse, see Jenkins, 'Black O Connell', pp. 22–23, 38.

the United States in such employments as coal-mining, chimney-sweeping and charring were often racially as well as literally blackened, the adoption of blackface or the discussion of slavery *outside* the music hall or minstrel stage became a means of expressing and negotiating ambiguities in the highly racialized discourse of class.[52] In a transatlantic context masking, mimicry and minstrelsy can be seen as interrelated forms of tactical behaviour often linked to groups or sites in transition to modernity, yet retaining an affiliation to residual forms of premodern practice.

This was the milieu in which Douglass operated during the course of his transatlantic tour. His rhetoric from this period shows him to have been aware of the potency of racial imagery, counterfeit and burlesque both in crossing class lines and articulating categories of dissent outside the sphere of abolitionist ideology. It was a symbolism that he actively employed. At a speech given in Ayr, Scotland, on 24 March 1846, Douglass codified his social rise since escaping from slavery by indicating his distance from the debased and 'blackened' forms of labour he – then a skilled craftsman trained as a ship's caulker – was forced to undertake in his early days in the North. 'After my escape,' he explained, 'I arrived at New Bedford, where I was engaged rolling oil casks on the quay, and doing anything that presented itself; yes, ladies and gentlemen, you must know that the individual who now addresses you even occupied at that time the *elevated* position of a chimney sweep.'[53] In his 'Farewell Speech to the British People' of 1847, Douglass described the Evangelical Ecumenical Alliance, which had failed to exclude slaveholders from its ranks shortly before, as 'miserably deceived – misled by the jack o' lanterns from America', an image combining the painted grin of the minstrel mask with the lamp black sometimes used by minstrels instead of burnt cork to 'black up'.

Earlier in the same speech, Douglass exhorted abolitionist crowds to 'adopt the motto of Pat', the popular Irishman of the Victorian stage and *Punch* magazine, as a 'principle of action'. Dale Cockrell remarks of the early minstrel stage in the United States that, significantly, 'more and more ... "Others" represented "Others," that representation itself bec[ame] politicised ... The Irish, who occupied a "low Other" social niche with black Americans, claimed triumph over blacks in issues of power and

---

52 Richard Moody makes the point that '[f]requently the very first entertainment seen by a new [immigrant] community was the minstrel show, whether performed by professionals or amateurs' (*America Takes the Stage: Romanticism in American Drama* [Bloomington, IN: Indiana University Press, 1955], p. 89).

53 Blassingame, *FDP* 1.l, pp. 199–200, emphasis original. Obviously Douglass is also punning on the social and literal meanings of 'elevated'.

control – representation! – on the stage and in the streets.'[54]

While the hallmark of minstrelsy was blackface, the form also relied heavily on the reproduction of black and other dialects as spaces of articulation. The implications of Douglass's use of dialect spaces will be dealt with in more detail in the following section. In this instance, however, Douglass, using Irish dialect to tell a British joke, is claiming jurisdiction over the symbolism of Irishness in a manner reminiscent of the representational authority assumed by minstrel performers over black subjects. 'Pat,' according to Douglass, 'upon entering a Tipperary row[,] [s]aid he, "Wherever you see a head, hit it!" [Loud cheers and laughter.]'[55] 'Pat and Mike' routines involved a cross-talk act in dialect, punctuated by bouts of violence by characters both stupid and, preferably, drunk. Irish acts were commonplace on the Victorian stage. Like minstrel shows, they created a permissive realm for their audiences, a space in which social norms regarding the use of violence, the expression of political opinion and so on, could be simultaneously violated and contained. By slipping into Irish dialect, Douglass crosses into the permissive realm of Irishness in which, according to the representational stereotype, such behaviour as drunkenness and violence is normalized. Despite the self-evidently negative connotations of the stereotype, however, particularly in an age bent on redeeming the working classes from the evils and excesses of alcoholic consumption, this portrayal also underlines the liberating potential of mimicry. For Douglass's representation of the Irish is one sanctioned by the imperial power (Britain) even as it acknowledges a population that is resistant to its regulatory stamp.

This instance of dialect usage illustrates the risks and opportunities of Douglass's use of 'Pat' as a stereotyped persona. The creation of a dialect space (which frequently occurs in Douglass's speeches) allows the speaker to enter the permissive realm of the subject of the mimicry, freeing the speaker himself from the strictures of the social and institutional space in which he is performing. Potentially, this can allow the articulation of ideas otherwise outside the discursive parameters of the social space. In this instance, use of the dialect space permits Douglass to suggest categories of resistance that transgress the abolitionist doctrines of non-violence

54 Dale Cockrell, *Demons of Disorder: Early Blackface Minstrels and Their World* (Cambridge: Cambridge University Press, 1997), p. 199 n43.

55 'Farewell to the British People', address delivered in London, on 30 March 1847 (Blassingame, *FDP* 1.2, pp. 19–52, excerpts pp. 31, 35). In this speech also Douglass quotes O Connell who 'once said, speaking of Ireland – *no matter for my illustration, how truly or falsely* – that "her history may be traced, like the track of a wounded man through a crowd"' (Blassingame, *FDP*, 1.2, p. 27, emphasis added).

and moral suasion, doctrines that, ironically, provide the moral legitimation underpinning his address ('Wherever you see a head, hit it!').[56]

Richard Bradbury has argued that, throughout his career, Douglass
vacillated 'between supporting moral force and physical force', concluding
that 'his work as a whole can be seen as an expression of the contradictions and tension of the reformer seeking to reform existing structures
while attempting to remain within [their] ... conservative logic'.[57] In a
letter to Francis Jackson from Scotland dated 29 January 1846, Douglass
confessed:

> My Soul sickens at the thought, yet I see in myself all those elements of
> character which were I to yield to their promptings might lead me to deeds
> as bloody as those at which my soul now sickens and from which I now turn
> with disgust and shame. Thank God liberty is no longer to be contended for
> and gained by instruments of death.[58]

Evidently Douglass was at this time drawn to, though never overtly
advocated, the recourse to physical as well as moral force as a means to end
slavery, an issue then dividing the transatlantic abolitionist movement. By
adopting the dialect space of Irishness, Douglass could suggest alternative strategies to the moral suasion advocated by Garrisonian abolitionists
without directly challenging their official non-violent stance. Mimicry of
another kind of other allowed him momentarily to exceed the authority
of the abolitionist frame in which he was speaking. By assuming the
identity of an undisciplined, external subject, who was both an unassim-
ilated other and a figure of public ridicule, he could disrupt that moral
authority while still maintaining the appearance of complete adherence.

It has become somewhat of a truism to say that like other subject
groups in Africa, Asian and the Americas, the Irish were during the
colonial period subjected to the disciplinary codes of imperial fantasy.
Unlike these other groups, the Irish presented a particular representational
challenge to British cultural and racial hierarchies in a period when the
British empire was expanding into Asia, Africa and Australia. In a letter
to his wife in 1860, Charles Kingsley infamously wrote of the Irish poor:

---

56 These doctrines are not quite restored in his subsequent statement that 'the
  abolitionists have resolved, that wherever slavery manifests itself in the United
  States, they will hit it. (Renewed cheering)' (Blassingame, *FDP*,1.2, p. 31).
57 Richard Bradbury, 'Douglass and the Chartists', in Alan J. Rice and Martin Crawford,
  eds, *Liverating Sojourn: Frederick Douglass and Transatlantic Reform* (Athens, GA,
  and London: University of Georgia Press, 1999), pp. 169–86 (173).
58 Frederick Douglass to Francis Jackson, Royal Hotel, Dundee, Scotland, 29 January
  1846, Boston Anti-slavery Collection, Ms.A.1.2 v16, p. 13.

But I am haunted by the human chimpanzees I saw along that hundred miles of horrible country. I don't believe they are our fault. I believe there are not only more of them than of old, but that they are happier, better, more comfortably fed and lodged under our rule than they ever were. But to see white chimpanzees is dreadful; if only they were black, one would not feel it so much, but their skins, except where tanned by exposure, are as white as ours.[59]

Representations of the Irish in the United States and Britain in this period typically cast them as low-browed threats to the political and racial order. The Irish, very different yet disturbingly the same, make obvious the arbitrariness of blackness as a racial sign. In the United States, it was the emergence of skin colour as a general category of difference that ultimately facilitated Irish American integration. In Kingsley, the 'white chimpanzees' disturb the binary oppositions of racialist discourse, though they confirm the necessity for colonial rule. By default, they generate a third category of representation, one in which the disturbance to the dominant symbolism of the colonial relationship can be contained. That contained rebellion against difference is present in Douglass's mimicry of Irishness, which allows him to exceed the parameters of abolitionist authority, by projecting ideological inconsistencies – recourse to modes of violent protest – onto the rhetoric of otherness.[60]

Yet, somewhat paradoxically, it also allows him to confirm his sameness to the British crowd. Alan Rice has argued that Douglass adopted a form of 'strategic Anglophilia'[61] while in Britain, by identifying with and promoting ideals of British racial liberalism. The strategic effect of this Anglophilia was that it facilitated Douglass's public acceptance in Britain and allowed for comparisons unfavourable to the United States to be made between the two countries.

There were of course significant differences in racial attitudes between Britain and the United States at this time, stemming from their respective

59 Cited in L. Curtis, *Anglo-Saxons and Celts: A Study of Anti-Irish Prejudice in Victorian England* (Bridgeport, CT: University of Bridgeport, 1968), p. 84.
60 Another disruption of the claims of moral suasion occurred when Douglass changed his position on the constitutionality of slavery as the possibility of a civil war increased. On this occasion, however, Douglass's position is more 'enlightened' than subversive, as it upholds the moral authority of the American nation-state and the legitimacy of state violence.
61 Alan Rice, '"The dogs of Old England know that I am a man." Or do they?', Paper given at the conference 'Frederick Douglass at Home and Abroad', Department of the Interior, Washington, DC, 13–16 September 1999. Rice's paper later appeared in revised form as chapter 7 of his *Radical Narratives of the Black Atlantic* (London and New York: Continuum, 2003).

political and economic agendas. Douglass was met not only with an apparent absence of racial prejudice (against black Americans), but with a form of class-based 'Negrophilia' which welcomed him into circles from which he might otherwise have been excluded. Well-spoken, intelligent and handsome, Douglass found himself relieved of the social requirements of family and economic privilege by the romance of his situation. He claims to have enjoyed 'nearly two years of equal social privileges in England, often dining with gentlemen of great literary, social, political and religious eminence'.[62]

To some extent this was a product of the moral prestige enjoyed by the abolitionist cause and the many adherents eager to establish their liberal principles. But Douglass enjoyed an unprecedented degree of social mobility in Britain and Ireland conferred on him by the upper and merchant classes with whom he consorted. And this mobility seems to have occurred by virtue of, rather than despite, his status as a black American and romantic fugitive. Thus while Douglass's professed Anglophilia, in the early years at least, certainly served strategic anti-slavery purposes, it was by no means limited to questions of direct political consequence. It was evident across a wide range of social and cultural issues, including his romantic interest in Scottish history and in the work of Walter Scott. It also emerged in his attitude to Ireland and, perhaps most importantly, was linked to the social mobility he enjoyed and the class affiliations realized during his stay in the United Kingdom in the years 1845–47.

The class profile of Douglass's audiences was to some degree determined by the venues at which he spoke, venues often arranged by local abolitionists, and therefore beyond his control. But socially, as his biographer William McFeely remarks, 'Douglass reached upward, rather than outward to labourers, one of whom he had been not so long ago.'[63]

This was evident as class preference in Britain in the same way it had been evident as ethnic and religious preference in Ireland. McFeely sees Douglass's attitude as mitigated somewhat by his contention that Douglass made a 'firm declaration of common purpose with the [British] Chartists', in Bristol on 25 August 1849. According to McFeely, Douglass

---

62 See Douglass, *Autobiographies*, p. 388.

63 McFeely, *Frederick Douglass*, p. 141; Blassingame, *FDP* 1.1, pp. 344–45. Douglass was more open to the use of the term 'white slavery' in the United States however. In *My Bondage and My Freedom*, he regrets the racism and fear which prevented white workers from making common cause with enslaved blacks, observing that 'both are plundered and by the same plunderers'. The passage is repeated in *Life and Times*. See Douglass, *Autobiographies*, pp. 330, 627–28.

made metaphoric use of the term 'slavery', and 'spoke of "political slavery in England"' and of 'slavery in the army, ... the navy, and, looking upon the labouring population, he contemplated them as slaves', going on to ask: 'Why does not England set the example by doing away with these forms of slavery at home, before it called upon the United States to do so?' This is a misreading of Douglass's speech on this occasion. In fact he was quoting from 'a paper [he had taken up] the other day', and went on to dispel any analogy between American slavery and the British working class, proclaiming 'that there was no more similarity between slavery, as existing in the United States, and any institution in this country'.[64]

But the tendency McFeely remarks on to 'reach upward' and away from any identification with manual labour and the working class is one of the strongest indications of Douglass's growing class affiliations during his overseas sojourn, affiliations that had racial implications. Insisting in a letter to the Lynn Anti-Slavery Sewing Circle that 'I am by no means unmindful of the poor; and you may rely upon me as one who will never desert the cause of the poor, no matter whether black or white',[65] Douglass nevertheless publicly underlined pauperism as a class status peculiar only to whites in the United States. In his 'Farewell Speech to the British People' Douglass contends that

> we do not have black paupers in America; we leave pauperism to be fostered and taken care of by white people; not that I intend any disrespect to my audience in making this statement. (Hear.) I can assure you I am in no ways prejudiced against colour. (Laughter.) But the idea of a black pauper in the United States is most absurd.[66]

Moreover, his repudiation of common cause with the British working class can be usefully contrasted with the stance of two of his contemporary fugitives, Lewis Garrard and Milton Clarke, brothers whose narratives were published in 1845 and 1846 respectively.[67] An appendix to an abolitionist compendium published in 1846 includes an essay entitled

---

64 A similar misreading is made by Richard Bradbury, who does, however, note Douglass's denial of any parallels between chattel slavery and wage slavery ('Douglass and the Chartists', p. 183). Douglass reiterated the denial of any similarity between wage and chattel slavery in a speech made in Bridgewater several days later.

65 Letter to the Lynn Anti-Slavery Sewing Circle, London, 18 August 1846, in Foner, *Frederick Douglass*, 1, p. 188.

66 Blassingame, *FDP*, 1.2, p. 37.

67 Lewis Garrard Clarke, *Narrative of the Sufferings of Lewis Clarke, during a Captivity of more than Twenty-five Years, Among the Algerines of Kentucky, Dictated by himself*, ed. Joseph C. Lovejoy (Boston: D.H. Ela, 1845), and Lewis Garrard and Milton Clarke, *Narratives of the Sufferings of Lewis and Milton Clarke, Sons of a Soldier of the Revolution ... Dictated by Themselves*, ed. Joseph C. Lovejoy (Boston: Bela Marsh, 1846).

'Facts: From the Personal Knowledge of Milton Clarke: Hired Slaves and Bagging Factories', dealing with the exploitation of factory workers and making common cause across the colour line within the parameters of class-based reform.[68] Such a comparison suggests that Douglass's Anglophilia was not an unqualified result of his need to delegitimize slaveholding in the American republic; it also involved carefully cultivated middle- and upper-class associations, and was markedly uninterested in popular socio-political movements.

In the context then, of an Anglophilia coupled with and qualified by an increasing middle- to upper-class identification, Douglass's frequent imitation of Irishness – a threat to British colonial and class configurations at the time of his visit as throughout the nineteenth century – acquires a more ambiguous cast. That ambiguity lies in what has been called mimicry's 'double consequence': the identification with the subject of the imitation, and, simultaneously, that subject's disavowal.[69] Bhabha also describes 'the effect of mimicry' as 'camouflage', going on to call mimicry, 'the sign of a double articulation, strategy of reform, regulation and discipline, which appropriates the other as it visualises power'.[70]

A reading of disavowal is consistent with Douglass's attitudes to the Irish peasantry while in Ireland, when he resisted any yoking of their plight with that of American slaves, a comparison which many Irish were wont to make. But by articulating Irishness, Douglass takes advantage of an anomaly in British racialist discourse, illustrating (in racial *and* class terms) his distance from a recognizable, and recognizably different, racial other. In this sense his rhetoric can be seen to participate in the production of race, but, as with his use of class metaphors, in ways which evidently cannot be understood solely as counter-responses to the racial paradigms of the United States and the slave–master relation which engendered them.

The African American Context

Certain difficulties attach to the critical evaluation of non-scripted performance in popular rather than formal theatrical domains. Despite the fact that Douglass and others were heavily involved in public speaking in

---

68 Appendix: 'A Sketch of the Clarke Family by Lewis Clarke', pp. 77–79; 'Question and Answers, by Lewis Clarke', pp. 79–84; 'Facts', pp. 96–98, in *Interesting Memoirs and Documents Relating to American Slavery* (London: Chapman, 1846).

69 See Blassingame, *FDP*, 1.1, pp. 34–130, and Jenkins, 'Black O Connell', p. 29. For a discussion of the basis of Douglass's attitudes to the Irish in anti-Catholic Nativism, see Hardack, 'Slavery in Romanism', pp. 115–40.

70 Bhabha, *Location of Culture*, pp. 85–86.

the early 1840s, few US examples of abolitionist speechmaking or other performative spectacles remain from the period immediately prior to the first publication of the *Narrative*. While acknowledging the limitations of any historical approach to performance or its wider political impact, it is nevertheless important to maximize the historical materials that are available. What evidence there is of this stage of Douglass's performative life comes largely from the reports of his activities while overseas. The widespread early use of shorthand in newspaper reportage in Britain and Ireland where its use was commonplace several years before its introduction to the United States provides a rich source of historical documentation as well as a glimpse of Douglass's public persona in all its immediacy.

Blassingame's collection is particularly important in this respect, collating newspaper reports of meetings, speeches and interviews from the earliest stage of Douglass's career. Not only do these contemporary reports transcribe much of what was actually said, in many instances they record the performative gestures – visual and oral – of the speaker, general mood and tone, and spectator response. As such, many of these reports can function retrospectively as a collection of dramatic sketches, complete with stage directions and details of audience expectation and interaction. Indeed, the extent of the detail provided facilitates not just interpretative readings of rhetorical content or style, it mandates an analysis of the performative dynamic itself within the wider theatricality of public debate in an age disinclined to broaden democratic participation.

As such, what is required is a critical repositioning with regard to these documents from which they may be seen as snapshots of a particular performative dynamic within the broader context of their historical enactment. The African American element of that context for example, suggests that attention to traditional forms in the Afro-American folk tradition, specifically those associated with oral culture, are relevant here. In that folk tradition, the character of the trickster emerges as a figure of resistance to the slave system in the rural South. An obvious example of this function is evident in the picaresque slave narratives, which, unlike the autobiographical rationality of the form pioneered by Douglass, rely on episodic sketches featuring the author as the central character in a battle of wits with those higher up the racial or class ladder. Typically in these narratives, middle-class morality – the rights and wrongs of stealing, lying, sabotage and so on – goes out the window in tales privileging wiliness as a tactic of survival, with the trickster's talents often hidden behind a façade of stupidity or ignorance.

The trickster figure in African American folk culture has counterparts in Native American and other oral literatures. Through time and contact, the trickster emerged in blackface minstrelsy, combining humour, popular racism and social criticism in one. The element of social criticism existed above and beyond the desire to distinguish between free and slave labour, or the related categories of race and ethnicity, and was directed at those higher up the class and economic ladder, normally bosses, factory owners and so on. As in the picaresque slave narrative therefore, the artlessness of slave characters in minstrelsy often masked a capacity for cunning that belied their apparent stupidity. It is this craft of disingenuity, the capacity to provide a vehicle for social criticism from behind the veil of submission, which makes the trickster figure an important actor in the public staging of political debate during the period.

In much of his early speechmaking, Douglass played with popular minstrel portrayals of the trickster figure. In this way, he was able to straddle class as well as ethnic divisions in his public addresses, simultaneously marshalling popular as well as elite forms as tools of protest and debate in the international arena.

Though overshadowed by the negative impact of pervasive racial stereotypes, then, the significance of the trickster as a shifting emblem of popular resistance in Afro- and American culture as a whole is well established. In his twentieth-century essay 'Change the Joke and Slip the Yoke',[71] Ellison wrote of the problematic image of the African American generated through popular stage stereotypes, and warned of the dangers of reading the trickster figure in African American literature and folklore through the lens of white American culture. 'In the entertainment industry,' Ellison states, 'the Negro is reduced to a negative sign that usually appears in a comedy of the grotesque and the unacceptable,' concluding that, because 'the fact of Negro slavery went to the moral heart of the American social drama, ... [s/he] was too real for easy fantasy, too serious to be dealt with in anything less than a national art.'[72]

The development of that national art form has been understood in its first phase, (the mid to late nineteenth century) as the province of white performers creating a culture of consent around the issue of Southern slavery. While this is largely the case, a blanket understanding of mid-century performance as the province of white performers with specific political motivations neglects the intricate dynamic of individual performances and the performers themselves. It also runs the risk of sidelining the broader use of performative modes by black and white

71 Ralph Ellison, 'Change the Joke and Slip the Yoke', in Nellie McKay and Henry Louis Gates Jr, *The Norton Anthology of African American Literature* (New York and London: Norton, 1997), pp. 1541–49.
72 Ellison, 'Change the Joke', pp. 1542–43.

alike in a period notable for its level of political activism and interest in ethical discourse.

Douglass frequently engaged with the image and mask of the trickster and minstrel. Far from being reduced to the 'negative sign' Ellison remarks upon, however, Douglass actively engaged with oral forms of parody in his public speaking, retaining, even at the end of his life, a tendency to ironize the 'social drama' of identity formation those forms more typically implied. For example, in a speech delivered in 1887 in Washington, DC at a reception held in honour of Arthur O. Conner and Thomas Gratton Edmonde, Frederick Douglass related the following anecdote, allegedly taken from his forty-five years of experience as an abolitionist speaker and activist:

> Speaking in Ohio, some time ago, a good Irishman, after I had got through, walking behind me, said to another Irishman:
> 'Jimmie, what do you think of that?'
> 'Faith,' said he, 'he is only a half nagur.' (Laughter.)
> 'Ah but,' said he, 'if half a nagur could make a speech like that, what could a whole one do?' (Great laughter.)[73]

Ellison contends that later minstrel performances by black Americans are subversions of the original intent of blackface, arguing that 'the Negro's masking is motivated . . . by a profound rejection of the image used to usurp his identity'.[74] These subversions are not limited to blackface performance. Moreover they are in evidence throughout the nineteenth century, existing in constant dialogue with broader political fora in which the politics of identity played a key role. An earlier instance of Douglass's use of a variation of this anecdote occurs in a speech given in Coventry, Britain, on 2 February 1847.[75] In this example from the 1880s, he manipulates his own self-portrayal by appropriating the voice of his racial critics (Irish Americans), transforming the meaning of blackness as debasement in minstrel performance, into blackness as an indication of linguistic achievement. In doing so he challenges the racial profile of performative mimicry in the United States, reversing the negative image of African Americans created by blackface minstrelsy and playing on other signifiers of difference, specifically dialect, through which the ethno-racial codification endemic to nineteenth-century minstrelsy, and part of the particularization of identity in the United States in the nineteenth century, occurred.

---

73 Blassingame, *FDP*, 5, p. 267.
74 Ellison, 'Change the Joke', p. 1547.
75 Blassingame, *FDP*, 1.2, p. 7.

Most notable in Douglass's rebuttal of populist racial stereotyping is this iteration of a dialect space, a clearly audible signifier of both ethnicity and class. For the purposes of this discussion, a dialect space is defined as a space of identification; an expression of the speaker (or character's) position on the socio-linguistic continuum; an indication of ethnicity, class, region or even gender. As the reports of his performances indicate, Douglass frequently adopted verbal masks, using dialect, an established yet overdetermined sign system, as a means of staging and controlling public debate.

In the example given above, Douglass and his audience view one another other across 'the racial joke' identified by Ellison as being at the heart of understanding of what is valid or true about US experience and identity. For Douglass's performance has farther-reaching implications than a somewhat doubtful humour; he plays with the tradition of the trickster yet shifts the character's typical ethnic profile from African to Irish American. In doing so, Douglass suggests his own indeterminacy, slipping, through his use of dialect, from black- into white-face (or voice). The nature of this performance, the facility with which Douglass adopts another linguistic mask, complicates the exclusive nature of signifiers, such as whiteness, blackness or class. Moving within another dialectically created identity by momentarily casting himself as a member of an Irish American audience who, despite his naivety, can recognize quality when he sees it, Douglass underlines the inherent stagedness of voice, image and identity, *and* the essentially hybrid nature of the American condition.

For Douglass reproduces, then breaches historio-cultural codes of racial representation through a combination of ventriloquism – the projection of the voice of another – and cultural creolization. The latter sees the redefinition of identity as an ongoing process of interaction and negotiation across ethnic or class boundaries. Identity then does not stem from essentialist criteria, nor become ossified by hierarchical structures of social control in which representative power is the exclusive domain of particular ethnic groups.

Clearly, the kind of subversion involved in the appropriation, arguably even the inversion of African and Irish American identities from Douglass's late performances, is related to the theatrical displays regulating the class and cultural politics of the antebellum period. Indeed, Douglass's reference to his own mixed racial heritage ('half a nagur') in the late phase of a career spent as a writer, abolition advocate, Union war correspondent and critic of Reconstruction underlines the degree to which the issue of identity politics continued to saturate late nineteenth-century discursive fields. Douglass's performance confirms the importance assumed by masking in the representation and appropriation of political agency in the late nineteenth century, for African Americans, as for other sections of US society.

Two major issues arise in considerations of Douglass's iteration of US identity in all its guises. First of these is Douglass's use of dialect spaces, an important element of his early speeches. In the context of the nineteenth century (and indeed much of the twentieth), dialect, or the deviation from standard (English) is understood as a marker of difference; an expression of the margins and, as a result, a space less subject to regulation and control, more open to the play of language and meaning.

Second is the question of audience composition, expectation and interaction. Regardless of their level of rhetorical prowess, public speakers and performers were never entirely in control of the subject matter under discussion at public gatherings. Aside from the pressures imposed by the vested interests of individual organizers – abolitionists for example – each audience constituted a new challenge, for its composition, political orientation, motivation and expectations could vary significantly from venue to venue, as could its readiness to engage directly with the speakers themselves. Each performance, then, can be to some extent considered an original, with the input, or potential input of the crowd itself a key actor in the staging of, and debate around, key issues. The level and kind of Douglass's interaction with his audiences will be discussed here, as will his ability to engage with issues of identity formation by working with rather than against the apparently limiting expectations of those audiences.

Context and Engagement

Today, Douglass is perhaps best known for his three autobiographies, which detail his life in slavery, flight to freedom and emergence as a public figure. These carefully crafted, textual acts of self-creation have ensured Douglass's place in western historical and literary canons, where he is now generally recognized by US historians as the representative African American of the nineteenth century.[76] Despite (or perhaps because of) the exceptional nature of his life, Douglass is seen as the man best epitomizing the capacity of the African American character to overcome adversity, adhere to principles of social justice and attain social, economic and political success; in other words to create himself within the parameters of US subjectivity and to resist the category of 'other'. One of the key imports of the autobiographies derives from this position: in the course

76 Blassingame, *FDP*, 1.1, p. xi.

of charting Douglass's life, the autobiographies also profile the development of American history from a critically engaged perspective of racial exclusion.

Despite the obvious importance of the autobiographies, however, it is important to note that much of the efficacy of Douglass's activism sprang from the popularity he enjoyed as a public speaker, his command of the platform, ability to capture and hold the attention of large crowds, and sway them with his rhetorical prowess. According to Blassingame, '[d]ramatic skill contributed heavily to Douglass's success as an orator. On the platform, he was a tragedian, a comic, a mimic and an occasional singer.'[77] The centrality of written documentation to Douglass scholarship, whether literary or historical, indicates a certain hierarchy in the academic and cultural focus, a tendency to view the past as evidenced only through certain kinds of texts. But accounts of Douglass's eloquence testify not only to his abilities as a public speaker, but to the importance of the role of performance and spectacle in his work: as modes of communication, as core elements in the politics of representation and in manipulating popular engagements with official discourse and ideology in the public sphere.

In the nineteenth century, public image and interaction were important vehicles to political participation. In anti-slavery politics, the figure of the black abolitionist was a form of testimony, confirming, through spectacle, the physical reality of the slave. For Northern US and European audiences, Douglass supplied a tangible, real-world referent to what was for most the virtual world of the slave South, a space lying beyond their personal knowledge or experience. Aside from this, although now extant only as transcriptions, much of Douglass's early speeches resist categories of class and ethnicity that conform to western prioritizations of literacy and text.

In this respect, the content of Douglass's oratory differs significantly from that of the *Narrative*, which constructs a rational subjectivity within the parameters of the American politics and the literary tradition. The importance of the role of literacy in Douglass's path to freedom has been much remarked upon, due in large part to the centrality of literacy in the *Narrative*. Despite its role in Douglass's economic and social advancement, however (the link is made compellingly by Douglass himself), the importance of literacy or textuality as an indicator of subjectivity can be overstated. Indeed, 'linking reading and writing inextricably with

77 Blassingame, *FDP*, l.1, p. xxxi. See also *Liberator*, 18 February 1842; William Wells Brown, *Three Years in Europe* (London: n.p., 1852), p. 260.

social development' is, as Valerie Smith acknowledges, 'to display an inherent bias toward Anglo-American uses of language'.[78] Smith is referring specifically to the moment in Douglass's *Narrative* at which 'the white man's power to enslave the black man', the power of the white man over the written word and its interpretation, is revealed. Even a work that privileges literacy to the extent demonstrated in the 1845 *Narrative*, however, includes descriptions of non-literary, non-abolitionist modes of resistance in the slave culture Douglass describes.[79] But Douglass's use of popular modes in performance more clearly illustrates the extent to which forms of alternative cultural practice influenced his rhetoric, as well as providing insight into the social dynamics of abolitionism itself.

Douglass's rhetoric and performance in the period from his initiation as an anti-slavery speaker while still a fugitive in 1841 to his manumission in 1847, corresponds to a period in which, as Gilroy writes, Douglass's 'consciousness of "race," self and society were profoundly changed'.[80] That shift in consciousness marked the beginning of Douglass's self-authorization as representative US man. It was a period during which he engaged politically with a variety of social sectors. The period was also key to Douglass's self-construction as a major actor in abolitionist politics.

And although characterized by an almost unprecedented class rise, this phase of Douglass's career also shows evidence of an interest in populist representations of African American identity. That interest was specifically in 'non-modern' performative practices, namely, verbal masking and minstrelsy. David Lloyd has described the non-modern as 'a space in which the alternative survives, in the fullest sense of that word, not as a preserve, or an outside, but as an incommensurable set of cultural formations historically occluded from, yet never actually disengaged with, modernity'.[81] The prioritization of literacy and of the rational rhetoric of post-enlightenment subjectivity has tended to overshadow those forms of alternative practice, or engagements with cultural formations present in Douglass's work that do not support his current canonical or histor-

---

78 Valerie Smith, *Self Discovery and Authority in Afro-American Narrative* (Cambridge, MA: Harvard University Press, 1987), p. 4.

79 Jenny Sharpe notes the significance of the incident of the magical root, remarking of the episode, which is coincidental with Douglass's confrontation with the slave-breaker, Covey, that '[it] is ... present in the text as the marker of a resistance to slavery that did not originate in the anti-slavery movement' ('"Something Akin to Freedom"': The Case of Mary Prince', *Differences: A Journal of Feminist Cultural Studies*, 8.1 [1996], pp. 31–56 [34–35]).

80 Gilroy, *Black Atlantic*, p. 132.

81 Lloyd, *Ireland after History*, p. 2.

ical profile.[82] According to Henry Louis Gates Jr, for example, Douglass 'seems to have given priority to the spoken word over the written word', concluding that Douglass is 'Representative Man because he was Rhetorical Man', following the western model of developmental masculinity. An understanding of Douglass's performative persona as inherently 'rhetorical' in this sense neglects the presence of mimicry, politically informed, class-based engagement, and audience interaction. Each of these elements influenced his performances, in ways not necessarily coterminous with those outlined in their subsequent historicization.

Imitation also occurs in Douglass's written work, through the process of signifying. But Douglass's rhetorical employment of alternative strategies of political negotiation in his speechmaking merits some attention. Those strategies included the incorporation of elements of what Mikhail Bakhtin describes as 'carnival', namely, ritual spectacle and comic verbal composition.[83] Douglass's use of a racially overdetermined vocabulary of class and the centrality of mimicry to his public performances are themselves acts of resistance; enactments of his intellectual and ideological freedom that extend the space of participation within anti-slavery as a whole.

His performances also posit an (albeit tense) relationship to a concurrent, racialized mode of cultural representation, that of blackface minstrelsy. Although the importance of minstrelsy within the United States derives primarily from its role in the formation of a white working-class identity, the form also had significant impact on popular performance in the transatlantic arena. Douglass's performances were moulded by the encounter between the official, controlled spaces of abolitionist activism and the contested zones of carnival, in which minstrelsy was a notable player, illustrating the degree to which he was, in the 1840s, able to engage in strategic dialogue with a range of constituencies within and without the province of liberal reform. Those dialogues were as much lampoons of the ideological and representative control exerted by the abolitionist movement as attacks on the institution of slavery itself.

And, as Sexton notes of minstrelsy, 'blackface convention rendered permissible topics that were difficult to handle on the Victorian stage or in print'.[84] Although generally performing before the staunchly respectable – unquestionably polite if not exclusively élite audiences – Douglass occasionally used the abolitionist platform in a way that transgressed the norms of genteel morality by exploiting the slippage between black

---

82 See Gates, *Figures in Black*, pp. 106–08.
83 Concept of 'Carnival' described by Mikhail Bakhtin in *Rabelais and His World* (1965), trans. Hélène Iswolsky (Bloomington, IN: London University Press, 1984).
84 Sexton, *White Republic*, p. 166.

and blackface in the public sphere. In Limerick on 10 November 1845, for example, Douglass indulged his audience in the spectacle of whips, manacles and leg-irons, conjuring up visceral images of abuse and the grotesque. According to the *Limerick Reporter*, Douglass, towards the end of his speech,

> proceeded to exhibit some of the implements used in torturing the slaves, among which was a collar taken from the neck of a young woman who had escaped from Mobile. It had so worn into her neck that her blood and flesh were found on it (sensation). After showing the fetters used in chaining the feet of two slaves together, he exhibited a pair of hand-cuffs taken from a fugitive slave who escaped from Maryland into Pennsylvania. He knew the man well. He was being brought in custody to his master by a constable – he saw a sharp rock before him, and with one mighty effort he raised his hands, and, striking the hand-cuffs against the stone, broke them, and at the same time his left wrist (sensation). He fled and was overtaken, but with the unbroken hand he drew a dirk from his breast, and cut down his pursuer (cries of 'bravo') ... Mr Douglas[s] then went on to exhibit a horrid whip which was made of cow hide, and whose lashes were as hard as horn. They were clotted with blood when he first got them. He saw his master tie up a young woman eighteen years of age, and beat her with that identical whip until the blood ran down her back. ... (cries of 'horrible').[85]

On many occasions, Douglass openly referred to beatings and brutality, even going so far as to claim that he carried the scars of whippings he received beneath his shirt, although he is never recorded as having displayed them in public. The carnivalesque elements of this display, notably the revealing details concerning the outrages perpetrated on women slaves and the exhibition of the implements that scored their flesh, exceed the norms of polite debate, gratuitously evoking the spectacle of the mutilated female body. Blassingame notes that the story that accompanies the 'horrid whip', the last item displayed by Douglass, refers to the whipping of Douglass's disabled cousin, Hester, recounted in the *Narrative* and a subject of scandal even in its written form. In Limerick, one of the few recorded occasions on which Douglass produced these items for display, and the venue at which he made a strong declaration against blackface representations playing in parallel with his own appearances, narrative and performative carnivalesque mesh in the image of Hester's mutilation, in an exhibition owing more to the circus or fairground than

---

85   Blassingame, *FDP*, 1.1, pp. 85–86. Perhaps the most famous exhibitor of the implements of slave torture and bondage was the ex-slave Henry 'Box' Brown, who engaged in more populist spectacle and performance during his British tour.

the solemnity of the Independent Chapel, Bedford Row.[86]

This was not the only use to which Douglass put his talent for mimicry, carnival or humour, however. Another form of ideological contest appears in Douglass's famous imitations of the Southern slaveholding preacher providing a lesson on obedience to an imagined audience of servants. This imitation was a great favourite of Douglass's early transatlantic tour. It sheds interesting light on the context of his performative engagement with a range of representational strata, and on his ability to mobilize class, ethnicity and race as signifiers of resistance.

As his self-configuration within British class and colonialist structures and within the parameters of official abolitionist doctrine illustrate, Douglass often played on modes of differentiation that took the form of racialization and excess. In the preacher sketch, Douglass occupies, through dialect, a range of subject positions that cross and re-cross the line of racial difference – hereditary bondage – instituted and upheld by the legal apparatus of the United States.

The lesson revolves around the errancy of 'Sambo', a plantation slave caught napping on the job by his master, who then whips Sambo so severely that he cannot work for a week. Sambo, the loyal, trusting black servant in the play The Patriot, had made his singing debut on the minstrel stage in a comic role in 1834, when he danced about and sang, 'Weel about – turn about – do just so, and eb'ry time weel about, Jump Sambo.'[87] In Douglass's account, Sambo reappears in and between narratives and counter-narratives of social formation. Douglass presents Sambo as an ingenu, a foil to both the bombast of the slaveholder and the worldliness and intellectual sophistication of Douglass himself. At the beginning of the performance, puffing out his chest and adopting what the editorial describes as the 'exaggerated attitude and drawling manner so characteristic of the American preachers, amid the laughter of all present', Douglass – articulating whiteface – asks:

---

86 Coincidentally perhaps, Limerick was also one of the few places in Ireland with a record of a black servant being kept by the gentry, unlike Britain where black servants or slaves were considered a mark of prestige. The Limerick Chronicle of 27 July 1803, contains the death notice of this man: 'DIED – Yesterday at Clonmakin, the seat of Mrs Palmer, his Mistress, after a lingering illness, which he bore with Christian patience, Robert St George, (a Black); – it was he who so gallantly defended the late Rev Edward Palmer's house, (his then Master) against a desperate gang of robbers on the night of the 6th January, 1792, and shot dead, with others, the principal of the party.' The said robbers, the report of the original incident records, arrived at the Palmers' house in blackface.

87 Toll, Blacking Up, p. 28; Moody, America Takes the Stage, pp. 68–69.

You servants, To what was this whipping traceable[?] [T]o disobedience, and
if you would not be whipped, and if you would bask in the sunshine of your
master's favor, let me exhort you to obedience. You should also be grateful
that God in his mercy brought you from Africa to this Christian land.[88]

Significantly, the dialect space of slavery apologism is overlaid on the
work of one of Douglass's precursors, Phillis Wheatley, whose 1772
poem, 'On Being Brought from Africa to America', carries the opening
line, "Twas mercy brought me from my *Pagan* land.'[89] Marking the limits
of élite moral and social apologetics, the preacher's remarks – or rather
Douglass's ventriloquizing of them – invoke the developmental narrative
of Enlightenment progress as rationale for the social and political status
quo. It is possible that Douglass is identifying an unwonted irony in
Wheatley's voice, but it seems more likely that this instance of Signifying
is both more problematic and more ironic. It undermines Wheatley's
ethical position on the opportunity for moral advancement that American
Christianity provides. It also ironizes the degree to which the rhetoric
of slavery and anti-slavery are mutually entangled, acknowledging the
common origin of much Afro- and Anglo-American literary production.
Thus, like the slave narrative, Douglass's rhetoric indirectly foregrounds
the issue of creolization, pointing to the degree of cultural transfer at
work in American society as a whole. Additionally, Douglass's revision
of Wheatley's construction of America as the site of her salvation, and
slavery as the vehicle of its achievement, implicates Wheatley herself in
the articulation of whiteface representations of the slave-subject.

Embedded in Douglass's parody of bourgeois rationalism, which
incorporates African American as well as slaveholding accents, is the
naive voice of Sambo, upholding the slaveholder's view: 'Me hear a good
sermon today, de Minister make ebery thing so clear, white man above a
Nigger any day.'[90] Sambo's inclusion underlines the shift in the narrative
axis of the performance towards the realm of the popular. Conversely,
Sambo's borrowing from the minstrel stage allows him to be understood
as an ironic articulation of blackface in this debate, that is, an imitation
of an imitation – and serves to distance Douglass, the authentic representative of blackness, from the ventriloquized counterfeit. Symbol of
arrested development rather than civilized progress, Sambo is presented

---

88 Blassingame, *FDP*, 1, p. 43, speech given in Cork, Ireland on 14 October 1845.
89 Phillis Wheatley, 'On Being Brought from Africa to America', in Nellie McKay and
    Henry Louis Gates Jr, eds. *The Norton Anthology of African American Literature*
    (New York and London: Norton, 1997), p. 171, emphasis original. Thanks to Stephen
    Matterson, TCD, for pointing out this overlap.
90 Blassingame, *FDP*, 1, p. 43.

as linguistically and intellectually stunted by the experience and institution of slavery, which replaces the Christianity of Wheatley's account as the promise of the Middle Passage.

Sambo's naivety, then, coupled with Douglass's incursion into the dialect space of white supremacy, simultaneously reproduces and undermines the discursive dominance of élite whiteface and populist blackface representations of the slave-subject. Use of dialect spaces enables a critique of the cultural legitimacy of these representations. By undermining any symbolic authority they may hold in the official or popular spheres, Douglass discloses the moral poverty of these representations and the political positions they characterize. For the conjunction of the views of both master and slave in the Sambo sketch produces an accord that is constitutively contradictory, with the logic of the pro-slavery argument brought to a conceptual impasse by this performative critique of rational reasoning and monologic discourse. This critique simultaneously questions the role of the slave-subject (and the African American moral élite) in the production of a non-imitative image of the African American iterative self.

So, by reinventing the minstrel stage as a site for understanding and deconstructing the rhetoric of enslavement, Douglass can manipulate white working-class forms of culture and practice, and revise the work of his African American precursors, without falling prey to either élite or populist representative hegemonies. Douglass's appropriation of the carnivalesque production of blackness endemic to the minstrel stage (the voice of Sambo) indicates, despite his protestations, the ongoing potential of blackface imitation as a mode of political dialogue, and his interest in appropriating the form to his own ends.

Just as blackface minstrelsy can then be said to involve a degree of cultural transfer, so too can Douglass's polemical appropriation of what he has clearly identified as a white working-class form. Moreover, the articulation of black- and whiteface subject positions within the same speech-frame initiates a dialogue of opposites, mediated through the voicing of multiple personae. This process of transfer and synthesis underlines the degree of creolization at work in the United States and Atlantic culture of the period, for Douglass's articulation of blackface and whiteface together creates a third space of representation that marks the interface between models of class-based cultural forms and their racial paradigms.

Houston Baker has remarked on Douglass's tendency to privilege standard English rather than black vernacular forms in his writing, but in the early phase of Douglass's public career he often staged himself through performative flirtations with the vernacular form.[91] Notably, this flirtation occurred at a time when Douglass was still beholden to the abolitionists, who prized him above all else for his persuasive and rational eloquence – an eloquence measurable by its distance from black planta-tion vernacular. Speaking of the relationship between Douglass's written and rhetorical voice and abolitionist attitudes to them, Henry Louis Gates notes: 'Douglass' oral testimony ... authenticated his *Narrative*. ... It was this spoken and written "voice" that abolitionists wanted to exploit, as the audible and visible signs of *reason*, to connect the members of the slave community to the whole of the human family.'[92] Douglass's early non-literary voice, however, shows a particular interest in vernacular forms and non-modern strategies more often associated with subaltern or non-rational modes. In his early career at least, the textual Douglass often seems very much at odds with his performative counterpart. Indeed, though complicated by the class dynamics of his own social rise, Douglass's evasion of the prohibitions of official language achieved through adopting the medium of a popular form he claimed to despise, and concurrent critique of the distortions of social reality endemic to racialist representation and official truths, allow many of his speeches from this period to be viewed as folkloric presentations of slave culture *in dialogue* with the official discourses of pro-slavery and abolition camps *and* the unofficial, carnivalesque white culture of blackface minstrelsy.

The tendency on the part of abolitionists and indeed of later critics to lionize Douglass's staging of a rational, enlightenment, textual self at the expense of attention to non-literary, carnivalesque elements of his rhetoric, in particular his manipulation of vernacular forms, might be compared with the mixed reception given to Paul Lawrence Dunbar's work. Famed in his lifetime primarily for his writing in the black vernac-ular, Dunbar's dialect poetry is frequently considered a romantic sop to white audiences seeking an unthreatening image of happy rural black folk. The problematic use of the black vernacular in some of his poetry is described by one critic as lending 'an air of apparent authenticity to the stories he told of quaint, amusing, and contentedly dependent blacks in the prewar and postwar South'.[93] Like Douglass's work, Dunbar's poetry falls into two linguistic categories: his dialect work, which includes some experimentation with Irish American, German American and regional as well as African American vernaculars; and his work in standard English.

91 Houston A. Baker Jr, Introduction to Frederick Douglass, *Narrative of the Life of Frederick Douglass, an American Slave* (London: Penguin, 1982), p. 3.
92 Gates, 'From Douglass to Wheatley', pp. 61–62.
93 McKay and Gates, *Norton Anthology*, p. 885.

The sentimentalism of some of Dunbar's dialect work has led to his placement within the minstrel tradition, with the result that his work is sometimes considered representative of *in*authentic blackness.

But Dunbar was clearly conscious of the representative sway held by blackface minstrelsy by late century and demonstrated his capacity to harness and expand the metaphoric import of the form's representative trope, namely, that of the blackface mask, in both streams of his poetry. His 1895 poem 'We Wear the Mask' figures minstrel masking – and by extension poses black vernacular speech in its performative mode – as an imposed form constantly at odds with, yet providing a useful disguise for, black reality.[94] Conversely, the poem 'An Ante-Bellum Sermon', from the same year, appropriates minstrel parodies of plantation idiom by posing as religious rhetoric in the black vernacular. Demonstrating the subversive capacity of blackface/blackvoice masking by encoding a prophecy of Jubilee in the dialect space of the black sermon, the poem enacts a further creolization of the minstrel form, which takes a step towards authentic blackvoice. Insisting, after thirty-six lines of thinly veiled sedition, that

> fu' feah some one mistakes me,
> I will pause right hyeah to say,
> Dat I'm still a-preachin' ancient,
> I ain't talkin' 'bout to-day,

the slave preacher goes on to caution his listeners: 'Now don't run an' tell yo' mastahs / Dat I's preachin' discontent.'[95] Through his tactical deployment of religious narrative – the Old Testament account of the exodus of the Israelites from Egypt – Dunbar fuses the 'atavism' of Southern black culture – the folk vernacular – with its non-modern, urban counterpart – the minstrel mask, retracing the process of white appropriation of black vernacular forms. Such deployments are absent from Dunbar's other dialect work, which rely on folksy sentimentality and humour, rather than on the irony that characterizes much of his Negro dialect work.

In *The Book of American Negro Poetry* of 1931, J.W. Johnson was to claim that 'in ... [Dunbar's] books the two channels through which black poetry emerged in America – the literary and oral traditions – begin to come together'.[96] Yet the double voice of Dunbar's poetry, what

---

94 Paul Lawrence Dunbar, "We Wear the Mask", in Nellie McKay and Henry Louis Gates Jr, *The Norton Anthology of African American Literature* (New York and London: Norton, 1997), p. 896.

95 McKay and Gates, *Norton Anthology*, pp. 891–92.

96 J.W. Johnson, ed, *The Book of American Negro Poetry* (Poe, NY: Harcourt, Brace & Worley, 1931), pp. 35–36.

Henry Louis Gates has called 'mask in motion',[97] finds a precedent in
Douglass's early oratory, particularly in his engagement with class-based
forms of racialized rhetoric and struggle with representative authenticity. Indeed 'An Ante-Bellum Sermon' provides a striking reminder of
Douglass's use of the same theme, though Dunbar's piece posits itself in
different dialogic relation to the black folk and (largely white) reading
public than does Douglass's multi-voiced performance. Ironically, while
Douglass owed much of his political success to his proficiency in standard
English, exemplary in his oratory and writing of 'the highest intellectual
culture',[98] Dunbar claimed, 'I've got to write dialect poetry, it's the only
way I can get them to listen to me.'[99]

Joanne Braxton concludes that for Dunbar 'the masked language of
black dialect was part and parcel of the larger American experience' (and
points out that his black dialect verse was as popular among black as white
folk audiences).[100] But it is also clear that Dunbar's use of the African
American vernacular was influenced by pressure from the marketplace.
Similar pressures were brought to bear on Douglass in his early years
as an abolitionist agent, as he took part in the closely fought battle for
discursive superiority in the public sphere. Indeed, the ongoing necessity for dialogue between official, folkloric and popular forms generates
a persisting overdetermination in Douglass's early rhetoric, with concurrent appeals across a range of socio-political positions.

Douglass's slaveholder's sermon in particular remains overdetermined
in this respect, with its corresponding critique of slavery and the plight
of wage workers in Britain and the United States. Conscious of their
economic oppression, workers adopted the vocabulary of slavery as a
means to indict their exploiters, describing themselves as 'wage' or 'white
slaves'. In Douglass's imitation, labour discipline is linked to salvation, as,
in the voice of the Southern preacher, he urges slaves to

97 Gates, *Figures in Black*, pp. 88–117.
98 *Anti-Slavery Bugle*, 22 August 1844, p. 4. Quoted in Gates, 'From Douglass to
    Wheatley', p. 61.
99 Quoted in Dickson D. Bruce Jr, '"Jingles in a broken Tongue": Dunbar's Dialect
    Poetry and the Afro-American Folk Tradition', in Jay Martin, ed., *A Singer in the
    Dawn* (New York: Dodd, Mead & Co., 1975), p. 94. This assertion is borne out by the
    poet Alice Dunbar (briefly married to Dunbar), who claimed that 'it was in the pure
    English poems that the poet expressed *himself*. He may have expressed his race in the
    dialect poems; they were to him the side issues of his work.' Alice Dunbar, quoted in
    David J. Nordoh, ed., *Paul Lawrence Dunbar* (Boston: G.K. Hall, 1979). pp. 89–90.
100 Joanne M. Braxton, ed., *The Collected Poetry of Paul Lawrence Dunbar* (Charlottes-
    ville, VA, and London: University Press of Virginia, 1993), p. xxiii.

labor diligently to make your calling and election sure ... Servants, be obedient onto your masters. Look at your hard, horny hands, your strong muscular frames, and see how mercifully he has adapted you to the duties you are to fulfil! ... while to your masters, who have slender frames and long delicate fingers, he has given brilliant intellects, that they may do the *thinking*, while you do the *working*.[101]

Though directed at racialized paradigms which insisted on the fitness of the races for certain employments based on their alleged physical and mental characteristics, this rhetoric could as easily apply to class distinctions made on much the same lines. In fact, at a time when conditions for free workers were deteriorating in the cities, and labour was becoming increasingly entangled in the contradictions of republican language, symbolism and social reality, Douglass's speech appeals across the colour line by activating the class dynamics of popular struggle in Britain and in the industrial North of the United States.

Significantly much of the contestatory rhetoric involving parody, dialogism and mimicry in Douglass's oratory corresponds to the years beginning with his initiation as an anti-slavery speaker in 1841 (he had escaped slavery in Maryland in 1838) and ending with his return from Europe, a free man, in 1847, after his freedom had been purchased by British friends.[102] As noted, little evidence remains of Douglass's speeches in the period up to the publication of the *Narrative* and his departure for the United Kingdom. But the latter years of that rhetorical populism, 1845–47, involved a profound renegotiation of Douglass's relationship with the abolitionist movement and US state formations. That renegotiation was staged in the shifting form of his literary work, which saw Douglass appropriating individual literary and moral authority. His oratory, however, also reveals the fluctuations between polite and popular forms, and appeals to hegemonic and non-modern modes, that this transitional period produced.

Though many of Douglass's speeches were reported in the press and several of his public letters to Garrison published in the *Liberator*, this period in Douglass's career predates the founding of the *North Star*, of which he became editor, and hence of a sustained, interactive relation with the written word and the reading public. It also marks a transitional period in Douglass's move from slavery to freedom. Escape to the North had turned Douglass from a slave into a criminal fugitive overnight. Speaking in 1844, Douglass described himself as 'not a fugitive *from*

---

101 Blassingame, *FDP*, 1.1, p. 17, emphasis original.
102 The money was raised by Anna and Ellen Richardson.

slavery – but a fugitive *slave*. He was a fugitive, he said, not *from* slavery
– but *in* slavery.'[103] The influence of the institution of slavery, according
to Douglass, exceeded its literal geographical and legal reach, allowing
him to posit the existence of another subjective category that is neither
enslaved nor free. Somewhere between bondage and freedom, the fugitive
occupies a moral and representational space that cannot be defined by
convenient binary oppositions. Escaped but not yet free, subject but no
longer enslaved, Douglass acquires an alternative identity that cannot be
contained by the victim/enlightened individual dichotomy allowed by
abolitionist convention.

This fugitive identity complements the dialogic mode of much of
Douglass's oratory at this time, which negotiates between structures of
oppression and appeal. The 'Farewell to the British People', delivered as
Douglass was about to embark for the United States, a free man, in 1847,
was the culmination of a period of rhetorical, literary and personal transition, at the beginning of which Rice, writing of the *Cambria* incident,
notes 'the racial world was turned upside down'.[104] Publication of
the 'Farewell' in pamphlet form in London in 1847 marked the end of
Douglass's improvisational engagement with carnival and his entry to
more mainstream, textualized approaches to political debate.[105] All told,
however, the rhetoric from the early period of Douglass's public life breaks
down the formalities of a linguistic hierarchy based on ideological conformity and initiates a dynamic of play with often competing discourses of
racial and class identity. These plays create categories of representation
undergoing constant redefinition in changing structures of social control,
and opens up avenues into contested zones in the politics of agency.

Conclusion

Enjoying a precarious existence on an interface at once transnational,
interethnic and interclass, in the period 1841–47 Douglass engaged in a
cultural politics which can be understood in terms of its negotiations of
overdetermined, fluctuating and competing forms of non-literary repre-

103 Blassingame, *FDP*, 1.1, p. 24.
104 Rice and Crawford, 'Triumphant Exile', p. 3.
105 As noted in Chapter 1, many of Douglass's letters to Garrison during his sojourn
    abroad were published in the *Liberator*. Unlike the *Narrative* and 'Farewell', these
    were absorbed into the highly controlled and in Douglass's view increasingly
    confining space of official abolitionist (Garrisonian) discourse. The 'preacher' parody,
    which was predominant in Douglass's early speaking career, was repeated again and
    again throughout his visit to Britain and Ireland. The parody fell out of usage on his
    return to the United States, when the tone of his speeches changed.

sentation. Many of his early speeches employ the racialized rhetoric of minstrelsy to produce a discourse of class that finds an echo in Douglass's own upward social mobility. In addition, Douglass's parodies of the slave–master relationship in the United States exploit the popularity of the minstrel shows while contesting their representative authority.

Moreover, his use of mimicry operates on the interface of United States racial and class politics and on that of popular enactments of British–Irish colonial relations. In these enactments, Irish stereotypes from the Victorian stage were sometimes invoked to provide a counter to Douglass's own racial difference and to challenge the prevailing authority of the abolitionist movement. Correspondingly, Irish subaltern movements developed strategies that relied for their effect on the high international profile of the anti-slavery cause, using adaptations of blackface to indicate subjection and dissent. These adaptations illustrate the counter-hegemonic as well as hegemonic potential of performative mimicry.

In his own performances, Douglass was dependent on the actual or imaginary presence of the carnival or 'marketplace crowd',[106] a collective capable of understanding and challenging the interrelation of his rhetorical performance to the diversity of forms operating in the transatlantic arena. Thus, Douglass engaged in dialogue with competing representational strains, in a struggle for representational agency and discursive superiority in the debate concerning slavery and abolition, and with the extended collective that gave it meaning and force. His oratory provides a focal point through which the rhetorical potential of folk culture, the carnival audience and the play between non-modern and Enlightenment invocations of politico-cultural space may be examined.

Finally, by exploiting the ambivalences of racialized discourse and manipulating its social authority, Douglass produced a dialogic form of popular interaction that found expression in both his rhetorical performances and later in his fiction, *The Heroic Slave*. That dialogue opened a space between élite and populist forms of political negotiation in which the class, racial and moral identity of the idealized nation-subject and his intended audience could effectively be imagined.

106 Bakhtin, *Rabelais and His World*, p. 188.

Chapter 6

Race, Civilization, Empire

Douglass's early overseas experience indicates the importance of transnational encounters to the formation of black American subjectivity, complicating claims to either US or African American exceptionalism in the mid-nineteenth century. The writing and rhetoric of the British–Irish tour exemplifies the potential for the creation of an enabling myth for the African American subject in spaces where the racial hegemony of the United States could safely be contested.

Equally revealing are the international experiences at the latter part of Douglass's career. In 1886, Douglass toured Europe and North Africa with his second wife, Helen Pitts. He was later appointed as US minister to Haiti from 1889 to 1891, and subsequently engaged as organizer of the Haitian pavilion at the 1893 Columbian World's Fair in Chicago.

The circumstances of these overseas experiences could not be more different from those of the early sojourn. Rather than seeking asylum or advocating resistance, Douglass travelled as a tourist or a representative of state. Additionally, by the end of the nineteenth century, Egypt and Haiti were important spaces in the political and cultural imaginary of western empire and black nationalism. Douglass's views on each country afford a glimpse of his attitudes to important elements in the American and African American cultural imaginary of the period. His writings reveal some of the complexity of the African American relationship with Africa and modernity, particularly as that relationship reflected the rise of the United States as an imperial power. It also provides an example of an often unacknowledged dimension of that relationship: the degree to which African American discourse, in its attempt to inscribe Africa and Africans into the logic of western historicism, became complicit in contemporary discursive practices of colonialism and imperialism.

The Egyptian Tour

The tour undertaken by the Douglasses in Europe and North Africa in 1886 was in many ways, as one of Douglass's biographers notes, 'the most conventional of upper-class trips abroad'.[1] Indeed the circumstances of

1 McFeely, *Frederick Douglass*, p. 324.

the trip could not have been further from those that obtained on his previous two trips, when he left the United States a fugitive and was severely restricted as to the countries he was allowed to visit. This time, instead of fleeing the 'shadow of the American eagle', Douglass travelled under its protection, carrying that symbol of republican democracy and empire on the US passport previously denied him by George M. Dallas, on the grounds that he 'was not and could not be an American citizen'.[2] His adoption of the guise of the American tourist is, then, as Kenneth Warren notes, 'fraught with significance ... His trip abroad ... an affirmation of his American citizenship – he tours the world as an American.'[3]

Douglass had achieved not just political and cultural recognition and established himself as one of the most easily recognizable and important Americans of the nineteenth century, he had acceded to the upper echelons of US society. In many ways the trip was confirmation of his class status as well as his citizenship, casting 'the black traveller, in the role of the civilized and élite traveller of the period',[4] part of the American gentry of the Gilded Age for whom 'European tourism became one of the chief means ... to establish its place in the world'.[5] Moreover, '[i]n deciding to undertake his own grand tour,' as Robert Levine writes, 'Douglass as representative black leader hoped to make his and, by extension, African Americans' claims to the world of culture'.[6] For, broadly speaking, 'the social élite of this period tended to identify its social superiority with what it alone possessed, namely its cosmopolitan exposures and artistic and cultural initiations'.[7] The literary production of the late tour therefore places Douglass within the bourgeois tradition of (African) American letters, confirming his ascension to the ranks of the US élite.

It also places the 'black traveller' within the larger context of the US imperial imaginary and transnational migration. In the United States, European immigrant groups developed a variety of ethnic identities without sacrificing the social value of whiteness, while those further up the class ladder could avail, at their leisure, of the same cultural consum-

---

2 Douglass, *Autobiographies*, p. 587.
3 Kenneth W. Warren, 'Frederick Douglass's *Life and Times*: Progressive Rhetoric and the Problem of Constituency', in Eric J. Sundquist, ed., *Frederick Douglass: New Literary and Historical Essays* (Cambridge: Cambridge University Press, 1990), pp. 253–70 (264–65).
4 Robert S Levine, 'Road to Africa: Frederick Douglass's Rome', *African American Review*, 34.2 (2000), pp. 217–31 (219).
5 Richard Brodhead, Introduction to *The Marble Faun: Or, The Romance of Monte Beni*, by Nathaniel Hawthorne (New York: Penguin, 1990), pp. ix–xxix, xiv.
6 Levine, 'Road to Africa', p. 220.
7 Brodhead, Introduction, p. xiv.

ables as their European counterparts. By the late nineteenth century, attitudes to Europe, Africa and the East, and their expression, became an important indicator of national identity and confirmation of cultural kudos for well-to-do US Americans. The claims to the world of culture that ensued included the appropriation of narratives of identity that looked to ideals of European civilization, including teleologies of empire and high culture, traced back to North Africa and western Asia.

Such narratives existed in tension with the contemporary political realities of the colonial presence and its attendant moral logic, which cast subject peoples, regardless of past glories, as culturally backward. Compounding this were several decades of Pan-Africanist theorizing on the part of black New World intellectuals seeking a cultural rationale for a political enterprise. Like their white counterparts, these early Pan-Africanists had, as Appiah argues, 'inherited a set of conceptual blinders that made them unable to see virtue in Africa, even though they needed Africa ... as a source of validation'.[8] For Douglass as a black American, North Africa, as a symbolic domain of cultural meaning, was complicated by a range of US domestic and transnational factors, including existing discourses of imperialism, racial oppression and class.

Until recently, critiques of nineteenth-century colonialism have focused almost exclusively on Europe, with little attention paid to US expansion in either its continental or overseas phases. Amy Kaplan and Malini Johar Schueller have challenged the exceptionalist position within US American Studies, citing the ideology of imperialism as key to the creation and sustenance of an ideal of the nation as empire that emerged in the late eighteenth century.[9] Part of that process involved the creation of figurative as well as real power discrepancies in the external world. These reinforced the image of the nation as vibrant, youthful, masculine and progressive in ways frequently mirroring the regenerative capacity of frontier encounters in the continental phase of expansion.[10]

Resistance to the mechanisms of power that maintained the United States as empire has, however, also existed in the Americas themselves

8 Kwame Anthony Appiah, *In My Father's House: Africa in the Philosophy of Culture* (New York: Oxford University Press, 1992), p. 5.
9 Amy Kaplan, 'Introduction: Left Alone with America', in Amy Kaplan and Donald Pease, eds, *Cultures of United States Imperialism* (Durham, NC: Duke University Press, 1993); Schueller, *US Orientalisms*. For a discussion of the United States as empire in the twentieth century, see R.W. Van Alstyne, *The Rising American Empire* (Chicago: Quadrangle, 1960).
10 See Richard Slotkin, *Gunfighter Nation: Regeneration through Violence; The Mythology of the American Frontier, 1600–1860* (Middletown, CT: Wesleyan University Press, 1973).

since the nineteenth century, if not before. Internally, these critiques have come from Native, African American and Chicano commentators, who have also occupied 'borderland' sites on the racial, cultural and territorial edges of the United States. External challenges have surfaced throughout the hemisphere, particularly in Latin America and the Caribbean. Disciplinary tendencies to reflect Anglocentric hegemonies in US culture may account for the neglect of both the strength and persistence of these critiques in discussions of US imperialism to date. But there is also a degree to which any address to US imperialism must also challenge the exceptionalism of African American positions regarding sites in the Caribbean, Africa and beyond.

Douglass's relationship to these sites is a case in point. His late writing on Egypt, Europe and Ireland, some of which was integrated into his last autobiography, *The Life and Times of Frederick Douglass*, is typically read within an introspective framework of black nationalism, racial uplift and cultural retrieval. In the nineteenth century, Africa provided a source of anxiety and optimism for many African American intellectuals, with many advocating black emigrationist schemes as a means of resolving the problems caused by slavery and segregation, and the perceived underdevelopment of Africa, in one fell swoop. For Douglass, who persistently opposed such schemes, complaining, as Bernard Boxill notes, 'that emigrationism encouraged the majority to "hope that by persecution or by persuasion the Negro can finally be dislodged and driven from his natural home"',[11] Africa, and Egypt in particular, was nevertheless crucial to an understanding of African American identity, in which Anglo-American cultural hegemonies, privileging European sites of imperial civilization, were creolized by Egyptological or Africanist accounts of western progress.

Within contemporary historiography, ancient Egypt was generally cast as the well-spring of western culture. Douglass viewed contemporary Egypt as a racial and cultural borderland, an opportunity for the articulation of his views on racial mixing and cultural hybridity.[12] Waldo

11 Frederick Douglass, 'The Folly of Colonization', in Howard Brotz, ed., *African American Social and Political Thought: 1850–1920* (New Brunswick: Transaction Press, 1992), p. 330. Quoted in Bernard R. Boxill, 'Douglass against the Emigrationists', in Bill E. Lawson and Frank M. Kirkland, eds, *Frederick Douglass, a Critical Reader* (Oxford: Blackwell, 1999), pp. 21–49 (29).

12 The issue regarding whether or not the Ancient Egyptians were a European or African/Afro-Asiatic people is still being contested. For a revisionary discussion of ancient civilization as of Afro-Asiatic origin, and of the appropriation of 'Classicism' to the European civilizationist narrative to the exclusion of those Afro-Asiatic roots, see Martin Bernal, *Black Athena: The Afroasiatic Roots of Classical Civilisation*, 2 vols (London: Vintage, 1991). For an evaluation and rebuttal of many of Bernal's claims, see Mary R. Lefkovitz and Guy MacClean Rogers, eds, *Black Athena Revisited*

Martin suggests that Douglass early 'explored ... ideas on the relationship among Europeans, Africans, Euro-Americans and Afro-Americans
... as part of his ethnological reflections on the unity and equality of
mankind. To Douglass the ethnologist, the question of the racial identity
of the ancient Egyptians represented a vital issue impinging upon both
African and Western identity, culture and history'.[13] 'Greece and Rome,'
Douglass claimed, articulating the dominant view, 'and through them
Europe and America – have received their civilization from the ancient
Egyptians'.[14] As for other cultural spokesmen of the period from across
the racial spectrum, for Douglass the ancient world was the origin of
modern, enlightened US culture, a source from which significant contemporary meaning could be generated. At stake was the legitimacy of the
African presence in the US national narrative of civilized progress and
manifest destiny, which relied on understandings of culture inherited,
in a direct line, from the greatness of the ancient world and in righteous
fulfilment of Christian scripture.[15] As a result, control of the semantic field
through which the European relationship to North Africa and western
Asia ('the Orient')[16] was mediated, was hotly contested by conservative
and reforming US sections of the establishment alike.

Though geographically part of Africa, Egypt, the 'cradle of western
civilization' was argued by nineteenth-century ethnologists, seeking to
maintain the racial status quo within the United States, to have been the
province and product of European, understood as white, rather than
African, understood as black, society. For the African American intellectual, a black Egypt would negate claims of African and African American
inferiority and provide Afro-America with what Douglass called the

---

(Chapel Hill, NC: University of North Carolina Press, 1996).

13 Waldo E. Martin Jr, *The Mind of Frederick Douglass* (Chapel Hill, NC: University of
   North Carolina Press, 1984), p. 203.
14 Blassingame, 'The Claims of the Negro Ethnologically Considered', *FDP*, 1.2, pp.
   497–525 (508).
15 The idea of 'Manifest Destiny' was first proposed by John Fiske in a lecture of that
   name that formed part of a series entitled *American Political Ideas: Viewed from the
   Standpoint of Universal History*, published, with an introduction by Spencer Clark
   (Boston: Houghton Mifflin, 1911). For Perry Miller's influential model of Puritan
   origins, see *The New England Mind: The Seventeenth Century* (New York: Macmillan,
   1939), and Perry Miller, *Errand into the Wilderness* (New York: Harper, 1956).
16 Edward Said describes the discursive processes by which the West created a syncretic
   Orient as 'Orientalism', which 'can be discussed and analysed as the corporate institution for dealing with the Orient – dealing with it by making statements about
   it, authorizing views of it, describing it, by teaching it, settling it, ruling over it:
   in short, Orientalism as a Western style for dominating, restructuring, and having
   authority over the Orient' (*Orientalism* [New York: Vintage, 1979], p. 2).

'moral support of Ancient Greatness'.[17] Like his contemporaries Martin Delaney and Edward Blyden, Douglass sought to celebrate ancient Egypt as an inclusive African rather than exclusively European cultural achievement,[18] rejecting 'the hellenomaniacal excision of Africa from the narrative of civilization's development'.[19] Douglass differed from these colleagues, however, in two important respects. Firstly, he did not, as noted, advocate the 'back to Africa' emigrationist approach proposed as a final resolution of the racial problem in the United States, though he was not averse to imperial expansion or civilizing mission. More importantly, his celebration of ancient Egypt characterized Egyptians, past and present, as Afro-European. In doing so he could posit an identity that, like his own, confounded the exclusivity and exclusion of the US model.

It would be a mistake, then, to read Douglass's declarations of racial affinity and lionisation of African cultural achievement as radical expressions of Pan-Africanist sensibility in which either European or US sociocultural hierarchies are significantly challenged. It was not his intention to dispute the hegemony of western imperial modernity, for he wished rather to rid it of its racial hierarchies. Robert S. Levine reads Douglass within a western liberal framework, contending that he 'resisted what could be termed an Afrocentric celebration of origins, and in *Life and Times* he presents instead a more progressive narrative of all roads leading to and from Africa'. Indeed in *Life and Times*, as Levine points out, Douglass's emphasis is 'ultimately less on locating and celebrating the black sources of Western civilization than on exploring the multiracial origins and development of the West'.[20]

Similarly, Douglass's famous speech, 'Claims of the Negro Ethnographically Considered' uses the racial indeterminacy of the Egyptian, who 'would ... have no difficulty in getting himself recognized as a negro',[21] to collapse US racial absolutes in favour of 'a composite American nationality' derived from mutual membership of the great family of man. The speech, given as a Commencement Address to the literary societies of Western Reserve College on 12 July 1854, argued that academic scholar-

---

17 'Diary of Egyptian and European Tour', 1886, Microfilm, Reel One, Box One, Frederick Douglass Collection, Library of Congress Manuscript Division, Washington, DC. A transcription of the diary is available in Alasdair Pettinger, ed., *Always Elsewhere: Travels of the Black Atlantic* (New York: Cassells/Continuum, 1998).

18 See , Martin, *Mind of Frederick Douglass*, p. 303.

19 Robert S. Levine, *Martin Delaney, Frederick Douglass and the Politics of Representative Identity* (Chapel Hill, NC, and London: University of North Carolina Press, 1997), p. 10.

20 Levine, 'Road to Africa', p. 220. Levine himself seems to become entangled here in the same progressivist vocabulary as Douglass.

21 Blassingame, *FDP*, 1.2, p. 509.

ship reflected the prejudices of wider society. The speech contradicted the claims of much racialist ethnographic research, which had gained currency in the United States during the nineteenth century, with the publication of Samuel George Morton's *Crania Americana* and *Crania Aegyptica* in 1839 and 1844 respectively. *Types of Mankind* by Josiah C. Nott and George R. Gliddon, published in 1854, compounded the essentialism of these earlier works, claiming in the introduction that, 'in the broad field and long duration of Negro life, not a single civilization, spontaneous or borrowed, has existed, to adorn its gloomy past'.[22]

The trip to Egypt, then, in the description of which Douglass insists on a hybrid racial origin for the progenitors of western civilization, underlines his determination to tackle an important political aspect of the cultural tourism of the late nineteenth century. The grand tour of Europe constituted an end to US cultural isolation, and conspicuous confirmation of cultural and material elevation. For Douglass, citizen of a nation predicated on the internal colonization of Native and African Americans, the grand tour also provided the opportunity for an ethnological fact-finding mission, the results of which could be used to contest the semantics of race in the United States. It was, for Douglass, a means by which culture – of a particular kind – could be consumed, then re-presented, under the aegis of American imperial identity, as an external reflection of the internal power dynamics of the United States.

By the second half of the nineteenth century, the North African Orient had become the subject of intense western scrutiny and archaeological investigation. Tensions had existed in US attitudes to the region since early century, when American sailors were held captive in Algiers, ironically reversing the racial paradigm governing US slavery and exacerbating the racial anxieties that underpinned it. But it was Egypt that was to provide the testing ground of racialist theorizing, initiating the debate as to whether the ancient Egyptians were of European or African stock. Aside from its impact on issues surrounding internal US racial organization, the new science of Egyptology had another important political

22 Nott and Gliddon, Introduction to *Types of Mankind* (1854), written during Glidden's time as US consul at Cairo. In a letter to his son Lewis from Paris, Douglass wrote that he 'had long been interested in ethnology, especially of the North African races. I have wanted the evidence of greatness, under a colored skin to meet and beat back the charge of natural, original and permanent inferiority of the colored races of men. Could I have seen forty years ago what I have now seen, I should have been much better fortified to meet the Notts and Gliddons . . . in their arguments against the negro as a part of the great African race' (quoted in McFeely, *Frederick Douglass*, p. 330). For a discussion of the discursive interrelationship between race and culture, see Ronald Takaki, *Iron Cages: Race and Culture in Nineteenth-Century American Culture* (New York: Knopf, 1970).

function, 'legitimat[ing],' as Schueller writes, 'the role of the West as cultural authority for and about the Orient'.[23] As well as embodying the rival epistemologies of élite western culture then, the Orient presented an opportunity for imperial expansion, a space into which western nations could extend their dominion through the mystification of imperial knowledge as control. As Said observes, '[w]hat German Orientalism had in common with Anglo-French and later American Orientalism was a kind of intellectual *authority* over the Orient within Western culture'.[24] Emblematic of the ideology of empire, in both its European and US modes, was the figure of the white male archaeologist, one of the major actors in the 'transmission of white male power [and] ... the emergence of a new global order of cultural knowledge'.[25] For imperialism, as well as 'the invention of race', which dominates US discussions of cultural hegemony in the nineteenth century, 'were fundamental aspects of Western industrial modernity'.[26]

In his assumed role of both US tourist and cultural detective, Douglass, despite his colour, in many ways typified the western presence in Egypt; although he confounded the racial model of the imperial agent, he nevertheless conformed, in his rhetoric, self-construction and ideological positioning, to the imperial archetype.[27] In his late autobiography, *The Life and Times of Frederick Douglass*, he appears as representative US subject in the Orient, though his ethnological intentions are perhaps less contentious and more clearly defined. 'The more [the American tourist] has seen of modern [European] civilization,' Douglass writes, 'the more he will want to see traces of that civilization which existed when these countries of Europe were inhabited by barbarians' But he goes on to confess that

> my desire to visit Egypt did not rest entirely upon the basis thus foreshadowed. I had a motive far less enthusiastic and sentimental; an ethnological purpose in the pursuit of which I hoped to turn my visit to some account in combating American prejudice against the darker colored races of mankind ... I had a theory for which I wanted support of facts in the range of my own knowledge.[28]

23 Schueller, *US Orientalisms*, p. 77.
24 Said, *Orientalism*, p. 874.
25 McClintock, *Imperial Leather*, pp. 1–2.
26 McClintock, *Imperial Leather*, p. 5.
27 The Orient was also a site of interest for other US writers at this time, including those of the American Renaissance. For a discussion of the impact of the Orient on the imagery and philosophy of Transcendentalism, see Arthur Christin, *The Orient in American Transcendentalism* (New York: Columbia University Press, 1932); for an account of the Oriental travels of other US writers see Franklin Walker, *Irreverent Pilgrims: Melville, Browne and Mark Twain in the Holy Land* (Seattle: University of Washington Press, 1974).
28 Douglass, *Autobiographies*, p. 1006.

Laudable as his intentions may be, Douglass is nevertheless implicated
in the quest for imperial knowledge; ultimately, his deracinated Orient
is manufactured in the interests of and for consumption by narratives of
western progress. Moreover, his stance is also that of the trans-cultural
consumer, who 'view[s] ... other cultures ... not as independent social
realities but as sites for travelling Americans to "take in"'.[29] In ways
comparable to contemporary travel and other US works of non-fiction,
then, Douglass uses the Orient to exalt the nation as empire and provide
existential ground to the figure of the US nation-subject.

For although the accounts of Egypt and indeed Europe in *Life and
Times,* and in Douglass's personal diary challenge US *racial* hierarchies,
they also reproduce many of the salient assumptions of western bourgeois
culture and Anglo-American imperial culture in particular. Little is made
of the British imperial presence in Egypt, for example, though Douglass
did attend a parade of troops in Cairo in March 1887, remarking in his diary
that the Egyptians 'are probably better off with [the British] than they
would be without them',[30] and presumably witnessed other incidences of
British dominion during his tour. Rather than condemning British imperialism, which did after all involve the subjugation on grounds of race of
colonized peoples, including Africans, Douglass merely confirms Egypt
as a contested site of (European) imperial power, referring to 'the motive
and mainspring of English Egyptian occupation and of English policy',
the Suez Canal, through which their ship passes 'smoothly and noise-
lessly between two spade-built banks of yellow sand, watched over by
the jealous care of England and France'.[31] According to Martin, Douglass
believed that, despite the oppressive nature of the their presence, 'the
British effort to bring Egypt political peace, social progress, and economic
prosperity – not to mention other innumerable "blessings" of English
culture – was laudable', concluding that in Douglass's view, '[t]he critical
English advantage ... was their hegemony'.[32]

The Orient, therefore (and indeed Europe), was constructed as a site
of ethno-racial and cultural, rather than social or political interest, and
it was to the élite American cultural hegemony that Douglass looked for
authorization of his new imperial identity. For despite his attacks on the
legitimacy of the racial profile of western narratives of cultural origin,
Douglass's celebration of Egypt is, like contemporary white accounts, an
explicit lionization of empire. It retains the élitist framework that traces

29 Brodhead, Introduction, p. xv.
30 'Diary', Library of Congress Microfilm.
31 Douglass, *Autobiographies*, p. 1008.
32 Martin, *Mind of Frederick Douglass*, p. 200.

the lineage of civilization from Pharaoh through Rome, Britain, and ends in the United States, to the exclusion of those neither absorbed nor elevated by the sweep of empire.

The position of the United States at the end of this narrative of imperial progress often goes unacknowledged. However, as Schueller points out, nineteenth-century US writers

> maintained a dialogue with or strove to create an indigenous Orientalism premised on the idea of civilization and empire moving west, from Asia, through Europe, to culmination in the New World. The New World thus displaced Britain as empire. ... [and] the Orient was seen as the new frontier against which the United States ... could define itself in terms of virtue and world mission.[33]

This 'indigenous Orientalism' differed, according to Schueller, from its European counterpart in that it could be used to construct imperialism 'more benevolently, as teleology'.[34] That teleology is evident in Douglass's writing on North Africa, though it is not confined to this locale. The progressivist rhetoric that characterizes his early Irish rhetoric, for example, later resurfaces in his discussions of Ireland and Haiti. Arguably indeed, Douglass found an easier subject in these racially uncomplicated spaces than on the uncertain racial ground of the United States and North Africa, a proposition which will later be discussed. Be that as it may, in his European and Egyptian rhetoric Douglass complicates and expands the perimeter of the Orient, merging Indic Orientalism, Egyptology and spectres of Old World decadence in a mystification of selfhood which becomes firmly embedded in, even as it revises, the radical US narrative of discovery, regeneration and empire.

In the latter stages of his career, the battle over slavery having been won, Douglass perhaps sought to refashion himself within a masculine paradigm derived from the ideal of the New World Adam.[35] Since Columbus, the Americas had been characterized as a prelapsarian space of infinite promise, one in which man's true potential could be fully realized. That promise was, in the United States, expressed in ubiquitous tropes of exploration and conquest, myths of encounter, Puritan origins

---

33 Schueller, *US Orientalisms*, p. 4.
34 Schueller, *US Orientalisms*, p. 9.
35 J. Lee Greene describes this as the first of the US permutations of the myth of America as Eden, a myth which, until the end of the nineteenth century, went through three distinct phases, including: America as earthly paradise; America as civil utopia; and the South as plantation idyll. For the reaction of African American writers to these mythologies, see J. Lee Greene, *Blacks in Eden: The African American Novel's First Century* (Charlottesville, VA, and London: University Press of Virginia, 1996).

and manifest destiny.[36] Early descriptions of the Americas also character-ized the Native American as a noble savage, an innocent counterpart to a fallen European civilization. Arguably, the discourse of the Americas derived from an early Orientalist narrative which formed part of European regeneration, or Renaissance, after the stasis of the Middle Ages, origi-nating in Columbus's initial search for the westward passage to India, and driven by the soon-to-be-raced and already gendered imperatives of first European and later American empire.[37]

Always implied in constructions of American masculinity, and there-fore nationhood, then, is the Orientalist vision of a supine, fertile and available space, strategically refashioned as depopulated wilderness. The latent racial instabilities of this model, which negated the presence of Native American peoples and African American slaves, led to two major forms of counter-racialization. The first involved, as Richard Slotkin demonstrates, the repeated enactment of the frontier experience: violent border encounters with Native Americans in which the masculine character of the new American subject was confirmed, and his relation-ship to the landscape naturalized; the second saw the construction of an image of the African American as a shadow presence, whose repre-sentative blackness provides ground to an otherwise indeterminate, volatile cultural whiteness, anxiously seeking subjective definition and normative status.[38] The American Renaissance saw a further synthesis of the relationship between the American and his natural environment, reinventing (Indic) Orientalist tropes of selfhood in the aesthetics of nineteenth-century Transcendentalism.

For obvious reasons, reinventing himself as Renaissance man provided Douglass with particular challenges. It is no coincidence that the locus

36 Miller's influential model has retained its currency in literary and cultural studies of the United States. However, Kaplan has shown that this model was formulated in the imperial context of Miller's presence in the Congo on an oil tanker, and, contrary to the generally held belief, is therefore implicated in colonial/imperialist construc-tions of the US American self. According to philosopher and historian John Fiske, the discovery of the Americas saved Europe from being consigned to Asian lethargy. Fiske also proclaimed: 'In the United States of America a century hence we shall … have a political aggression immeasurably surpassing in power and dimensions any power that has yet existed.'

37 See Schueller, *US Orientalisms*, pp. 7–13.

38 Slotkin, *Gunfighter Nation*. In the later works of his frontier trilogy, Slotkin shows how the myth of the frontier was adapted in the later phases of US empire to justify the US presence in the Philippines and Vietnam, and used as an analogy for the explo-ration of space. Using examples from Poe, Hemingway and others, Toni Morrison reveals the tropological importance of the black presence as an othering device to normative figurations of the white American subject (*Playing in the Dark: Whiteness and the Literary Imagination* [London: Picador, 1993]).

of that reinvention, which, unlike his earlier self-fashioning, is existen-
tialist rather than directly political (though it does of course impinge on
the politico-subjective status of African Americans and signify upon and
repeat tropes of high imperialism), is not the United States, but the Orient.
Ireland and Britain had provided a liberating space for Douglass, one in
which his early battles for American selfhood could be enacted free from
the symbolic as well as political shackles of the contemporary representative paradigm. The ratification of this final phase is similarly displaced,
this time to Egypt, a place where ideologies of race could more easily be
questioned, and where Douglass could stage a credible encounter with
the myth of American origins.

That mythological origin was, in Douglass's late work, constructed
in his own image. His Egyptian travelogue had a precedent in the work
of the African American writer David F. Dorr, who published his travel
narrative *A Colored Man Round the World* in 1858, following an alleged
tour of world's major cities in the 1850s with his master, Louisiana plantation owner Cornelius Fellowes. The work is critical of white Egyptology,
though its albeit sometimes parodic mobilization of Orientalism is lacking
in irony and is ultimately used as a means of legitimating the cultural
and moral privilege of the narrating subject.[39] Particularly notable in
Douglass's account is his representation of the North African as original
man. The 'children of the desert' he observes are, like Douglass himself,
'half brothers to the negro'. Yet they are located at one end of a teleology
of progress, with Douglass, the representative subject, at its civilized
American end. Childlike and unspoiled, the Egyptians of Douglass's
account – like the (now somewhat romanticized) American slaves of the
not-too-distant past, who work 'best and hardest when it is no longer
work but becomes play with joyous singing' – perform 'their tasks in a
like manner, amid shouts of laughter and tricks of fun, as if their hard
work were the veriest sport. In colour,' Douglass continues,

> these Arabs are something between two riding saddles, the one old and the
> other new, ... a little lighter than one and a little darker than the other, I did
> not see a single fat man among them. They were erect and strong, lean and
> sinewy. Their strength and fleetness were truly remarkable. They tossed the
> heavy bags of coal on their shoulders and trotted on board our ship with
> them for hours without halt or weariness. Lank in body, slender in limb,
> full of spirit, they reminded one of blooded horses ... [T]hese people seemed
> about as much at home in the water as on the land, and gave us some fine
> specimens of their swimming and diving ability. Passengers would throw

39 David F. Dorr, *A Colored Man Round the World*, 1858, ed. and intro. Malina Johar
Schueller (Ann Arbor, MI: Univeristy of Michigan Press, 1999).

small coins into the water for the interest of seeing them dive for them; and this they did with almost fish-like swiftness, and never failed to bring from the bottom the coveted sixpence or franc ... and to show it between their white teeth as they came to the surface.[40]

The description applauds the Arab – for his physique, his industriousness, and for the unquestioning, childlike spectacle he provides for his western admirers. This is the Egypt of the writing present, fallen from previous greatness, yet providing Douglass with a point of comparison that confirms a teleology of progress that reveals the US subject as the new paradigm of civilization, and, by extension, empire.

Notably, in Douglass account, these 'sable children' bear many of the hallmarks of the noble savage, though they are pictured not in an exotic landscape, but in the context of willing if difficult labour of a decidedly industrial cast. In a letter to his son Lewis, Douglass described his reaction to the scene: 'It was wonderful to see how this dirty and disagreeable work was done,' he wrote. 'The men seemed to revel in it. As I looked upon them, I thought of the time when in New Bedford I was, nearly fifty years ago, glad to do the same kind of work.'[41] This private correspondence indicates that Douglass's concern to establish a shared origin for black and white American was more than élite posturing, although it does reproduce teleological notions of progress, and continues self-referentially to replicate Douglass's favoured self-image as representative, African American, self-made man. For the hybrid (primitive) origins of the US nation-subject find modern correlation in the African American labourer, indirectly characterized as an asset rather than a threat to US industrialization and development.

The projection of the black US self into the Orient, then, is used by Douglass to neutralize anxieties of race in the domestic sphere, while retaining intact the logic of cultural progress crucial to understandings of national identity. Yet the distinctions drawn between viewer and viewed, writer and subject, undermine the ideological integrity of an account that negates racial hierarchies, indicating that Douglass could not unequivocally celebrate Egypt present, as opposed to Egypt past, as an African American cultural signifier. Racial blurring exacerbates rather than obviates the need for a distinctive figuration of the western subject in terms of his difference from, rather than proximity to, his representative object. Undoubtedly this difference exists, although it is outside the normative dichotomies underpinning white, male, Anglo-American structures of selfhood. Rather than an inappropriate and unavailable

40 Douglass, *Autobiographies*, p. 1007.
41 Quoted in McFeely, *Frederick Douglass*, p. 330.

racial distinction between modern spectator and anachronistic spectacle, or recourse to heteronormative configurations of empire which rely on passive female figures to confirm the potent masculinity of the active, imperial subject,[42] Douglass activates a temporally grounded discourse of manhood. As a result, his description of the Egyptians involves subtle regendering of the encounter, in which they are infantilized by their playground behaviour, and produced in homosocial relation to the imperial spectator, the mature gentleman traveller.

Schueller notes that Douglass's ethnological arguments were repeatedly prefaced by statements concerning the 'manhood' of African Americans, and suggests that that 'contextual usage of the term ... suggest[s] that it operates more as a gendered signifier than as a signifier for general humanity', concluding that 'African American manhood is further validated by the findings of Egyptology'.[43] The gendering of the late Egyptian writing differs significantly from the oppositions in Douglass's early arguments concerning the racial equality of African Americans, which favoured the victimization of women rather than the emasculation of men. Here, the Arab provides external opposition to African American manhood that confirms Douglass's place within bourgeois American masculinity, which, as Richard Yarborough notes in a different context, 'Douglass was unable or unwilling to call into question.'[44] The authorization of African American masculinity at the expense of that of the Arab signals Douglass's manipulation of the gendered trope of empire in the creation of an Afro-American, or black Orientalist perspective.

Douglass's trip to the Old World retraced, in fact and in representation, the steps of his earlier journeys, recalling his earlier visit to Britain and Ireland, when 'the famine of 1845 was doing its ghastly work, and the people not only of Ireland, but of England and Scotland, were asking for bread',[45] and re-establishing Douglass within the paradigms of statesmanship represented by O Connell, Gladstone and so on. As Kenneth Warren astutely observes, '[t]he melancholy litany of absent faces [listed in Douglass's account of his late transatlantic journey] is not meant to

---

42 See McClintock, *Imperial Leather*, pp. 21–74. There was some precedent for this in Douglass's earlier writing. Jenny Franchot writes: '[S]lavery provides [Douglass with] that feminine object with which his subjectivity could commune and assert its necessary mastery' ('The Punishment of Esther: Douglass and the Construction of the Feminine', in Eric J. Sundquist, ed., *Frederick Douglass: New Literary and Historical Essays* [Cambridge: Cambridge University Press, 1990], pp. 141–65 [159]).

43 Schueller, *US Orientalisms*, p. 107.

44 Richard Yarborough, 'Race Violence and Manhood: The Masculine Ideal in Frederick Douglass's *The Heroic Slave*', in Eric J. Sundquist, ed., *Frederick Douglass* (New York and Cambridge: Cambridge University Press), pp. 166–88 (182).

45 Douglass, *Autobiographies*, p. 985.

distance Douglass from his past. Rather [it] serves to distinguish Douglass as one of the few remaining representatives of a heroic age.'[46] This is confirmation indeed of his heroic manhood. The trip also revised the path of imperial progress from the Old World to the New. The quest for origin therefore represents a movement forward in space and backward in time, a movement, incidentally, mirrored in the progressive blackening of the people Douglass encounters. 'As the traveller moves eastward and southward ... he will observe an increase of black hair, black eyes, full lips and dark complexions,'[47] Douglass wrote of a journey which carried him from the east coast of the United States, the industrial frontier of western modernity, to the 'colossal ruins that speak to us of a civilization that extends back into the misty shadows of the past, far beyond the reach and grasp of authentic history'.[48] The Arabs Douglass views and appropriates to his counter-discourse of race are, like himself, the descendants of ancient greatness. But for all their past glory, which, in the absence of contemporary indicators of greatness must be mystified and placed beyond the reach of authentic, progressive, linear history, the Egyptians occupy a form of anachronistic space, signalling their distance from the adult manhood Douglass embodies as bearer of US national ideology.

Douglass's strategic rehistoricization of discursive formations of race dramatizes his resistance to the reality and rationale of internal colonization. That resistance is, however, not without its contradictions, as Douglass, seeking final confirmation of American manhood, becomes complicit in a related discourse of US empire. Much of the ambivalence of his position may be explained by the ongoing ambiguity in the relationship of the black subject to the United States, and the tension caused by that ambiguity in external sites of cultural identity inhabited by racially equivalent, but politically and culturally distinct groups. Though seeking racio-cultural legitimation for the African American population of the United States, Douglass is, in North Africa, also questing for that American imperative fundamentally incompatible with indigenous culture of any kind: the *tabula rasa* of the Columbiad vision.[49] This

46 Kenneth W. Warren, 'Frederick Douglass's *Life and Times*: Progressive Rhetoric and the Problem of Constituency', in Eric J. Sundquist, ed., *Frederick Douglass: New Literary and Historical Essays* (Cambridge: Cambridge University Press), pp. 253–70 (264).
47 Douglass, *Autobiographies*, p. 989.
48 Douglass, *Autobiographies*, p. 1006.
49 The Columbiad myth has retained its attractions, for African American critics as well as writers. A recent compilation of literary and critical work edited by Henry Louis Gates Jr, Maria Diedrich and Carl Pederson, which in fact calls for greater application of postcolonial theory to critiques of African American experience and literature, is titled *The Black Columbiad: Black Imagination and the Middle Passage* (New York: Oxford University Press, 1999).

tension is implicit in his characterization of Egyptian Arabs, which echoes Columbus's description of landfall at Guanahaní, and first encounter with the indigenous people of the Americas. 'In order to win their good will,' Columbus wrote,

> I gave them some of the red hats and glass beads that they put round their necks ... with which they were very pleased and became so friendly it was a wonder to see. Afterwards they swam out to the ship's boats where we were and brought parrots and balls of cotton ... and they bartered with us for other things which we gave them. ... They go as naked as their mothers bore them, even the women, though I saw only one girl, and she was very young. All those I did see were young men, none of them more than thirty years old. They were well built, with handsome bodies and fine features. Their hair is thick, almost like a horse's tail, but short. ... Some of them paint themselves black, though they are naturally the colour of Canary Islanders, neither black nor white; and some paint themselves white, some red and some whatever colour they can find.[50]

In his own journal, Douglass describes the boarding of his own ship in Port Said, a modern Babel, where 'the few houses that make up the town look white, new and temporary, reminding one of some of the hastily built wooden towns of the American frontier',[51] by 'a perfect swarm of Arab laborers, frocked, hooded, or fezed, barefooted and barelegged to the knees ... What a wild clamour – what a confusion of tongues all going at once and endeavoring to drown the voice of the other.'[52] His published description of Egyptian labourers bears many of the hallmarks of the encounter with original man, marking the beginning of Douglass's self-affirmation as a heroic, masculine subject brought into being on territorial or aesthetic frontiers. As distinct from much US Orientalist writing at this time, the encounter does not promote the standard vision of a vigorous, youthful United States penetrating a spent and dissipated Orient: to the contrary in fact, Douglass is characterized as an elder statesman casting a paternalistic eye over a vibrant, exotic source of both culture and, notably, labour. But in its early stages, the journey to Egypt takes the form of a reverse Columbiad in which the territory of origin (Europe and North Africa) and US imperial intention (the Orient) can only be partially reclaimed for its cultural descendants.

For, as the journey proceeds, the debt to both Orientalist and Columbiad visions becomes increasing apparent. Douglass's ship passes through

---

50 Christopher Columbus, *Journal of the First Voyage (Diario del primer viaje), 1492*, ed. and trans. B.W. Ife (Warminster: Aris & Phillips, 1990), pp. 29–31.
51 Douglass, *Autobiographies*, pp. 1006–1007.
52 'Diary', Library of Congress Microfilm.

the Suez canal under the jealous eyes of European sentinels and cultural rivals, Britain and France, to an empty frontier space, 'to which the eye, even with the aid of the strongest field-glass, can find no limit but the horizon'.[53] 'Nothing in my American experience,' Douglass claimed, 'ever gave me such a deep sense of unearthly silence, such a sense of vast, profound, unbroken sameness and solitude, as did this passage.'[54] Inevitably, and in hindsight, this passage from the known to the unknown subverts the Columbiad fantasy by evoking the foundational experience of New World peoples of African descent, the Middle Passage. More deliberately perhaps, Douglass gestures towards the transcendentalist, Indic Orientalism of Emerson, signifying upon the empowered American vision of Emerson's 'transcendental eyeball'. This is an Orientalism which sees the construction of a contingently 'free' imperial body – Douglass – through the erasure of the native presence and its racial implications, and the characterization of the landscape as a passive, disembodied, ahistorical and spiritual other, without its own agency, against the figure of the American nation-subject imagined as active, masculine and whole. Douglass was soon to fall foul of the body–spirit dichotomy of the Indic framework, when his decision to climb the Great Pyramid with 'two Arabs before me pulling, and two at my back pushing', left him in a state of near collapse, and, due to his advanced age, 'unable to recover from the strain in less than two weeks'.[55] But his immediate reaction to the desert landscape was to extol its virtues as the locus of existential self-discovery, a

> wide waste, under this cloudless sky, star-lighted by night and by a fierce blazing sun by day, where ever the wind seems voiceless, it was natural for men to look up to the sky and stars and contemplate the universe and infinity above and around them; the signs and wonders in the heavens above and in the earth beneath.

'In such loneliness, silence and expansiveness,' Douglass declares, in direct accord with the Transcendentalist view, 'imagination is unchained and man has naturally a deeper sense of the Infinite Presence than is to be felt in the in the noise and bustle of the towns and men-crowded cities' (*Autobiographies*, p. 1009).

Douglass also uses the desert, however, to signify upon the Columbiad fantasy of discovery, and contemporary literary engagements with whiteness. He looks out from the deck of ship to an expanse 'where neither tree, shrub nor vegetation of any kind, nor human habitation breaks the view', bearing striking resemblance to the open sea, a 'flat,

53 Douglass, *Autobiographies*, p. 1008.
54 Douglass, *Autobiographies*, pp. 1007–1008.
55 Douglass, *Autobiographies*, p. 1012.

broad, silent, dreamy and unending solitude'. In her analysis of what she calls the 'complex and contradictory situation in which American writers found themselves during the formative years of the nation's literature', Toni Morrison, using the example of Poe's *The Narrative of Arthur Gordon Pym*, describes 'the visualised but somehow closed and unknowable white form that rises from the mists at the end of the journey', noting that images of whiteness occur in American narrative 'after [that] narrative has encountered blackness ... figurations of impenetrable whiteness that surface in American literature whenever and Africanist presence is engaged'.[56] Like his literary antecedents, Douglass engages with the symbolism of race, counterpoising, despite his ongoing attempts to deconstruct racial dichotomies in favour of composite or hybrid accounts, images of whiteness with shadows of an Africanist presence. Echoing Melville and Poe, Douglass describes something that 'appears occasionally away in the distance [–] a white line of life which only makes the silence and solitude more pronounced' (*Autobiographies*, p. 1008); a form, in other words, of existential self-empowerment that assists in the visual conquest of the landscape and suggests a connection with the 'Infinite Presence' itself. Immediately *succeeding* this self-characterization within the American Renaissance ideal, a North African figure appears; an image of incoherent selfhood, destabilizing the tranquillity of the landscape and potentially the identity of the spectator. From nowhere, this 'sign of life' emerges

> wholly unlooked for, and for which it is hard to account. It is the half-naked, hungry form of a human being, a young Arab, who seems to have started up out of the yellow sand at his feet, for no town, village, house or shelter is seen from which he could have emerged; but here he is, and he is as lively as a cricket, running by the ship's side up and down the sandy banks for miles and for hours with the speed of a horse and the endurance of a hound, plaintively shouting as he runs: 'Backsheesh! Backsheesh! Backsheesh!' and only stopping in the race to pick up the pieces of bread and meat thrown to him from the ship. (*Autobiographies*, p. 1008)

Even compared to that which preceded it, this is a highly ambivalent account of the Egyptian native. Indeed, perhaps the most notable element of his characterization is the 'nativeness', which distinguishes him so starkly from Douglass himself. Gone is the empathy that characterized the earlier descriptions, to be replaced by a fascination with the bizarre young Arab, whose unaccountable presence undermines the integrity of the otherwise tranquil *tabula rasa*. His sudden, almost supernatural appearance, manic pursuit of the ship, evident hunger and eerie mantra

56 Morrison, *Playing in the Dark*, p. 32.

provide an image of a less wholesome relationship with the Oriental presence, and more clearly, if unintentionally, define the true nature of the imperial relationship with the North African other. More immediately, the encounter posits a form of racial anxiety, provocatively deployed on the boundary of imperial space, and belying the racial proximity earlier referred to by Douglass. Like the mirage that simultaneously appears in the far distance, 'now ... a splendid forest and now a refreshing lake', and which travels in parallel to the moving ship, though 'its distance from the observer remains ever the same', the young Arab illustrates Douglass's cultural distance from, if ongoing racial proximity to, an unstable, under-developed native presence. Indeed, although the description of the Arab presence in effect disrupts constructions of both the United States and a spiritualized Orient as *terra nulla,* awaiting the inscription of the potent, American self, it also eerily anticipates the river scenes in Conrad's African work of fifteen year later.[57] One critic has argued that Douglass's racial and cultural vision was always limited, suggesting that he 'never broke through his North African or Mediterranean approach to Africa'. Douglass's repeated characterization of black Africans as essentially barbarians has led Martin to suggest that, 'he found it easier to identify with North Africa, where the people more closely resembled mulattos and

57 Joseph Conrad, *Heart of Darkness* (London: Penguin, 1995). Conrad's works also illustrates the overdetermined nature of discourse concerning Euro-African relations in the late nineteenth and early twentieth centuries. Chinua Achebe contends that 'Conrad was a bloody racist', and that 'white racism against Africa is such a normal way of thinking that its manifestations go completely undetected', concluding that 'Africa [is] a setting and back drop which eliminates the African as a human factor'. Wilson Harris, on the other hand, sees *Heart of Darkness* as a critique of rather than apologetic for European colonialism, asserting that Achebe's reading does not recognize 'the novel form as a medium of consciousness that has its deepest roots in an intuitive and much, much older self than the historical ... conditions ... that bind us to a particular decade or generation or century', going on to suggest that 'this ... matter may arouse incomprehension in Africa where, by and large, tradition tends towards homogenous imperatives'. M.M. Mahood contends that 'Conrad ... was responsible for three stories about the Congo. The first, "An Outpost of Progress", is a clear, hard picture of the harm done to black and white alike by the colonial intrusion. The last . . . has for subject the harm done by such exposure when it is undertaken for questionable motives,' and '[b]etween these ... "Heart of Darkness" an intensely personal and autobiographical tale, in which the drive to draw upon both first-hand experience and recent agitation in order to enlarge upon the protest of "An Outpost of Progress" is shot through with doubts' (Chinua Achebe, 'An Image of Africa', in Robert Hamner, ed., *Conrad: Third World Perspectives* [Washington, DC: Three Continents Press, 1990], pp. 119–30 [124]; Wilson Harris, 'The Frontier on Which *Heart of Darkness* Stands', in Hamner, *Conrad*, pp. 161–67 [161–62]; and M.M. Mahood, *The Colonial Encounter: A Reading of Six Novels* [London: Collins, 1977], p. 35).

the gap between Western and African cultures seemed smaller and less significant'.[58] His Egyptian writing, however, indicates an antipathy to the North African, whom Douglass is inclined to characterize as a culturally degenerate 'native' rather than a potentially integrable hybrid.

It may be that Douglass's attempts to recuperate Egypt as a site of Afro-European hybridity and thereby rehabilitate the African American presence in the US national imaginary were always compromised by his apparently unshakable belief in established cultural hierarchies and the logic of progress. Even his most profound existential reverie, for example, is interrupted by the 'the startling whistle of the locomotive and the sound of the rushing train' (*Autobiographies*, p. 1010), symbol and agent of US modernization and territorial expansion.[59] His bizarre encounter with the Arab however, indicates that, despite his racial egalitarianism, Douglass too was prey to prevailing US tendencies that sought legitimation in external sites of empire and through signification on the bodies of culturally anachronistic others.

It seems almost certainly true that, as Martin asserts, 'it has been difficult, if not impossible, for Western blacks, like Western whites, to escape widespread anti-African images'.[60] This, however, does not fully account for Douglass's ambivalence towards the Arab, who, after all, provided Douglass with his most important, credible and comprehensive cultural counterpoint in the external world, and who was never understood as African in white racial discourse. Perhaps it was Douglass's very Americanness that prevented his identification with those he willingly deemed racial equals but whose current cultural profile he could neither celebrate not understand. For example, Douglass predictably recoiled from Catholic clergy in Rome, characterizing them in terms of Oriental decadence and decay, and in equal measure from the 'howling and dancing dervishes' of Cairo. 'Both,' he claimed,

> seemed equally deaf to the dictates of reason. The dancing and howling dervishes often spin around in their religious transports till their heads lose control and they fall to the floor sighing, groaning and foaming at the mouth like madmen, reminding one of scenes that sometimes occur at our own old-fashioned camp-meetings. (*Autobiographies*, p. 1013)

58 Martin, *Mind of Frederick Douglass*, pp. 205–07.
59 Warren too reads the whistle of the train as 'a note of progress', though he ascribes it to Douglass's antipathy to religion rather than to the activation of an Orientalist trope of potent Western masculinity, arguing that for Douglass, 'though the religious world may be beautiful and moving, it is not a world on the move. ... Douglass finds [in] the ruins of a great civilisation a scene inimical to human progress, a scene that underscores "the vanity of all things"' ('*Life and Times*', p. 267).
60 Martin, *Mind of Frederick Douglass*, p. 208.

That Douglass may have been witnessing the source of some form of African American religious custom is lost in his determination to police cultural propriety, rigidly insisting on conformity to rational western forms of religious practice.[61] And, although he had words of praise for Islam, declaring that 'I can easily see why the Mohomidan [*sic*] religion commends itself to these people, for it does not make color the criterion of fellowship as some of our so called Christian churches do. All colors are welcome to the faith of the Prophet,'[62] his condemnation of the circumstances of Muslim women reveals the extent to which his cultural beliefs were embedded in Amerocentric ideas of liberty, gender and human dignity. 'In Cairo,' Foner notes, 'Douglass was depressed by the "squalor, disease and deformity — all manner of unfortunate beggary"',[63] in direct recall of the scenes he described forty years earlier in some of his Irish writings. More tellingly, Douglass confided to his diary his concern at the 'pitiful' daily encounter with 'hooded and veiled women'. 'It is sad,' he explained, 'to think of that one-half of the human family should be thus cramped, kept in ignorance and degraded, having no existence except that of minister[ing] to the pride and lusts of the men who own them as slaves are owned.'[64] Schueller describes the importance of the figure of the degraded Eastern woman in the nineteenth century as a means to certain kinds of social power for US women. Missionary activity in particular, the conversion of the heathens in the East (itself an element of the Columbiad fantasy), provided women adventurers with the opportunity to 'transgress the defined sphere of domesticity ... and embody the nation as empire by distinguishing themselves from the raced bodies of Oriental women'.[65] For liberal, enlightened and independent US women, then, North African women became the emblem of their relative liberation, sexual integrity, and confirmation of moral and cultural superiority. Travelling as he was with his second wife, Helen Pitts, and indebted to feminine, bourgeois US society for much of his ideology, readership and ongoing support, Douglass seemed unable to resist the popular image of Muslim women as passive, suppressed and in need of rescue. Indeed, scripted as they are within the logic and vocabulary of US slavery, these women appear as the most needful of western cultural enlightenment, and in this may even act as a metonym for a syncretic Orient.[66] Inter-

---

61 For a discussion of Douglass's antipathy to the black preaching voice, see Warren, '*Life and Times*', pp. 253–70.

62 'Diary', Library of Congress Microfilm.

63 Foner, *Frederick Douglass*, 4, p. 125.

64 'Diary', Library of Congress Microfilm.

65 Schueller, *US Orientalisms*, p. 78.

66 Readings of Douglass by (exclusively male) American critics have tended to repro-

estingly, the veil, which frustrates the scopic drive of the US traveller, is the greatest signifier of oppression in Douglass's cultural vocabulary, triggering a fantasy that categorizes unseen, and ultimately, for westerners, unknowable relationships within the notoriously abusive framework of master–slave sexual relations. Douglass's reading of the veil is a far cry from the radicalism of Fanon, who points to its subversive, often revolutionary potential. More recently, Islamic feminists have underlined the radical cultural and political meanings of the veil, as well as its power to signify a different understanding of a self, one grounded in models of privacy, modesty and resistance.[67] But in Douglass's North African observations, the veiled women, like the young native, illustrate the limitations of a liberal western vision seeking to collapse discrete, indigenous forms into hybrid global understandings of culture and human subjectivity. Ultimately, it is the North Africans themselves, and not white racialist discourse, that provide the greatest challenge, and resistance, to Douglass's liberal, western embrace. His inability adequately to represent them is confirmation of the insularity of even the most liberal myths of US American origin, which continue to privilege the modern hybrid state, and its imperial landscapes, at the expense of non-western, non-modern, frequently 'native' cultural matrices.[68]

There is also another form of cultural inscription operating within Douglass's account of his Egyptian experience. This draws on more radical African American tendencies towards territorial separatism, or at least the mystification of extraterritorial sites as mythical emblems of cultural origin, religious salvation or eternal reward. Remarkably at odds with the racial imperatives of Douglass's quest is the scriptural reference which everywhere underpins his account, and which merges at times with the quotidian life he describes around him. Images of Egypt as Zion abound, with the land repeatedly pictured 'as it was in the days of Abraham and Moses',[69] in a manner derivative of African American folk and vernacular forms. Particularly notable is the preponderance of biblical reference to

---

duce Douglass's attitude, implicitly empathizing in their readings with Douglass's view.

67 A certain cross-fertilization with Dorr's narrative, which frequently dwells on veiled Oriental women, is also occurring here. An example of the signifying play in African American letters is provided by the chapter in Dorr's work on Constantinople, entitled 'The Dogs Provoke Me, and the Women are Veiled' (1858). Douglass was fond of commenting on the perspicacity of British dogs during his first sojourn (1845–47) a trope then manipulated by Dorr, who is subsequently re-signified upon by Douglass in his own work.

68 See Martin, *Mind of Frederick Douglass*, pp. 212–14, with regard to Douglass's attitudes to Native America.

69 Douglass, *Autobiographies*, p. 1009.

the captivity of the Israelites in Egypt. 'In passing through the land of Goshen,' Douglass writes,

> I experienced a thrill of satisfaction in viewing the scene of one of the most affecting stories ever written – the story of Jacob: how his sons were compelled by famine to go into Egypt to buy corn; how they sold their young brother Joseph into slavery; how they came with a lie upon their lips to hide their treachery and cruelty; how the slave boy Joseph gained favor in the eyes of Pharaoh; how these brothers who had sold him were again by famine brought face to face with Joseph who stipulated that the only condition upon which he could again see them was that they should bring their young brother Benjamin with them; how Jacob plaintively appealed against this arrangement by which his grey hair might be brought down in sorrow to the grave, and finally, through the good offices of Joseph, the happy settlement of the whole family in this fertile land of Goshen ... here was the land of Goshen, with fields yet green, its camels still grazing and its corn still growing as when Jacob and his sons with their flocks and herds were settled in it three thousand years ago.[70]

In parallel with the ethnological interest Egypt holds for Douglass is its overarching, biblically based Judaeo-Christian meaning, a meaning everywhere inscribed on the landscape. In the Christian paradigm through which Douglass reads this space, and despite the dominance of Islam in the region as a whole, Egypt is already encoded with and appropriated as a site of western religious significance. Understandings of that metaphorical significance, as of biblical meaning more generally, differed sharply in the United States. Puritan belief figured North American expansion as 'Manifest Destiny', while biblical exegesis had been widely used throughout the life of the nation as justification for slavery, citing African American genealogical inferiority and alleged descent from the biblically damned Ham. As discussed in Chapter Five, the appropriation and creative misrepresentation of racial apologists in the guise of Southern preachers formed an important part of Douglass's early rhetorical intervention in vernacular forms of slave resistance. His flirtation with folk and vernacular forms engaged with a much wider African American cultural process that generated radically liberational readings of Christian doctrine. Even at this late stage of his career, Douglass's ongoing relationship with that folk culture, and the black preaching voice in particular, is clearly present. In a letter to his son Lewis, he wrote, 'You did not think, I did not think, nobody thought, that I would venture so far from home as I am this Sunday morning. "Go down Moses, way down in Egypt land and tell old Pharaoh to let my people go."'[71] His journey

70 Douglass, *Autobiographies*, pp. 1010–11.
71 'Diary', Library of Congress Microfilm.

is not merely an élite source book for Douglass's ethnological arguments, then, but a return to the Promised Land of Canaan, a manifestation of a long-held belief in a personal destiny, early frustrated by slavery, but now righteously fulfilled. 'I had strange dreams of travel even in my boyhood days,' Douglass writes.

> I thought I should some day see many of the famous places of which I heard men speak, and of which I read even while a slave ... A few years back my Sundays were spent on the banks of the Chesapeake bay, bemoaning my condition and looking out from the farm of Edward Covey, and, with a heart aching to be on their decks, watching the white sails of the ships passing off to sea. Now I was enjoying what the wisest and best of the world have bestowed for the wisest and best to enjoy. (*Autobiographies*, pp. 1013–14)

Witness to the wonders of the ancient world is confirmation of spiritual as well as material success, even in the face of significant adversity. Latent in this Zionist vision of return is, of course, the Babylon of slavery. Lying dormant rather than being actively pursued in Douglass's writing, therefore (he prefers to find frequent personal analogy in Paul), is a reconception of the New World as a land not of promise but of corruption, indicating the presence of a counter-discourse that indirectly characterizes America as fallen, an understanding more in line with African American and indeed Caribbean folk and religious figurations of the New World as exile. And the implications of the counter-discourse do not end here. For though Douglass allegedly seeks cultural and ethnological validation in Egypt, the metaphorical alliance created by the scriptural overlay is with the Israelites, for whom Exodus, or escape from Pharaoh, marked the first step on the journey to the Promised Land.[72] Suggestion of scriptural analogy thus not only counters internal US racial hierarchies, although

---

72 Bernal contends in *Black Athena* 1 that the seventeenth century saw 'Greek studies [brought] into alliance with Christianity ... During the first centuries of the Christian era the main struggle was between Christians and pagans ... [who] saw the distinctions between Egypt, the Orient and Greece as relatively unimportant. Jews ... on the other hand, scored points against the Greeks by pointing out the lateness and shallowness of Greek civilization in comparison with those of the Egyptians ... and ... the Israelites. ... The possibility of pitting Greeks against Egyptians ... in defence of Christianity, did not occur until the Renaissance ... After the Reformation, and the break away from *Roman* Catholicism, the relationship [between German and Greek culture and language] became much stronger, with the new image of Greek and German as the two languages of Protestantism ... [A] feeling developed that the Teutonic-speaking peoples were "better" and more "manly" than the Romance-speaking nations of France, Spain and Italy and that their languages as a whole were superior to Latin and on a par with Greek' (Bernal, *Black Athena*, 1, pp. 192–93). Arguably, Douglass's view of Egypt is mediated through an English-speaking, Judeo-Christian/Protestant lens.

it retains the imaginary availability of North Africa as an external locus of cultural meaning; its language also provides a critique of imperial structure and progressivist accounts of human history per se. Such is the duplicity of this rhetorical mode that it can simultaneously celebrate the destiny made manifest in Douglass's literal presence in the Holy Land, and negate the claims of 'African' culture at the core of Douglass quest for legitimation. Ultimately, however, the Zionist undercurrent posits the truly important people of Douglass's journey as mythological rather than real. Egypt becomes less a symbol of successful creolization than of the divided self, warring against itself in the search for an enabling myth that can fully integrate the African American presence to the myths of American origin and destiny, without negating the realities of oppression, past or present.

From early on in his career, Douglass had attempted to construct bridges of cross-racial cultural solidarity with North Africa. In 'Claims of the Negro', he maintaining of the ancient Egyptians that, though 'it may not be claimed that [they] were negroes, – viz:- answering in all respects, to the nations and tribes ranged under the general appellation, negro; still it may safely be affirmed, that a strong affinity and a direct relationship may be claimed by the negro race, to THE GRANDEST OF ALL THE NATIONS OF ANTIQUITY, THE BUILDERS OF THE PYRAMIDS'.[73] Despite the strength of his black nationalist views however, there can be little doubt that, unlike the Pan-Africanists of his generation, Douglass's concern was never Africa, but America. His ethnological opinions, and his autobiographical form, privilege racial hybridity in the construction of a 'representative' US American subject, advocating a 'melting pot' approach to understandings of a US national identity formed of a composite of European and African roots, and the eventual creolization of more recent immigrant groups, such as Asians. Douglass's discourse on Egypt illustrates the competing tendencies in the anti-racialist rhetoric of Afro-America, and the extent to which it too is implicated in the discourse and practice of empire. His late image as American Renaissance man captures the strengths and shortcomings of the national cultural imaginary.

---

73 Blassingame, *FDP*, 1.2, p. 517.

Chapter 7

Models of Progress:
Ireland, Haiti and the Atlantic

The extended version of Frederick Douglass's *Life and Times* was published in 1892 with chapters additional to those of the earlier editions.[1] These later chapters deal with Douglass's tour of Europe and North Africa, and with his Haitian diplomatic experiences. Their inclusion in the final version of his last autobiography illustrates the importance of Douglass's engagement with the realities of US expansion and the underpinning myths of empire to his construction of nationhood and representative identity. Another autobiographical publication of Douglass's latter years was a text that reworked his early transatlantic experience, entitled 'Thoughts and Recollections of a Tour in Ireland'. Published in the *AME Review* in 1886, just before he embarked on the journey that would retrace and extend the path of his earlier travels, this piece is more or less contemporaneous with Douglass's Egyptian writing. It reveals some of the political views that fed into his autobiographical project at the time. It also allows for a comparison between Douglass's political stance on Irish Home Rule, and his views on Haiti, to whose history and current condition Douglass had previously compared Ireland.

For Douglass, the issues of emancipation, racial equality and citizenship were directly and inextricably linked to questions of nationhood and identity. The traditions and tropes in which that identity was encoded were also crucial to his own self-fashioning throughout his career. The contrary, however, was also true: in his role as fugitive, cultural tourist and diplomatic emissary, Douglass was instrumental in mediating transnational sites of US interest, and defining their place in the American cultural imaginary. This was as true of his early overseas experience in Ireland as it was of his later position as agent and representative of state in Haiti.

1 The text was originally published in 1881, and was a commercial failure. It was published in a new edition in 1882 but sales continued to be slow. An expanded edition was published in 1892 including chapters on Douglass's European tour, Douglass's support of John Sherman in the US presidential campaign of 1888, his appointment as US minister to Haiti and the controversy over the Môle St Nicolas. For a chronology of the text's publication see Douglass, *Autobiographies*, pp. 1072–77.

'Thoughts and Recollections' forms part of Douglass's journalistic contribution to American public life, in the early stages of which, Shelley Fishkin Fisher and Carla Peterson contend, he established the 'we' behind his Emersonian 'I' as a demarcation of those within and outside the abolitionist community.[2] This dynamic of inclusion and exclusion permeates Douglass's writing: well after the formal abolition of slavery at the end of the Civil War, he continued in this binary mode – which was based on élite, civilizationist models of morality – particularly in discussions of international politics.

The title of the 1886 piece, 'Thoughts and Recollections', refers to Douglass's first transatlantic crossing in 1845, a journey that began an association with the United Kingdom that was to last for fifty years. In 1859, shortly after John Brown was hanged and one year before the outbreak of the American Civil War, Douglass returned to Britain for another lecture tour. His 1886–87 trip abroad covered Britain (and France, Italy and Greece) as well as Egypt. By the time of writing, Douglass had established himself as a figure of national and international stature, whose intervention in the narrative of nationhood was ongoing. Earlier in his career, Douglass had challenged the racial exclusivity of the US model of national identity by activating the moral logic of nativism, an anti-immigrant attitude privileging the position of the 'native-born' in the US, and normally adopted by native-born white Protestants. Irish Catholics became a major focus of anti-immigrant feeling from the early nineteenth century, although its political importance diminished as the issue of slavery became a dominant American concern. With the increase in immigration in the late nineteenth century, nativist sentiment regained some of its political currency. In the mid 1840s, Douglass had invoked a nativist counter-representation of the Irish peasantry and urban working class, stressing their moral incompatibility with insular abolitionist and nativist views of constituency, and casting himself, almost by default, as an idealized nation-subject. Nativism continued to have an attraction for Douglass, possibly because of its potential for racial inclusion, indicative as it was of birth and a particular set of political and cultural norms, rather than necessarily skin colour. For Douglass, a strategic reading of nativism could provide a viable template for both Afro- and Euro-American identity based on an understanding of the citizen as an American creole.

The integrity of the nativist position was, in the second half of the nineteenth century, coming under increasing pressure, as the presence

---

2 Shelly Fishkin Fisher and Carla Peterson, '"We Hold These Truths to be Self-Evident": The Rhetoric of Frederick Douglass's Journalism', in Eric J. Sundquist, ed., *Frederick Douglass: New Literary and Historical Essays* (Cambridge: Cambridge University Press, 1990), pp. 189–204 (190).

of an ever-growing number of immigrants, eager both to assimilate to mainstream US society and to retain particular ethnic identities, began to displace the internal cultural boundaries of national subjectivity. The panacea for this threatened internal displacement had always been the frontier, against which the nation could express itself as a coherent political unit. This coherence was hugely compromised by the internal colonization of African and Native Americans, neither of whose cultural profile was acknowledged by the Anglo-American hegemony. But, at a time when national, cross-continental consolidation had been all but achieved and the United States was entering a phase of overseas expansion, the national cultural imaginary, too, turned outwards in search of new sites of cultural validation.

These sites were used to stage important debates in US culture of the time, the political, racial and cultural dynamics of which they were stage-managed to reflect. The North African Orient was attractive to Afro- and Euro-Americans alike because of the richness and indeterminacy of its racial and cultural profile. For Douglass it became the site of his self-legitimation as American Renaissance man. As Schueller puts it, 'the very existence of complex racial dilemmas in the United States reproduced in the imaginative literature of the country a far greater concern with racial dynamics within Orientalism than existed in the literature of their European counterparts'.[3] The same might also be said of the existence of internal cultural dilemmas other than race, such as religious affiliation and practice, moral norms, class, and the assimilation of large numbers of immigrants of diverse cultural and linguistic backgrounds. These too prompted a range of literary and journalistic output which sought to resolve internal contradictions by appropriation and inscription of external populations with the imperial logic of US cultural codes.

'Thoughts and Recollections', which takes as its subject the debate around British colonialism and Irish Home rule, is one such exercise. It illustrates discrepancies in conventional understandings of representative power based on a black-white racial divide in the nineteenth century. For, as Daniel Brantley notes,

> Douglass's participation in worldwide reform movements may be cited in support of the proposition that blacks, through their leaders, exercised influence on a global scale at a time when most of them were enslaved in the South, few could vote, and none of them were regarded as United States citizens nor served in any foreign service posts.[4]

3 Schueller, *US Orientalisms*, p. 94.
4 Daniel Brantley, 'Black Diplomacy and Frederick Douglass's Caribbean Experiences, 1871 and 1889–1891: The Untold Story', *Phylon: The Atlanta University Review of Race and Culture*, 95.3 (1984), pp. 196–209 (196).

Early in his career Douglass had established himself as witness and mediator of overseas spectacle for a US abolitionist audience, though he never went so far as to proffer opinions on the contemporary political situation while in Ireland or Britain. But the 'Irish question' was an issue that retained its international currency throughout Douglass's career. In many ways the position of the Irish in the United Kingdom mirrored the state of internal colonization that obtained for Native Americans and, post-emancipation, African Americans, in the Southern States. Such was Douglass's antipathy to Irish Americans, however, and the antebellum importance of retaining the focus of the transatlantic human rights debate firmly on the issue of slavery, that he resisted attempts to analogize the Irish as 'slaves' or make common cause with the Irish peasantry or urban working class during his British–Irish tour. Instead, Douglass saw a closer relation between Irish and Haitian history, an analogy he drew publicly in his speech at the Columbian World's Fair in Chicago in 1893.[5]

The debate regarding Irish de-colonization occurred at a time when the cults of domesticity and empire were at their height in Britain, and native civilizationism, black nationalism and overseas expansion were assuming increasing importance in the United States.[6] Concurrent growth in US immigrant communities, particularly the Irish who, according to Douglass, 'control ... New York, and dictate the policy of the Pacific States in relation in relation to Chinamen and other competing labourers',[7] further politicized US ethnic identity, as well as raising the profile of international issues, such as Irish separatism. Moreover, the emergence of distinctive ethnic communities at the end of the century was placing increasing pressure on previous ideals of what it meant to be

---

5 'It was once said by the great Daniel O Connell that the history of Ireland might be traced, like a wounded man through a crowd, by the blood. The same may be said of Haiti as a free state' (*Lecture on Haiti*, World's Fair, Chicago, 2 January 1893, in Foner, *Frederick Douglass*, 4, p. 483). Other, more explicit comparisons between Ireland and Haiti were made by Douglass throughout his career.

6 In 1887, Douglass heard Gladstone speak to the British parliament on the question of Irish Home Rule and lectured on this subject in Washington after his return to the United States in the same year. See also the radicalization of his position on Ireland late in his career in the article written for the *New National Era*. For a discussion of (British) domesticity and empire, see McClintock, *Imperial Leather*, pp. 22–74. For an overview of the intellectual history of nineteenth-century Black Nationalism, see Wilson Jeremiah Moses, *The Golden Age of Black Nationalism* (New York: Oxford, 1978).

7 Douglass, 'Thoughts and Recollections', n.p. Original manuscript in Frederick Douglass Collection, Manuscript Collection, Library of Congress, Washington, DC. Quotations taken from original manuscript and noted in the text using the abbreviation 'TR' followed by page number.

a US American. Race, as a political concept, was becoming more complex, with immigrants from Ireland, Southern and Eastern Europe (initially racialized as non-white), and China, posing a challenge to monolithic, Anglo-American models of native identity and requiring a response that acknowledged the increasing cultural diversity of the nation. For these new US Americans, already established ethno-cultural spaces and forms of representation were proving inadequate. But, although they destabilized the master narrative of the US American hegemony, they also demanded that they be embodied in its representative paradigms.

Throughout his career, Douglass had fought for African American inclusion in that hegemony. This late autobiographical piece sees him once again seizing the opportunity to influence the meaning and position of particular sections of US society in the national cultural imaginary.[8] In a manner that draws on contemporary modes of US cultural understanding, notably those tropes of United States imperialism, nation-building and overseas travel, Douglass's late reworking of his first overseas experience is an attempt to categorize, map and control extra-territorially, those subjects now causing internal disruption to nativist discourse.

The argument re-advances Douglass's early experience in Europe, which had provided a transnational dimension to his identity and writing, as a representative experience. The journey he had taken in 1845 had retraced the historical and geographical route of enslavement, from Europe and Africa to the Americas, and reactivated the transatlantic narrative of discovery, conquest and black slavery severed by Independence and its subsequent ideology. Alan Rice and Martin Crawford characterize Douglass's Atlantic crossing as the 'refiguring of … a historically enslaving experience into a literally liberating one'.[9] But, uncharacteristically, the subject of 'Thoughts and Recollections' is not slavery, but the issue of Irish Home Rule, a movement that attempted to establish political autonomy for Ireland through ongoing lobbying for repeal of the Act of Union of 1800, which had abolished the Irish parliament in Dublin. Though technically part of an imperial government, whose territory included large sections of Africa, Asia, Australasia and America, Ireland was in reality a place of widespread and endemic poverty, oppression, disenfranchisement and ongoing political agitation. Ireland was therefore uniquely placed: it was an emerging nation-state, and a colony of the world's largest empire. In the United States, Ireland reflected the stasis, poverty and corruption of the European past. Simultaneously its

---

8 For a discussion of Douglass's attitudes to and representations of Asians, see Martin, *Mind of Frederick Douglass*, pp. 214–15.

9 Rice and Crawford, 'Triumphant Exile', p. 3.

large migrant population constituted a fragment of the American present. In British colonial terms, Ireland continued to be underdeveloped and overexploited, with labour eventually emerging as the country's primary export, an important resource in British and US industrialization, and in westward migration.

Douglass's interest in Ireland then was both historical and contemporary: Ireland had in the past provided him with a refuge from re-enslavement; but changes in US social structures caused by emancipation and immigration demanded that he modify his tendency to privilege Anglo-American norms in culture and politics. Irish Americans presented new challenges to the structure and definition of American subjectivity, although they had undergone what Theodore Allen calls a 'sea-change' during their westward migration.[10] Irish immigrants destabilized nativism, later confirming themselves within its boundaries by adopting a 'white' identity that differentiated them from African Americans, the lowest rung on the US class and racial ladder. The issue of Irish nationalism was one that Douglass treated with some ambivalence for reasons tied to anti-black racism in the United States in which Irish Americans were implicated. In addition, Douglass's long-standing Anglophilia, his class and cultural identification with Anglo-America, re-enforced the jaundiced view he was inclined to take of the Irish population and its political ambitions.

The central theme of black autobiography had always been 'the demand for the recognition of black manhood',[11] and much of Douglass's writing restates the link between autobiographical writing and the project of self-creation and liberation. Early in 'Thoughts and Recollection', Douglass establishes the by now familiar autobiographical nature of his work:

> If I am asked by your respective readers, as I probably shall be, for most of them are, I doubt not, under forty years of age, why I made the voyage to the United Kingdom of Great Britain and Ireland, I suppose I should muster courage to tell them, however humiliating it might seem. I was a slave, a fugitive slave. (TR, p. 6)

One of the achievements of the slave narrative was to produce a counternarrative of US identity, through which the history of the United States was represented anti-heroically as a process of enslavement rather than liberation, contradicting élite versions of the United States as a liberating space. Douglass's placement of American overseas relationships within

10   Allen, *Invention of the White Race*, 1, p. 159.
11   John W. Blassingame, 'Black Autobiography as History and Literature', *The Black Scholar*, 5.4 (1973), pp. 2–8 (2).

this vernacular history of slavery, with its black-specific narrative of slave memory, re-centres the American cultural imaginary in the Atlantic passage and on uncomfortable historical realities. For although the subject of this address is to be the Irish political situation, Douglass is also at pains to establish a moral hierarchy that prioritizes African American experience, positing the existence of a grand narrative in which the slave trade is the defining component. Though his subsequent political analysis is one that indisputably privileges the world-view of the United States, Douglass is also destabilizing core principles of the Anglo-American vision by displacing Columbiad and Puritan myths of European origin and American rebirth with a founding myth of the Middle Passage and an absent Africa.

In this, the text is comparable to Douglass's Egyptian writing, which activates teleologies of race and culture in order to challenge and debunk white racialist ethnography, and establish African American claims to the world of high culture within the United States. The Irish text goes a step further, by confirming the centrality of the Atlantic as an external site of subjective enactment for Douglass, the representative (African) American nation-subject; historically linking the slave who 'went abroad [not] as a gentleman and a scholar ... [but] for the purpose of finding liberty and shelter denied me at home' (TR, p. 6) with the now public figure and man of letters. Despite the shift to a black Columbiad vision, then, Douglass continues to corroborate the progress narrative that informed US attitudes to the Old World, and globalizing, expansionist tendencies within western culture as a whole.

Yet Douglass's self-historicization also has other, more pragmatic ends. Self-inscription within the morally prestigious, transatlantic context of abolitionism allows him to mark out a space from which he can intervene in the debate regarding Irish nationhood without apparent trespass on the territory of British Empire. As such, this strategic re-narrativization of his own life allows Douglass to adopt a position that appears to transcend national boundaries and affiliations, and invert normative understand-ings of the historical relationship between Europe and the Americas. 'The going away of a man from a republic in search of liberty in a monarchy,' as Douglass claims of his early voyage, 'was a striking commentary upon the institutions of both countries and the inappropriateness of names as signifying things' (TR, p. 6). For the United States, rather than Europe, is the site of past oppression, from which, through black struggle and European example, it has fortunately advanced.

In this late example from his writings, then, Douglass uses his original journey across the Atlantic to fuse political and spatial landscapes in the writing present in order to establish his interpretative authority. He subsequently sets his early motives against contemporary reasons for transatlantic travel, primarily that of the Grand Tour of Europe undertaken by Americans, 'to enlarge . . . [our] . . . stock of knowledge by observation and study of the peoples, countries and civilizations older than our own' (TR, p. 6). It was a trip on which Douglass was himself soon to embark. In the record of the North African leg of that journey, Douglass would activate US Orientalist tropes of discovery, empire and American manhood, and contest white racialist accounts of Egyptian civilization by promoting a version of western progress and US American nationality that stemmed from hybrid, Afro-European origins. This text, however, is politically rather than culturally motivated. It therefore challenges other premises of insular US national ideology, notably the Monroe Doctrine of 1823, which severed political links with the outside world, positing in its place the international scope of a representative self wielding the extraterritorial influence the United States was already in fact exercising in Africa, the Caribbean and the Pacific.

Acknowledgement of the degree of overseas contact US citizens actually enjoyed allows Douglass to confront the illusion of an insular and insulated United States through a strategy of reversal that plays on the plural or hybrid nature of modern subjectivity.[12] Contrary to the familiar utopian image of the United States as a new Eden, the end point in a teleology of empire, Douglass extends the expansionist trope by presenting a reverse diaspora, which, he suggests, allows Americans to be 'found in all lands and languages', even going so far as to describe his countrymen as prey to a 'migratory habit ... much in excess of a wise moderation' (TR, p. 2). This undercuts contemporary reactions to non-white or new immigrant groups within the United States, which figured cross-cultural and cross-racial contact in terms of contagion. It also differs from twentieth-century Caribbean configurations of the black diaspora in Britain, described as 'colonization in reverse',[13] which characterize mass movements of people and the subsequent 'settlement' of the once imperial centre by former slaves and colonial subjects. Brodhead observes that 'American authors after the Civil War knew that they had to define themselves first off in

12 See Bhabha, *Location of Culture*, p 23.
13 This is also the title of a forty-four line poem by the Caribbean poet Louise Bennett, the first stanza of which runs:

> Wat a joyful news, Miss Mattie,
> I feel like my heart gwine burs
> Jamaica people colonizin
> Englan in reverse.

(Louise Bennett, 'Colonization in Reverse', in Paula Burnet, ed., *The Penguin Book of Caribbean Verse in English* [London: Penguin, 1986], pp. 32–33 [32].)

relation to the matter of Europe in order to situate themselves for prospective American audiences'.[14] For Douglass, the relocation of US identity outside national borders and in Europe positions him within élite, nativist culture, illustrating an ever-increasing confidence in US identity as an exportable commodity, and a growing tendency to consume culture as spectacle. The imaginary US identity proposed, then, is given credence not only by its point of cultural and moral origin – the postbellum United States – but by being repeatedly restated in external destinations at the moment of the cross-cultural encounter.

Far from the isolationist pose adopted by many US politicians throughout the century, Douglass insists that 'men learn what is wisest and best by comparison of one thing with another, and ... [b]esides, men are made broad or narrow by their environments', underlining the value of cross-cultural encounters in providing useful images of national identity. In a country seeking to incorporate its diverse and expanding immigrant population to the myth of America, that encounter was itself a daily occurrence, proof of the dynamic of creolization through which the nation and its expanding native cultural imaginary were being created. Douglass had earlier described that process of transformation as, 'the change going on in the nation at large, – converting Englishman, Germans, Irishmen, and Frenchmen into Americans, and causing them to lose, in a common American character, all traces of their former distinctive national peculiarities'.[15] The immigrant population, however, also confirmed the logic of progress that lay at the heart of the imperial venture. Freedom and citizenship, the goals of a transatlantic (if not transpacific) migration now uncomplicated by slavery, confirmed the progressivist stance of a nation that had been expanding westwards since Independence. In sharp contrast to this idealization was the ongoing reality of racial oppression, the central tropes of which were being reworked in Orientalist sites of US empire, both imaginary and real.

In common with his later defence of Haiti at the World's Fair, however, Douglass, in his discussion of the Irish situation, activates a progressivist logic based on primitivist rather than Orientalist ideas, and which privileges an increasingly hegemonic US world-view, even as it dismantles national racial hierarchies. Much is made of Ireland's 'proximity, and our increasing facilities for intercourse with her'. Ireland is 'the land that lies nearest us that has the deepest and strongest hold upon our affections' (TR, p. 1). The paternalism of this language signals the shift in direction undergone by the United States in its expressions of territorial desire.

14 Brodhead, Introduction, p. xv.
15 Blassingame, *FDP*, 2, p. 515.

For Douglass's manipulation of the trope of transatlantic voyage to create the vision of a black Columbiad also allows him to displace the imaginary centrality of the western frontier as the site of American subjective emergence, and produce another emblem of national transition and potential self-fashioning. The thesis offered by historian Frederick Jackson Turner in 1893, in his paper 'The Significance of the Frontier in American History', held that the US American character had been shaped by the encounter between civilization and depopulated wilderness, which had transformed the European into 'a new product that is American'; it was the vacant frontier that had been the enabling condition of US democracy. With the 'closing of the frontier', according to Turner, Americans would be formed by new and different challenges.[16] In fact, as Slotkin shows, it was the repeatedly re-enacted violent encounter between civilized man and the primitive native that provided the founding myth of the continental phase of US expansion. In anticipation of the challenges posed by the removal of the western frontier experience, Douglass transposes the imaginary encounter between the civilized and primitive, shifting the frontier of knowledge from west to east. The Atlantic voyage and the shifting, illusory space of its enactment replace the wilderness expanse of western frontier as the primary site of US subjective emergence.

But it is the potential for the extension of the US progress narrative in sites that lie beyond that space that empower the characterization of the Atlantic as a frontier space. The 'new product' of the existential interval is the black nation-subject produced in the encounter with slave history and a new kind of native whose moral and domestic primitivism had been conventionalized in Douglass's earlier travel writing. In his Egyptian writing, Douglass would, in the course of establishing African Americans within the cultural hegemony of the United States, deliver an image of a new, 'Oriental' native, and proffer North Africa as a possible locus of further expansion and subjective enactment. In the text of 'Thoughts and Recollections', however, the triangular traffic of the slave trade, which linked, intermingled and dispersed the inhabitants and cultures of three continents, is used to appropriate the previously exclusive codes of the journey, both literal and metaphoric, from original identity to New World reconstructions of the self.

That new self will establish the rationalism and inevitability of the progress narrative, firstly in Ireland and later, in the final chapter of Douglass's public career and autobiography, in Haiti. 'Once her shores

---

16 For a discussion of the use of Turner's suggestion in US wars on Cuba and Puerto Rico, see Amy Kaplan, 'Black and Blue on San Juan Hill', in Amy Kaplan and Donald Pease, eds, *Cultures of United States Imperialism* (Durham, NC: Duke University Press, 1993), pp. 219–36.

were separated from us by months, now the separation is measured by days,' Douglass remarks of Ireland, in a geographical and temporal confla- tion of distance that will impact on his political analysis. For in Ireland, as in Haiti, Douglass adopted modern, imperialist conceptualizations of time that provided 'privileged vantage onto the global realm ... so that imperial progress is consumed at a glance'.[17] Although his intentions were undoubtedly to present a constructive critique, in both cases Douglass uses time as a geography of social power. His famous ethnological speech, 'Claims of the Negro', had seen him attack racialist representations of Africanist peoples. Of the popular ethnological 'family tree', in which anatomy was used as an analogy of progress, Douglass complained that

> the European face is [always] drawn in harmony with the highest ideas of beauty, dignity and intellect ... The negro on the other hand, appears with features distorted, lips exaggerated, forehead depressed – and the whole expression of the countenance made to harmonize with the popular idea of negro imbecility and degradation.[18]

In the same speech, as an example of the importance of environment and education on physical aspect, Douglass spoke of his attendance nine years earlier at a temperance convention in Ireland:

> Never did human faces tell a sadder tale ... I say, with no wish to wound the feelings of any Irishman, that these people lacked only a black skin and woolly hair, to complete their likeness to the plantation negro. The open, uneducated mouth – the long, gaunt arm – the badly formed foot and ankle – the shuffling gait – the retreating forehead and vacant expression – and, their petty quarrels and fights – all reminded me of the plantation.

Douglass concluded, in a description which suggests Stuart Hall's conten- tion that 'the object of identification is as likely to be that which is hated as that which is adored',[19] that:

> The Irishman educated, is a model gentleman; the Irishman ignorant and degraded, compares in form and feature with the negro.[20]

---

17 Dubbed 'panoptical time' by McClintock, a mode in which the trope of progress establishes secular time as the agent of a unified world history. Not only natural space but also historical time could be collected, assembled and mapped onto a global science of the surface (McClintock, *Imperial Leather*, pp. 32–37).

18 Blassingame, *FDP*, 1.2, p. 510.

19 Hall, '"Who Needs Identity?"', p. 3.

20 Blassingame, *FDP*, 1.2, p. 521. Douglass also claimed in the same speech that 'an educated man in Ireland ceases to be an Irishman; and an intelligent black man is always supposed to have derived his intelligence from his connection with the white race' (Blassingame, *FDP*, 1.2, p. 509).

Haiti and the World's Fair

Even as he criticized the racialism of social Darwinism, then, Douglass was inclined to reproduce its salient structures, and see economic and cultural backwardness reproduced in physiognomy or the result of specific environmental factors. His views in this respect made him a suitable candidate for appointment as the Commissioner of the Republic of Haiti pavilion at 'a world's fair celebrating the four-hundredth anniversary of Columbus's discovery of America'. 'In 1492,' McFeely writes, 'the explorer had set foot on Haiti's island, Hispaniola; in 1893 ... Chicago staged the World's Columbian Exposition ... to commemorate ... the blessedness of four hundred years of the New World.'[21]

The World's Fair was an occasion on which New World colonialism became a celebrated part of the narrative of western progress, with the idea of a unified world time reproduced as spectacle. Unquestionably, the United States represented the pinnacle of that colonial achievement, although the development of other regions of the hemisphere was far from uniform. Douglass's inaugural speech at the Haitian pavilion illustrates the racial solidarity he felt with the population of the black republic, as well as the symbolic importance Haiti continued to assume in African American cultural politics. 'Haiti,' Douglass wrote,

> was the first of all the cis-Atlantic world, upon which the firm foot of progressive, aggressive and all-conquering white man was permanently set ... She was the first to be invaded by the Christian religion ... Happily too she was the first of the New World in which the black man asserted his right to be free and was brave enough to fight for his freedom and fortunate enough to gain it.[22]

As far as the progressive logic of the westward sweep of European civilization, and the place of the black man within that narrative of progress was concerned, Haiti had not in the past been found wanting. Haiti symbolized the potential of black nationalist politics in effecting social change, providing confirmation of the doctrine of natural rights, the morality of the struggle against slavery and the favour of history. Questions regarding the Haitian future, as to whether 'it be civilisation or barbarism?' remained, however, to be answered. And Douglass was on hand to do so. 'In Port au Prince,' he claimed, 'I saw more apparent domestic happiness, more wealth, more personal neatness, more attention to dress, more carriages rolling through the streets, more commercial

---

21 McFeely, *Frederick Douglass*, p. 359.
22 Inaugural address of Haitian Pavilion at the Columbian World's Fair, 1893, in Foner, *Frederick Douglass*, 4, p. 478.

activity, more well clothed and well cared for children, more churches [etc.] ... than I saw there twenty years ago.'

In fact, Douglass's eye-witness comparison is a little misleading. He had visited Hispaniola in 1871 as a member of the Commission of Enquiry to Santo Domingo, and supported the Commission's calls for annexation of the Dominican Republic. In an undated account of the Commission's voyage, Douglass describes Port-au-Prince from the sea, from a ship en route to the city of Santo Domingo, but there is no evidence that he later crossed into Haiti.[23] In a piece entitled 'Santo Domingo Days', however, Douglass describes the landscape of the same voyage through the history of resistance and revolution, remarking on the 'heights of [the] promontory [from which] Toussaint L'Ouverture's eagle eye beheld the ships of France sent to reenslave a people whose own heroic efforts had achieved freedom.'[24] Despite his enthusiasm for Haitian statehood, however, Douglass's attitude to Santo Domingan independence was, in the 1870s, more ambivalent. He clearly had high hopes of the social and economic advancement that would follow annexation. Writing 'a few years' after the Commission's visit, Douglass recalled Santo Domingo:

> with her black and swarthy population, diminished and apparently still diminishing, beautifully blessed by nature but woefully [cursed] by man, ... trembling on the verge of civilisation, doubtful of her fate, debating the question whether she is to be saved to peace, progress and happiness or to fall away into the measureless depths of barbarism, has after her manner, and according to the measure of her importance in time and space, her claims to present, her appeal to make, and her story to tell.[25]

Given the experience of Reconstruction in the US South, Douglass's optimism about annexation seems, in retrospect, a little misplaced. Politically, however, and perhaps with Reconstruction still in mind, Hispaniola, the 'cradle of American beginnings',[26] and the Haitian republic in particular, retained, possibly even increased its political and cultural importance for African Americans at the end of the nineteenth century. Though not always inclined to distinguish Haiti and Santo Domingo from one another, Douglass was consistent in his interpretation of their combined symbolic importance in US racial politics. As the 'holy land of the new world',[27]

---

23 Frederick Douglass, 'Santo Domingo', Folder 5, Speech, Article and Book File, Frederick Douglass papers at the Library of Congress, nd, 1-2.
24 Frederick Douglass, 'Santo Domingo Days', Family Papers, Frederick Douglass Papers at the Library of Congress, n.d., p. 3.
25 Douglass, 'Santo Domingo', pp. 2, 4.
26 Douglass, 'Santo Domingo', p. 6.
27 Douglass, 'Santo Domingo', p. 9.

the 'recognised centre of a vast and powerful religious organisation, the influence of which extended into both Southern and Central America ... long before Plymouth Rock had yet a tongue',[28] the island represented, in Douglass's mind, the possibility of outcomes other than the ongoing racial conflict that characterized post-contact politics in the United States. Douglass had long urged his countrymen to, 'contemplate the island of Santo Domingo' from that 'higher, nobler side of heart and sentiment which rejoices in liberty and humanity', as a space appealing 'directly and powerfully to the poetic and best side of human nature, that side which disregards natural differences in color, fortune and features, and which makes a man's country the world, and his countrymen all mankind'.[29] The solidarity he consistently demonstrated with Haiti/Santo Domingo then, was rooted in his hope that the island's multiracial politics might eventually be reproduced in the United States. Ever the pragmatist, Douglass sought in the Caribbean images of New World, republican statehood, politically amenable to the US public, yet intended to dissipate the racial hostility that continued to define the post-bellum era.

In his inaugural speech at the World's Fair, that pragmatism, the racial solidarity that was central to much African American interest in Haiti, and his own experience as US minister to that country, combined to make Douglass's speech, indeed the Pavilion itself, emblems of resistance to the racial politics of the Fair, even as they confirmed its civilizationist agenda. As Commissioner and the most important African American of his generation, it was important that Douglass bear personal witness to Haiti's history of progress, even if doing so involved the occasional little white lie. Some of the same logic led him to downplay the country's economic underdevelopment. In his speech, Douglass defended Haitian industry, economic progress and republicanism, despite state corruption and underdevelopment, because of the underlying racial question the country begged as to whether 'it be true that the Negro, left to himself, lapses into barbarism'.[30] But, if his defence of Haiti was ultimately a defence of the race, his concern was less with Haitian material reality, past or present, than with the island's symbolic meaning for African Americans in post-reconstruction politics.

The contrast with his representation of Ireland, in which material reality assumed political and moral significance, is sharp. In Ireland, the people provided Douglass with 'the most distressing examples of ignorance, pauperism, and suffering' he had seen. Moreover, although

28 Douglass, 'Santo Domingo', p. 8.
29 Douglass, 'Santo Domingo Days', pp. 3–4.
30 Foner, *Frederick Douglass*, 4, p. 483.

Douglass expressed admiration for the struggle for independence that succeeded the abolition of slavery in Haiti, he was reluctant, in addressing the Irish situation, to abandon the Anglophilia that had been one of the mainstays of his political platform since the 1840s. '[A]n Irishman,' he contends, irrational 'under the influence of a sense of ancient wrongs, ... [finds it hard] to be entirely just in his judgement of measures proposed to remedy the wrongs of his country.' In contrast to his position on Haiti, paternalism is privileged over self-determination, perhaps as a result of Douglass's long-standing identification with British ethical culture. He was clearly reluctant to universalize his political judgements by extending the republican ideal to those beyond his political sympathies.

Douglass was, of course, in a closer, more compromising and more representative position with regard to Haiti than to Ireland. His relationship to the island of Hispaniola was a long-standing and complex one. Douglass was on the point of travelling to Haiti to explore its possibilities as a black emigrationist site when the US Civil War broke out and the trip had to be postponed.[31] On 28 January 1871, during his 1871 visit to the Dominican Republic, he addressed a meeting of some 200 descendants of African Americans resettled near Samana in 1825 by the American Colonization Society.[32] In Chicago, he took the platform as the former agent of the United States in both republics, and as Haitian Commissioner to the World's Fair, an appointment that seemed to some to stretch Douglass's loyalties thin. His term as US minister to Haiti had been fraught with controversy, as a result of the conflict that erupted over the Haitian port, the Môle Saint Nicolas, which the United States wished to acquire as a coaling station. Douglass's defence of Haitian sovereignty at the time led to questions regarding his national allegiance and even, Warren suggests, to Douglass 'being rhetorically divested of his American citizenship'.[33]

Much of the dispute centred around Douglass's support for the Haitian president, Hippolyte, who had come to power just before Douglass took up his appointment in a US-assisted coup in 1889. On appointment, Douglass 'was ... encouraged to capitalize on a revolution largely of American manufacture'.[34] But he refused overtly to bully the Haitian government into ceding the Môle to the United States, though he suggested the

---

31   For a discussion of Douglass's views on emigrationism, see Boxill, *Against the Emigrationists*, pp. 21–49.

32   Anon., 'Supplement', *Frank Leslie's Illustrated Newspaper*, New York, 11 March 1871, p. 1. On the question of annexation itself, the paper remarks, 'Dominica is not worth our having' (p. 1).

33   Levine, 'Road to Africa', p. 228; Warren, 'Life and Times', p. 268.

34   McFeely. *Frederick Douglass*, p. 339.

concession would be 'in the line of good neighbourhood and advanced civilization'.[35]

The opinion of Douglass's enemies was that his appointment to the post of Haitian Commissioner was 'a payoff for having taken Haiti's part ... in the negotiations for the [Môle]'.[36] There was certainly no small irony attached to the appointment of a US American as official spokesman for the first independent Caribbean nation, given the imperial designs of the United States on the country during Douglass's stint as minister. Hippolyte's recognition of Douglass's role during the conflict had other effects however. Hippolyte's flattery, McFeely argues, 'blinded the commissioner to the fact that [Hippolyte] was a ruthless dictator'.[37] In his desire to represent the race, Douglass became implicated in his support for a Haitian national élite, whose repressive measures had effects as materially harmful as those stemming from the ongoing protection of racial privilege that obtained in the United States.

The symbolism of race was everywhere present at the Chicago Exposition. The World's Fair, specifically designed as 'a metaphor for human progress', centred on the specially constructed and unfortunately named 'White City'. The exhibition was dubbed the 'whited sepulcher' by Ida B. Wells in her pamphlet *Why the Colored American is not at the World's Fair*,[38] written to protest at the absence of any African American repre-

---

35 Quoted in McFeely, *Frederick Douglass*, p. 249. The Caribbean became a site of strategic importance to the United States in the nineteenth century, as the country entered into competition with other Western powers holding overseas territories in the region, notably Britain, France and Spain. As an independent state, Haiti offered the opportunity for annexation without contest from European powers. Douglass had been appointed minister resident and consul general to Haiti in 1889, and served during the term of President Hippolyte, who came to power in a US-assisted coup d'état in that same year. The United States wished to acquire the Haitian port, the Môle St Nicolas, as a coaling station, an acquisition that would have given them a strategic military foothold in the Caribbean. Douglass was involved, with Rear Admiral Bancroft Gerardi, in the negotiations for the Môle, which were unsuccessful, with the Haitians refusing access to the United States on the grounds that it would infringe on Haitian sovereignty. For a full discussion and explanation of that relationship, see Rayford F. Logan, *The Diplomatic Relations of the US with Haiti, 1776–1891* (Chapel Hill, NC: University of North Carolina Press, 1941); Raymond F. Logan, *The Diplomat in Haiti: The Diplomatic Correspondence of US Minister Frederick Douglass from Haiti, 1889–1891* (Salisbury, NC: Documentary Publications, 1977); and Douglass, *Autobiographies*, pp. 1026–45.

36 McFeely, *Frederick Douglass*, p. 367.

37 McFeely, *Frederick Douglass*, p. 367.

38 The 'White City' and Wells's description of it marks another interface with Conrad, who characterized Leopold's Brussels, the imperial centre of the European mission in Africa, as the 'sepulchral city' (Joseph Conrad, *Heart of Darkness* [London: Penguin, 1995]).

sentation. But, although, like Wells, outraged at the exclusion of African Americans, Douglass was nevertheless broadly in accord with the logic of historical positivism that underpinned the Exposition. This logic was evident along the 'midway', the long strip leading up to the entrance to the White City. Along the walkway, a series of replicated villages, organized in sequence, provided a time line of human progress. A cluster of African grass huts (home to the 'savage Dahomede', according to Douglass), provided the starting point, with the most advanced cultural achievement represented by the Teutonic village at the opposite end.

Structurally, the Fair produced a temporal and cultural panorama that allowed peoples and cultures to be consumed as commodity spectacle. Writing of the nineteenth-century World's Fairs, Susan Buck-Morss describes the 'message of the exhibitions [as] the promise of social progress without revolution'.[39] Of the Crystal Palace Exhibition in London in 1851, McClintock notes that 'the panorama created produced the idea of democracy as the voyeuristic consumption of commodity spectacle … in an emerging national narrative that began to include the working class into the Progress narrative as consumers of national spectacle'.[40] In Britain and the US, related forms of spectacle were created in the interests of promoting a nationally accessible model of empire that could advance according to its own particular logic of democracy and progress. The Columbian World's Fair marks an early beginning to the American century. In Chicago, white US workers and new immigrants could feel included in the imperial nation, with the spectacle of their progress, achievement and their ambition acting as compensation for their low class and economic status. This may also help to explain the absence of representations of African Americans at the Fair. Aside from the embarrassment of having to re-create the spectacle of slavery in the land of the free, an African American exhibit would have complicated the racial thesis the Fair advanced, as well as illustrating the economics of oppression it had so neatly sidestepped.

Afro-America could, however, be represented by the Haitian pavilion. Douglass regarded his appointment as Haitian commissioner as a duty to represent 'our common race'. Yet for all its transnational black idealism, his dedication speech relies on much of the same logic as underpinned the Exposition itself. Douglass's identification with the US nation as empire had surfaced in his Egyptian writing. The ideas that informed that

---

39 Susan Buck-Morss, *The Dialectics of Seeing: Walter Benjamin and the Arcades Project* (Cambridge, MA: MIT Press, 1990), p. 128.
40 McClintock, *Imperial Leather*, p. 59. Though McClintock refers here specifically to the Crystal Palace Exhibition in London in 1851, many of the same conclusions can be drawn regarding the later Chicago show.

identification, notably those of the American 'new man' and the historical positivism of empire, intersect with those of his dedication address and find correlation in several of the conclusions expressed in his Irish essay. In his dedication speech, for example, Douglass activated a counternarrative of African progress in the Americas. Haiti presents itself as a New World twin to Old World Egypt, as the 'cradle in which American religion and civilization were first rocked'. Haiti, like Africa, had been proposed as an emigrationist site for African Americans, a proposition in which Douglass had shown some interest.[41] In common with the imperial eyes cast on North Africa, in the World's Exposition speech, the 'ethnologist observes [Haitians] with curious eyes, and questions them on the grounds of race; ... [S]cholar and philanthropist are interested in their progress, their improvement and the question of their destiny'. Like the Egyptians, 'the people of Haiti, by reason of ancestral identity, are more interesting to the coloured people of the United States than to all others'.[42] Douglass was claiming the Haitian people, as he had earlier done of the 'builders of the pyramids', as African American cultural property.

Commenting on the later nineteenth century, Brantley observes that

> there was an international aspect of the status of Negroes in the United States ... [B]lacks served on diplomatic missions and were federal foreign service officers who had been put in charge of American diplomatic and consular facilities located in the countries to which they were accredited ... [H]istory books have failed in relating the American foreign policy toward the Caribbean in the nineteenth century, to acknowledge that blacks made any contribution to that policy.[43]

Douglass's importance in the negotiations for the Môle is incontestable. Still more important, however, was his role in mediating Haiti, culturally and politically, as a site of US interest. In his speech at the inauguration of the Haitian Pavilion, Douglass describes Haiti as 'the original pioneer emancipator of the nineteenth century',[44] contradicting the country's dominant image as 'a society whose values were profoundly different from those of the western world',[45] and western tendencies to interpret images of black nonconformity to bourgeois values, out of context, as primitive savagery. Haitian children go naked because in Haiti 'people

41 See 'Haytian Emigration', in Foner, *Frederick Douglass*, 5, pp. 471–72.
42 Foner, *Frederick Douglass*, 4, p. 479.
43 Brantley, 'Black Diplomacy', p. 197.
44 Foner, *Frederick Douglass*, 4, p. 485. This positive appraisal is compromised, however, by Douglass's position as an agent of the Haitian dictator, Hippolyte, against whose regime Douglass did not speak out.
45 Charles Arthur and Michael Dash, eds, *Libéte: A Haiti Anthology* (London: Latin America Bureau, 1999), p. 317.

consider more the comfort of their children in [a warm climate] ... than any fear of improper exposure of their little innocent bodies'. It is 'not true that the people of Haiti are lazy as they are usually represented to be. There is much hard work done in Haiti, both mental and physical.' Charges of snake worship drew the response that the practice was

> as old as Egypt and is a part of our own religious system. Moses lifted up the serpent in the wilderness as a remedy for a great malady, and our Bible tells us of some wonderful things done by the serpent in the way of miraculous healing. Besides, he seems to have been on hand and performed marvellous feats in the Garden of Eden, *and to have wielded a potent and mysterious influence in deciding the fate of mankind for time and eternity. Without the snake, the plan of salvation itself would not be complete.* No wonder ... that Haiti, having heard so much of the serpent in these respectable and sublime relations, has *acquired* some respect for a divinity so potent and so ancient.[46]

It is difficult to avoid the suggestion of irony here in this somewhat radical rereading of the Fall in which the long-maligned serpent has his reputation rehabilitated as a key player in the narrative of Christian salvation. This aside, Haitian society and religious practice are cast within a logic that sees Christianity as enabling moral progress, and the creolization of non-Christian beliefs as a key context for the advancement of civilization. Paradoxically, Douglass legitimates Haitian belief-systems through the suggestion of Christianity's common origin in the overdetermined space of Egypt, at once the cradle of western civilization and the site of old testament slavery, but short circuits links to non-Egyptological African cultural practice. Culturally, writing Haiti in involves writing much of Africa out.

Politically, however, Douglass was keen to present Haiti as a dynamic, if underdeveloped, society, deeply embedded in and indebted to the same socio-cultural influences as the United States: in effect, as modern. Yet there are also some inklings of the attraction Haiti was to hold for the later artists and intellectuals of the Harlem Renaissance, such as Langston Hughes and Zora Neale Hurston. Despite their common aesthetic and cultural interests, their views on US imperialism in Haiti differed sharply, and both were sometimes ambivalent about Haitian political identity.[47]

---

46 Foner, *Frederick Douglass*, 4, pp. 482–83, emphasis added.

47 See Langston Hughes, 'White Shadows in a Black Land', *Crisis*, New York, 41 (1932), p. 157, and Zora Neale Hurston, *Tell My Horse* (New York: Harper and Row, 1938). Hughes, a witness to the final period of the US occupation of Haiti, described his own first encounter with the country as 'a new world, a darker world, a world where the white shadows are apparently missing, a world of his own people', though he finally decides that 'the dark-skinned little Republic ... has its hair caught in the white fingers of unsympathetic foreigners' (Hughes, 'White Shadows', p. 157). Hurston, who

That same ambivalence is latent in much of Douglass's writing and rhetoric, perhaps because, despite his support for Haitian sovereignty, his loyalties were ultimately to Anglo-American cultural and political values. Similarly, his attitude to Ireland underlines an increasing tendency, late century, to identify with elements of imperialism, specifically its positivist logic, a tendency that would find its fullest expression in the black Orientalism underpinning his writing on North Africa. In his writings on Ireland, that tendency coalesced with the Anglophilia that had long been the mainstay of his cultural politics. 'In Great Britain, as in this country,' Douglass argued in his analysis of the Irish question, 'liberty and civilization are thought to be safer in the Union than out of it – safer with the whole than with a part – with the mass of the people acting together under one common government than with a few acting in a separate government.' Aside from the somewhat rose-tinted appraisal of the United States and Britain as exponents of a republican ideal, this characterization of contemporary politics erases the history of oppression mentioned earlier in the piece. It also avoids recognition of a discrete political identity based on anti-colonial nationalism, advancing unity rather than democracy as a criterion for freedom. Conversely, Douglass did not hesitate to recognize the legitimacy of either the Haitian state or the revolutionary action that had brought it about. Aside from the necessity of violence in the fight against slavery, he considered the black republic as sufficiently anchored in the history and traditions of the west to merit the status of statehood and self-determination. As a result he sought to assimilate Haitian cultural practice to US convention, supported US neo-colonial ventures in the Caribbean region, and chose to neglect much of the material reality with which he had been confronted during his Haitian sojourn. This ambivalence to material reality had surfaced in his early Irish writings, though the rationale underpinning its representation, or the lack of it, was somewhat different.

Rationalizing Reality

An analysis of Douglass's writing, then, reveals both points of comparison and striking differences in his treatment of Ireland and Haiti, one an

---

conducted the first serious study of Voudou by a black American, shows little solidarity with Haitians in *Tell My Horse*. Her anthropological venture is also implicated to some degree in black forms of US cultural imperialism or symbolic appropriation. Commenting on Haiti's relationship with other countries in the hemisphere, Hurston notes: 'There is a marked tendency [in Haiti] to refuse responsibility for anything that is unfavorable. Some outside influence they say, usually the United States or Santo Domingo, is responsible for all the ills of Haiti' (Hurston, *Tell My Horse*, p. 105).

extant and the other a potential nation-state. Common to both representations however, is Douglass's projection of a normative US world-view
onto other spaces. In this late Irish piece, US national unity, the basis on
which the Civil War was fought and slavery abolished, is used to rationalize the contemporary profile of the United Kingdom. Beyond this, the
text mobilizes positivist views of the North–South divide in the United
States to explain cultural and economic differences in Ireland. According
to Douglass, 'Cork in the south and Belfast in the north, ... [are] the two
cities which may be well enough taken as typical of the civilisation of
each section'; the difference between them 'about as distinctly marked
as is the difference between the northern and southern sections of our
own country, and they show the same superior progress of the one over
the other'. There is a ready explanation for the internal disparity in the
United States, 'explained by one word:–Slavery' (TR, p. 9), or, more
properly for the time of writing, the social and economic inequities which
followed its abolition. Irish difficulties, however, are not explained by
the presence of injustice, nor by any natural disadvantage. For, though
'[t]he North seems to me far in advance of the South in all the elements
of progress ... [a]ll the natural conditions [in the South] seem favorable to
the development of wealth and prosperity'. The country is not cast, as
was Haiti, at an earlier point on the teleology of development, or as a site
where cultural difference can be understood in the context of creolization, with differing, apparently barbarous cultural forms discovered to
have related origins in a western civilizationist paradigm. The argument
is worth quoting at length. Irish underdevelopment is, Douglass writes,

> due ... to three causes: Religion; want of diversified food; and freedom from
> foreign admixture. The South is Roman Catholic; its people live mainly on
> potatoes, and the population is purely Irish. They are agricultural, strangers
> alike to manufactures and commerce. They attract to themselves neither a
> mixed diet, nor a mixed population. The great Hombolt [*sic*] has said, that
> while one acre of wheat will only sustain life in two persons during one year,
> an acre of potatoes will sustain life in eight persons during the same period,
> while one acre of bananas will support forty persons during a year. Now, the
> people in the South of Ireland, owing to the absence of other means of liveli-
> hood are compelled by high rents and enforced poverty, to live on small
> farms, and, as they generally have large families, they are obliged to raise
> and live on potatoes. Now, I believe it is demonstrated and admitted, that
> not only from the structure of the human body, but also from the teachings
> of experience, it is manifest that no people can be strong and flourish, either
> mentally or physically, upon a single article of diet. Equally does it appear
> that any race or variety of people will deteriorate which shall remain entirely
> apart from other races and varieties of men. In fact, it does not appear that

oneness, in population, oneness in the matter of religious belief, or oneness in diet, is favorable to progress. Contact, variety, competition, are essential to the life, both of individuals and nations. Uniform religious opinion brings mental quiet, and mental quiet brings mental stagnation, and mental stagnation brings death to human progress. (TR, p. 15)

Douglass's thesis corresponds with earlier characterizations of the Irish, which set them outside progressivist history. The south of Ireland is described, correctly, as pre-industrial, insular and destitute, locked into a cycle of poverty, ignorance and homogeneity. Not only has this 'oneness', a fatal mixture of ethnicity and religion, impeded progress social and economic progress, it is in fact the cause of endemic misery and deprivation. This extraordinary depoliticization of both history and governance confirms the degree to which Douglass continued to identify with British and Anglo-American values. His identification with Anglo-Protestantism in particular appears to have blinded him to social and economic realities, which, in another context, he might have been quick to condemn. His praise for the north of Ireland, where, although less numerous, the Irish Roman Catholic population was equally immiserated, illustrates an unwillingness to address social inequity in circumstances where the universalism of his own political views might have been open to question.

Although, as part of its French colonial inheritance, Haiti was nominally Catholic, and, in Anglo-American terms, culturally primitive, Douglass was able to identify examples of social and economic progress, as well as imagine a future in which that country would continue to flourish. Like other black New World intellectuals who came after him, Douglass viewed the Americas as the site of future salvation for black and white alike. According to this New World logic of progress, Haiti had set upon a road leading away from the primitivism of Africa while serving as a reminder of the roots of American modernity in African and European civilization. Hal Foster argues that 'the primitive is a modern problem, a crisis in cultural identity',[48] manifested in the simultaneous recognition and disavowal of difference. Haiti's character as a black, New World, post-revolutionary state, in which any potentially disruptive 'native' presence was markedly absent, allowed Douglass to celebrate a religious profile at considerable odds with his own beliefs, secular and otherwise,

---

48 Hal Foster, *Recoding: Art, Spectacle, and Cultural Politics* (Port Townsend, WA: Bay Press, 1985), p. 204. In his appointment as commissioner, as throughout his career, Douglass's words and actions tend to be read in celebratory mode. See Anna R. Paddon and Sally Turner, 'Douglass's Triumphant Days at the World's Columbian Exposition', *Proteus: A Journal of Ideas*, 12.1 (spring 1995), pp. 43–47.

and to overlook the shortcomings of a violent, corrupt and dictatorial political system. Ireland, whose people required only a 'black skin and woolly hair' to make them indistinguishable from the 'plantation Negro', bore too much structural and economic similarity to the plantation South for Douglass ever to be able to admit that Anglo-Protestant ethics were as likely a part of the problem as an element of the solution. In both cases, his tendency to opt for cultural rather than real politics as explanations for the status quo signals the degree to which he was committed to the principles of liberal democratic capitalism in a pluralist context as the only solution to disadvantage, real or perceived.

There is, then, continuity in the logic of representation informing characterizations of Ireland, Haiti, and even Egypt, in Douglass's late writing and rhetoric. In 'Claims of the Negro', Douglass observed, 'Those nations freest from foreign elements present the most evident marks of deterioration.'[49] His later work continued to advance a philosophy of hybridity, which, alongside the developmental dynamic of creolization, he saw as indicative of economic, social and racial progress. Indeed, it is on the issues of progress and hybridity that intersections in his arguments regarding transnational sites of American meaning are most apparent. Unlike the potential Douglass saw in Haiti and Egypt, however, the 'oneness' he witnessed in Ireland was anathema to modernity. His writing sees a retreat from the possibility of a viable national or cultural space that could not conform to the racial hybridity or ideological integrity of an idealized American model.

Throughout his writing, Douglass sought to destabilize the racial norms of the Anglo-American political hegemony while leaving its cultural profile more or less intact. This presents a problem for any discursive closure, however, in a piece that, by virtue of its subject – Home Rule – is forced to confront a reality both current and historical, namely colonialism. According to Hall,

> cultural hegemony is never about pure victory or pure domination; ... it is never a zero-sum cultural game; it is always about shifting the balance of power in the relations of culture; it is always about changing the dispositions and the configurations of cultural power, not getting out of it.[50]

In his late writing on Ireland, Douglass, faced with the realities of history and his own republicanism, shifted ground in order to retain his political

---

49 Blassingame, *FDP*, 1.2, p. 522.
50 Stuart Hall 'What Is This "Black" in Black Popular Culture?', in David Morley and Kuan-Hsing Chen, eds, *Stuart Hall: Critical Dialogues in Cultural Studies* (London and New York: Routledge, 1996), pp. 465–75 (468).

integrity without destabilizing the cultural hegemony he valued. Caught
in the contradictions of his own discourse, he presents Home Rule as an
act of mutual liberation for Britain and Ireland, the one political, the other
moral and perhaps economic. He is in favour of Home Rule for Ireland
'for two reasons:—First because Ireland wants Home Rule, and Secondly,
because it will free England from the charge of continued oppression
of Ireland'. His moral logic emphasizes the rights and responsibilities
of self-determination, invoking a duty to the future 'to work out their
own destiny without outside interference' (TR, p. 18), simultaneously
suggesting that British freedom depends on escape from its own history,
as well as from the economic pressures of colonial administration.

As is the case with his writings concerning Haiti and Egypt, Douglass's
publications and speeches about Ireland suggest he wielded some
authority as an interpreter of sites of US political and cultural importance.
Indeed, the international influence he exerted in the latter years of his
life, whether political or representative, indicates the increasing importance of the black American subject in mediating tropes of US imperial
identity in emerging spaces of US influence in Europe, Africa and the
Americas. Gregory S. Jay has remarked of Douglass that his 'new status
as a canonical figure originates not only in his race and class, and not
simply in his position as an historical-political actor as well as a writer,
but also in the kinds of texts he produced and the way they came into
being'.[51] Despite having provided an early experience of freedom outside
the racialized context of the United States, in Douglass's writing Ireland
comes in many ways to signify a premodern present, to illustrate the
dangers of remaining outside the cultural realms of empire. Haiti, on the
other hand, is represented as capable of integration to a black progress
narrative running in parallel to the culturally dominant Anglo-American
perspective.

Throughout his life, Douglass formulated historically viable forms of
representative US identity, frequently against a transnational rather than
US domestic backdrop. In doing so he reproduced many of the contemporary paradigms underpinning US understandings of the self, particularly
its positivism and embedded sense of imperial dominion. Thus, Douglass's
Egyptian writing produced black Orientalism as a compensatory rhetoric
that could absorb African Americans to the US cultural imaginary. Those
same tropes of American imperial identity were used to indicate the superiority of western modernity in Douglass's discussions of North Africa and

51 Gregory S Jay, 'American Literature and the New History: The Example of Frederick
    Douglass', in Donald Pease, ed., *Revisionary Interventions into the Americanist Canon*
    (Durham, NC: Duke University Press, 1994), pp. 211–42 (213).

other regions of the world. In this he was complicit in the creation of a self-image that reflected paradigmatic elements of US subjectivity, and involved the casting out, marginalization and misrepresentation of those outside his sphere of cultural understanding. His political vision, based as it is in liberal democratic pluralism, celebrates the modern as a political enterprise, but it nevertheless refuses a range of political realities that, like slavery, present problems to any unequivocal lionization of western ideals of human progress. In this, perhaps, Douglass became more representative than even he might have anticipated or wished.

Conclusion

From the outset of his public career, Douglass was confronted with the dilemma of representation in the complex social, cultural and political milieu of the nineteenth-century Atlantic world. His early trip to Ireland, and the changes to the *Narrative* that he implemented there, signal his first major reconfiguration of the anti-slavery debate. The central fiction of the narrative, the slave subject, is repositioned within an international Atlantic, rather than insular US discourse of western modernity. The Irish *Narratives* become the expressive locus of Douglass's economic success, social mobility and increasing ideological independence. They also mark his alliance with feminized political spaces of comparable class and moral intention, an alliance that was to continue throughout his career.

In this, Douglass's work was instrumental in consolidating a transnational ethical culture committed to liberal, Anglo-American values and the principles that underpinned them. Conversely, the preface to the new texts becomes the site of a counter-discourse, which posits slavery as the result of colonial process, though the radicalism of that position was soon to be lost with the emergence of Douglass's unequivocal Anglophilia. The *Narratives* also demonstrate the agency of the slave-subject in mediating images of the United States in an international context, and, indeed, Douglass's power over the economic and ideological success of transatlantic abolitionism.[1]

Ireland, a site on the margins of western discursive practice, was a space of empowerment for Douglass in the early years of his public career. The impact on his writing was such that it necessitates a re-evaluation of the apparent limitations of the slave narrative form. In its Irish incarnations, Douglass's *Narrative* demonstrates a generic and formal flexibility that attests to his increasing personal status and narrative authority, as well as confirming the recalibration of his socio-political stance. As such, the Irish editions, composed on the margins after an escape from the United States, might be considered an act of literary maroonage, with direct impact on contemporary hegemonic understandings of US

1 Douglass, *Narrative* (1845; 1846).

subjectivity and the American experiment as a whole.

In addition to the implications for generic understandings of autobiography within the American canon, or the exceptionalism of the African American narrative position, the Irish *Narratives* have repercussions for the now national space in which they were produced. Gayatri Spivak claims that 'there can be no grand theory of canons; rather canons must be thought of within specific institutional practices inscribed within particular historical moments and as securing specific positions of authority'.[2] The position of authority secured by Douglass during his British–Irish tour was one in which he redefined the context of the autobiographical act and claimed representative jurisdiction over the Irish peasantry and urban working class. As such, it can be seen in much the same light as liberal narratives of élite or colonial subjects written or observed within the same Irish national space – Swift, for instance. The institutional practice that includes such narratives in the Irish canon suggests that a comparable approach might be adopted to 'interface texts', such as the Irish *Narratives*, which illustrate and enact competing claims of race, class and national identity at decisive moments of cross-cultural encounter. Examination of that interface clarifies the separation of ethnic and political identity. In doing so it illuminates the levels of interaction and exchange attendant on the emergence of transnational politics, while confirming the integrity of the local for understanding material reality, individual and group agency, and political goals.

The textual negotiations undertaken by Douglass in the period from 1845 to 1847 saw him reconfiguring élite British and US technologies of selfhood. During the period, he also presented a complex performative self, often at odds with élite western understandings of modern subjectivity. Douglass's performances in Ireland and Britain demonstrate certain consistencies in the kinds of strategies they adopt: all operate on the interface of political discourse and subaltern resistance, and include manipulations of the discourses of colonialism and empire, class and race, modernity and tradition. Douglass's articulation of dialect spaces is particularly noteworthy. These illustrate his capacity to engage with and manipulate both dominant and subversive modes of contemporary representation and resistance. Despite his stated distaste for such practices, and indeed his own social mobility, Douglass appropriated certain elements of working-class, popular entertainment. Specifically, he engaged in dialogue with blackface minstrelsy, using his own performances to revise

2 Gayatri Chakravorty Spivak, 'How to Read a "Culturally Different" Book', in Francis Barker, Peter Hulme and Margaret Iversen, eds, *Colonial Discourse/Postcolonial Theory* (Manchester: Manchester University Press, 1994), pp. 126–50 (132).

its representative categories. These acts of subversion undercut many of
the contemporary representative hegemonies that had taken root in the
United States, freeing the black subject from symbolic bondage in the
white imaginary.

This raises a question regarding the relationship of the black subject
to western discursive structures. Henry Louis Gates has claimed that

> to attempt to employ a Western language to posit a black self is inherently to
> use language ironically. The relation of the speaking black subject to the self
> figured in these languages must by definition be an ironical relation, since
> that self exists only in the 'non-place of language,' or … [as] an absence.[3]

Douglass's performative dialogues with official discourse and unofficial
carnivalesque culture illustrate the levels of irony which underpinned any
self-iteration within the transatlantic discursive field during this period,
given that field's significant overdetermination by categories of difference
above and beyond those of black and white. However, his career also
indicates that to presume, even privilege such irony in cases where the
subject, in his self-construction, intention and stated belief does not see
any conflict between the words used and the things signified, may be
an oversimplification of intention and effect. Moreover, the fact that, as
Douglass's career progressed, he became increasingly more emblematic of
many of the characteristics lionized by US culture, and instrumental in
expressing its national discursive paradigms, limits the degree to which
we can read his work as continuing in the state of exclusion such an irony
presupposes.

It might be more useful to see Douglass's rhetoric and writing as a
negotiation of the terms of what in the Caribbean has been described
as 'nation-language'. The fact that Douglass's version of that language,
in the US instance, did not in the main reflect contemporary American
folk vernaculars, but rather élite, rhetorical constructions of selfhood
may only indicate the degree to which his concept of African American
nationhood was embedded in the greater US whole.

This is borne out by Douglass's late writing, which continued to seek
legitimacy, in external sites, for a self now constructed within the logic
of the United States as empire. For Douglass's autobiographical project
changed in accordance with his shifting role in US political life and the
cultural imperatives of the times. His reconstruction of the Atlantic as a
primary site in the (African) American cultural imaginary is an indication of the representative sway he held at the end of his life and, indeed,
the centrality of Europe and Africa as imaginary sites in his conception

3 Gates, *Figures in Black*, p. 117.

of American selfhood. His symbolic use of the Atlantic as an African American response to, or replacement of, the frontier encounter underlines the extent to which he had come to conceive of the United States, continentally and beyond, as empire.

This reconfiguration of the Atlantic as the space of US American subjective emergence removes the dialectical opposition created by the Native American presence on the western frontier. This had played an important role in the construction of the civilized self in the United States. Additionally, the native presence suggested, however ambivalently, that hope for a prelapsarian world of purity and promise remained intact. The positivism of Douglass's views was such, however, that he was inclined to look ever forward, to privilege liberal western values and economic development as ends in themselves.

This celebration of the modern at the expense of the native is evident in Douglass's writings on Egypt. In his determination to fabricate an inclusive myth of American identity for black and white alike, he activated many of the tropes of empire then informing US attitudes to the Orient. As a result, he produced an image of the Arab that, far from consolidating earlier claims of racial solidarity, produced a form of black Orientalism only marginally less ambivalent than its white counterpart. In his search for a self whose virtue and transcendence was proven in accordance with contemporary US paradigms of subjectivity, Douglass activated Columbiad and Orientalist tropes of empire. As a result, he was forced to abandon the scene of what could have been the site of his greatest dialectical victory to contemporary transcendentalist tropes of American manhood and Oriental spirituality. As in Ireland fifty years before, the native in Douglass's Egyptian writing is marginalized, judged according to western, progressive, hybrid versions of subjectivity and civilization that leave no space for alternative accounts of human subjectivity or cultural normativity.

In his representation of Haiti, a site without a native presence, Douglass sought to counteract negative images of that country in the United States. He defended Haitian cultural practice – though he reconfigured it within western Christian cultural paradigms – and defended that nation's right to self-determination. On the other hand, Douglass was also implicated in the appropriation and (mis)representation of Haiti as a potential locus of African American contribution to the expansion of the US cultural and territorial imaginary. His readings of Haiti anticipate the reactions of later African American intellectual to this and other Caribbean sites.

In Douglass's work, then, as this book has argued, both the potential and the realities of African American influence in international and imperial contexts of global modernity come into focus. His writing and rhetoric challenge and mark symbolic boundaries of nation and self-hood, and specialize in the production of often counter-hegemonic frontier effects. However, many of those effects indicate that, despite the double consciousness that continued to haunt internal figurations of the African American subject, the sensibilities of this most representative of American nation-subjects were always more western than otherwise.

Bibliography

Unpublished Primary Sources

Anti-Slavery Collection. Boston Public Library, Boston, Massachusetts, USA.
Frederick Douglass Collection. Manuscript Division, Library of Congress, Washington, DC, USA.
The Weston Papers. Boston Public Library, Boston, Massachusetts, USA.

Published Primary Sources

Anon. 'Supplement.' *Frank Leslie's Illustrated Newspaper*, New York, 11 March 1871.

Blassingame, John, ed. *Frederick Douglass Papers*, Series One, *Speeches, Debates, and Interviews*. 5 vols. New Haven: Yale University Press, 1979–86.

Braxton, Joanne M., ed. Introduction to *The Collected Poetry of Paul Lawrence Dunbar*. Charlottesville, VA, and London: University Press of Virginia, 1993.

Brown, William Wells. *Three Years in Europe*. London: n.p., 1852.

Clarke, Lewis Garrard. *Narrative of the Sufferings of Lewis Clarke, during a Captivity of more than Twenty-five Years, Among the Algerines of Kentucky, Dictated by himself*, ed. Joseph C. Lovejoy. Boston: D.H. Eli, 1845.

Clarke, Lewis Garrard, and Milton Clarke. *Narratives of the Sufferings of Lewis and Milton Clarke, Sons of a Soldier of the Revolution ... Dictated by Themselves*, ed. Joseph C. Lovejoy. Boston: Bela Marsh, 1846.

Columbus, Christopher. *Journal of the First Voyage (Diario del primer viaje), 1492*, ed. and trans. B.W. Ife. Warminster: Aris & Phillips, 1990.

Conrad, Joseph. *Heart of Darkness*, London: Penguin, 1995.

Conway, M.D., A Native of Virginia. *Testimonies Concerning Slavery*. 2nd edn. London: Chapman & Hall, 1865.

Dorr, David F. *A Colored Man Round the World*. 1858. Ed. and intro. Malina Johar Schueller. Ann Arbor, MI: University of Michigan Press, 1999.

Douglass, Frederick. *Autobiographies*, ed. Henry Louis Gates Jr. New York: Library of America, 1994.

——. 'The Folly of Colonization.' in *African American Social and Political Thought: 1850–1920*, ed. Howard Brotz. New Brunswick, NJ: Transaction Press, 1992.

——. *Narrative of the Life of Frederick Douglass, An American Slave, Written by*

Himself. Boston: Boston Anti-Slavery Society, 1845.

——. *Narrative of the Life of Frederick Douglass, An American Slave, Written by Himself*. 1st Irish edn. Dublin: Webb & Chapman, 1845.

——. *Narrative of the Life of Frederick Douglass, An American Slave, Written by Himself*. 1st Irish edn, variant. Dublin: Webb & Chapman, 1845.

——. *Narrative of the Life of Frederick Douglass, An American Slave, Written by Himself*. 2nd Irish edn. Dublin: Webb & Chapman, 1846.

——. 'Thoughts and Recollections of a Tour in Ireland.' *AME Church Review*, 3 (1886), n.p.

Dubois, W.E.B. *Black Reconstruction in the United States, 1860–1880*. New York: n.p., 1977.

——. *The Souls of Black Folk*. Chicago: A.C. McClurg & Co., 1903.

Dunbar, Paul Lawrence. 'We Wear the Mask.' In *The Norton Anthology of African American Literature*, ed. Nellie McKay and Henry Louis Gates Jr. New York and London: Norton, 1997, p. 896.

Dunne, Finlay Peter. *Mr Dooley in Peace and War*. Boston: Small, Maynard & Co., 1898.

Edgeworth, Maria. 'The Grateful Negro.' In *British Literature 1780–1930*, ed. Anne K. Mellor and Richard E. Matlock. Fort Worth, TX: Harcourt Brace College Publishers, 1996, pp. 546–55.

Ellison, Ralph. 'Change the Joke and Slip the Yoke.' In *The Norton Anthology of African American Literature*, ed. Nellie McKay and Henry Louis Gates Jr. New York and London: Norton, 1997, pp. 1541–49.

Foner, Philip S. *Life and Writings of Frederick Douglass*. New York: International Publishers, 1975.

——, ed. *The Life and Writings of Frederick Douglass*. 5 vols. New York: International Publishers, 1950.

Franklin, Benjamin. *The Works of Dr Benjamin Franklin: Consisting of Essays, Humorous, Moral and Literary, with His Life, Written by Himself*. London: J. Limbird, 1824.

Franklin, C.L. 'The Eagle Stirreth Her Nest.' In *The Norton Anthology of African American Literature*, ed. Nellie McKay and Henry Louis Gates Jr. New York and London: Norton, 1997, pp. 71–78.

Gates, Henry Louis, Jr, ed. *The Classic Slave Narratives*. London: Penguin, 1987.

——, and Nellie McKay, eds. *The Norton Anthology of African American Literature*. New York and London: Norton, 1997.

Hughes, Langston. 'White Shadows in a Black Land.' *Crisis*, 41 (1932), p. 157.

Hurston, Zora Neale. *Tell My Horse*. New York: Harper & Row, 1938.

Logan, Rayford F. *The Diplomat in Haiti: The Diplomatic Correspondence of US Minister Frederick Douglass from Haiti, 1889–1891*. Salisbury, NC: Documentary Publications, 1946.

Mellor, Anne K., and Richard E. Matlack, eds. *British Literature 1780–1830*. Fort Worth, TX: Harcourt Brace College Publishers, 1996.

Merrill, Walter M., ed. *The Letters of William Lloyd Garrison*, vol. 3. Cambridge, MA: Harvard University Press, 1973.

Pettinger, Alasdair. *Always Elsewhere: Travels of the Black Atlantic*. New York and London: Continuum, 1998.

Ripley, Peter C. *The Black Abolitionist Papers*, vol. 1, *The British Isles, 1830–1865*. Chapel Hill, NC: University of North Carolina Press, 1985.

Second Appeal from the Dublin Ladies' Association to the Females of Ireland. Signed Catherine Elizabeth Alma, Corresponding Secretary, Blackrock, near Dublin, 26 October 1837. Printer George Ridings, 34 Patrick Street, Cork.

Stowe, Harriet Beecher. *Uncle Tom's Cabin*. Boston: J.P. Jewett, 1852.

Thackeray, William M. *The Irish Sketchbook*. 1843. Dublin: Gill & Macmillan, 1990.

Virginia Minstrels, Dublin, Ireland, 1844. Programme, Harvard Theater Collection.

Wells, Ida B. 'Why the Colored American is not at the World's Fair.' Chicago: n.p., 1893.

Wheatley, Phillis. 'On Being Brought from Africa to America.' In *The Norton Anthology of African American Literature*, ed. Nellie McKay and Henry Louis Gates Jr. New York and London: Norton, 1997, p. 171.

Secondary Sources

Achebe, Chinua. 'An Image of Africa.' In *Conrad: Third World Perspectives*, ed. Robert Hamner. Washington, DC: Three Continents Press, 1990, pp. 119–30.

Allen, Theodore W. *The Invention of the White Race*. 2 vols. London: Verso, 1994.

Andrews, William. *To Tell a Free Story: The First Century of Afro-American Autobiography, 1760–1865*. Urbana, IL: University of Illinois Press, 1986.

——, ed. *Critical Essays on Frederick Douglass*. Boston: G.K. Hall, 1991.

——, ed. *Literary Romanticism in America*. Baton Rouge, LA: Louisiana State University Press, 1981.

——, ed. Introduction to *The Oxford Frederick Douglass Reader*. New York and Oxford: Oxford University Press, 1996.

Anon. *Paul Robeson Speaks*. London: Quartet Books, 1978.

——. 'The Theatre Royal in Dublin, from 1830–1831.' *Dublin University Magazine*, 72 (1870), pp. 454–71.

Appiah, Anthony. *In My Father's House: Africa in the Philosophy of Culture*. New York: Oxford University Press, 1992.

Arthur, Charles, and J. Michael Dash, eds. *Libéte: A Haiti Anthology*. London: Latin America Bureau, 1999.

Baggett, Paul. 'Transcending the Boundaries of Nation: Images and Imaginings of Frederick Douglass.' *In Process: A Journal of African American and African Diasporan Literature and Culture*, 2 (spring 2000), pp. 103–13.

Baker, Houston A., Jr. 'Autobiographical Acts and the Voice of the Southern Slave.' In *The Slave's Narrative*, ed. Charles T. Davis and Henry Louis Gates Jr. Oxford and New York: Oxford University Press, 1982, pp. 242–61.

——. *Blues, Ideology and African-American Literature: A Vernacular Theory*. Chicago: University of Chicago Press, 1988.

——. Introduction to Frederick Douglass, *Narrative of the Life of Frederick*

Douglass, an American Slave. London: Penguin, 1982, p. 3.

——. *Long Black Song: Essays in Black American Literature and Culture*. Charlottesville, VA, and London: University Press of Virginia, 1972.

Bakhtin, Mikhail. *Rabelais and His World*. 1965. Trans Hélène Iswolsky. Bloomington, IN: London University Press, 1984.

Barbour, Brian M., ed. *Benjamin Franklin, a Collection of Critical Essays*. Englewood Cliffs, NJ: Prentice-Hall, 1979.

Barker, Francis, Peter Hulme and Margaret Iversen, eds. *Colonial Discourse/ Postcolonial Theory*. Manchester: Manchester University Press, 1994.

Beames, Michael. *Peasants and Power: The Whiteboy Movements and Their Control in Pre-Famine Ireland*. Sussex: Harvester Press, 1983.

Bernal, Martin. *Black Athena: The Afroasiatic Roots of Classical Civilisation*. 2 vols. London: Vintage, 1991.

Bhabha, Homi. *The Location of Culture*. London and New York: Routledge, 1994.

Blackett, Richard. *Building an Anti-Slavery Wall: Black Americans in the Atlantic Abolitionist Movement, 1830–1860*. Baton Rouge, LA: Louisiana State University Press, 1983.

——. 'Cracks in the Anti-Slavery Wall: Frederick Douglass's Second Visit to England (1859–1860) and the Coming of the Civil War.' In *Liberating Sojourn: Frederick Douglass and Transatlantic Reform*, ed. Alan J. Rice and Martin Crawford. Athens, GA: University of Georgia Press, 1999, pp. 187–206.

Blassingame, John W. 'Black Autobiography as History and Literature.' *Black Scholar*, 5.4 (1973), pp. 2–8.

Blight, David W. *Frederick Douglass's Civil War: Keeping Faith in Jubilee*. Baton Rouge, LA, and London: Louisiana State University Press, 1989.

Boxill, Bernard R. 'Douglass against the Emigrationists.' In *Frederick Douglass, a Critical Reader*, ed. Bill E. Lawson and Frank M. Kirkland. Oxford: Blackwell, 1999, pp. 21–49.

Bradbury, Richard. 'Douglass and the Chartists.' In *Liberating Sojourn: Frederick Douglass and Transatlantic Reform*, ed. Alan J. Rice and Martin Crawford. Athens, GA, and London: University of Georgia Press, 1999, pp. 169–86.

Brantley, Daniel. 'Black Diplomacy and Frederick Douglass's Caribbean Experiences, 1871 and 1889–1891: The Untold Story.' *Phylon: The Atlanta University Review of Race and Culture*, 95.3 (1984), pp. 196–209.

Breiner, Laurence A. *An Introduction to West Indian Poetry*. Cambridge: Cambridge University Press, 1998.

Brodhead, Richard. Introduction to *The Marble Faun: Or, The Romance of Monte Beni*, by Nathaniel Hawthorne. New York: Penguin, 1990, pp. ix–xxix.

Brody, Jennifer Devere. *Impossible Purities: Blackness, Femininity and Victorian Culture*. Durham, NC: Duke University Press, 1998.

Brotz, Howard, ed. *African American Social and Political Thought: 1850–1920*. New Brunswick, NJ: Transaction Press, 1992.

Buck-Morss, Susan. *The Dialectics of Seeing: Walter Benjamin and the Arcades Project*. Cambridge, MA: MIT Press, 1990.

Butterfield, Stephen. *Black Autobiography in America*. Amherst, MA: University of Massachusetts Press, 1977.

Carretta, Vincent. 'Three West Indian Writers of the 1780s Revisited and Revised.' *Research in African Literatures*, 29.4 (winter 1998), pp. 173–87.

Chakrabarty, Dipesh. 'Minority Histories, Subaltern Pasts.' *Perspectives*, 13 (November 1997), pp. 37–43.

Christin, Arthur. *The Orient in American Transcendentalism*. New York: Columbia University Press, 1932.

Cockrell, Dale. *Demons of Disorder: Early Blackface Minstrels and Their World*. Cambridge: Cambridge University Press, 1997.

Crotty, Raymond. *Ireland in Crisis: A Study in Capitalist Colonial Underdevelopment*. Dingle: Brandon Books, 1986.

Crowley, John W. 'Slaves to the Bottle: Gough's Autobiography and Douglass's Narrative.' In *The Serpent and the Cup: Temperance in American Literature*, ed. David S. Reynolds and Debra J. Rosenthal. Amherst, MA: University of Massachusetts Press, 1997, pp. 115–35.

Curtis, L. *Anglo-Saxons and Celts: A Study of Anti-Irish Prejudice in Victorian England*. Bridgeport, CT: University of Bridgeport, 1968.

Davis, Charles T. and Henry Louis Gates Jr, eds. *The Slave's Narrative*. Oxford and New York: Oxford University Press, 1982.

Deane, Seamus. *Strange Country: Modernity and Nationhood in Irish Writing since 1790*. Oxford: Oxford University Press, 1997.

De Vita, Alexis Brooks. 'Escaped Tricksters: Runaway Narratives as Trickster Tales.' *Griot: Official Journal of the Southern Conference on Afro-American Studies*, 17.2 (fall 1998), pp. 1–10.

Dunbar, Alice. 'The Poet and His Song.' *AME Church Review*, 31 (1914), p. 124.

Earnest, John. *Resistance and Reformation in Nineteenth Century African American Literature*. Jackson, MS: University of Mississippi Press, 1995.

Ferreira, Patricia. '"All But a Black Skin and Woolly Hair": Frederick Douglass's Witness of the Irish Famine.' *American Studies International*, 37.2 (1999), pp. 69–83.

Fisch, Audrey. *American Slaves in Victorian England: Abolitionist Politics in Popular Literature and Culture*. Cambridge: Cambridge University Press, 2000.

———. '"Negrophilism" and British Nationalism: The Spectacle of the Black Abolitionist.' *Victorian Review*, 19 (summer 1993), pp. 20–37.

Fisher, Shelley Fishkin, and Carla Peterson. '"We Hold These Truths to be Self-Evident": The Rhetoric of Frederick Douglass's Journalism.' In *Frederick Douglass: New Literary and Historical Essays*, ed. Eric J. Sundquist. Cambridge: Cambridge University Press, 1990, pp. 189–204.

Fiske, John. *American Political Ideas: Viewed from the Standpoint of Universal History*. Boston: Houghton Mifflin, 1911.

Foner, Philip, and Ronald L. Lewis, eds. *The Black Worker: A Documentary History from Colonial Times to the Present*, vol. 1, *The Black Worker to 1869*. Philadelphia: Temple University Press, 1978.

Foster, Hal. *Recoding: Art, Spectacle, and Cultural Politics*. Port Townsend, WA: Bay Press, 1985.

Franchot, Jenny. *Roads to Rome: The Antebellum Protestant Encounter with Catholicism*. Berkeley, CA: University of California Press, 1994.

——. 'The Punishment of Esther: Douglass and the Construction of the Feminine.' In *Frederick Douglass: New Literary and Historical Essays*, ed. Eric J. Sundquist. Cambridge: Cambridge University Press, 1990, pp. 141–65.

Frey, Sylvia and Betty Wood. *Come Shouting to Zion: African American Protestantism in the American South and British Caribbean to 1830*. Chapel Hill, NC: North Carolina University Press, 1998.

Fulkerson, Gerald. 'Exile as Emergence: Frederick Douglass in Great Britain, 1845– 1847.' *Quarterly Journal of Speech*, 60 (1974), pp. 68–82.

Gates, Henry Louis, Jr. *Figures in Black: Words, Signs and the Racial Self*. New York and Oxford: Oxford University Press, 1987.

——. 'From Douglass to Wheatley: The Politics of Displacement.' In *Frederick Douglass: New Literary and Historical Essays*, ed. Eric J. Sundquist. Cambridge: Cambridge University Press, 1993, pp. 47–65.

——. *The Signifying Monkey: A Theory of Afro-American Literary Criticism*. New York and Oxford: Oxford University Press, 1988.

——, and Maria Wolff. 'An Overview of Sources on the Life and Work of Juan Latino, the Ethiopian Humanist.' *Research in African Literatures* 29.4 (winter 1998), pp. 14-51.

——, Maria Diedrich and Carl Pederson, eds. *The Black Columbiad: Black Imagination and the Middle Passage*. New York: Oxford University Press, 1999.

Giles, Paul. 'Narrative Reversals and Power Exchanges: Frederick Douglass and British Culture.' *American Literature*, 73.4 (2001), pp. 779–810.

Gilroy, Paul. *The Black Atlantic: Modernity and Double Consciousness*. London and New York: Verso, 1993.

Greenberg, Kenneth. *Honor and Slavery*. 1996.

Greene, J. Lee. *Blacks in Eden: The African American Novel's First Century*. Charlottesville, VA, and London: University Press of Virginia, 1996.

Griffin, Patrick. *The People with No Name: Ireland's Ulster Scots, America's Scots Irish, and the Creation of a British Atlantic World, 1689–1784*. Princeton, NJ: Princeton University Press, 2001.

Guha, Ranajit, ed. *Subaltern Studies: Writing on South Asian History and Society*. 5 vols. New Delhi: Oxford University Press, 1984.

Haggerty, George. *Gothic Fictions/Gothic Form*. University Park, PA: Pennsylvania State University, 1989.

Hall, Stuart, and Paul du Gay. 'What Is This "Black" in Black Popular Culture?' In *Stuart Hall: Critical Dialogues in Cultural Studies*, ed. David Morley and Kuan-Hsing Chen. London and New York: Routledge, 1996, pp. 465–75.

——. Introduction: 'Who Needs Identity?' In *Questions of Cultural Identity*, ed. Stuart Hall and Paul du Gay. London and Thousand Oaks, CA: Sage Publications, 1996, pp. 1–17.

——, eds. *Questions of Cultural Identity*. London and Thousand Oaks, CA: Sage Publications, 1996.

Hamilton, Cynthia S. 'The Gender Politics of Reform.' In *Liberating Sojourn: Frederick Douglass and Transatlantic Reform*, ed. Alan J. Rice and Martin Crawford. Athens, GA, and London: University of Georgia Press, 1999, pp. 73–92.

Hamner, Robert, ed. *Conrad: Third World Perspectives*. Washington, DC: Three Continents Press, 1990.

Hardack, Richard. 'The Slavery of Romanism: The Casting Out of the Irish in the Work of Frederick Douglass.' In *Liberating Sojourn: Frederick Douglass and Transatlantic Reform*, ed. Alan J. Rice and Martin Crawford. Athens, GA, and London: University of Georgia Press, 1999, pp. 115–40.

Harris, Wilson. 'The Frontier on Which *Heart of Darkness* Stands.' In *Conrad: Third World Perspectives*, ed. Robert Hamner. Washington, DC: Three Continents Press, 1990, pp. 161–67.

Harrison, Richard S. *Richard Davis Webb: Dublin Quaker Printer*. Cork: Redbarn, 1993.

———. 'The Cork Anti-Slavery Society, Its Antecedents and Quaker Background.' *Journal of the Cork Historical and Archaeological Society*, 97 (1992), pp. 69–79.

Hellwig, David J. 'Patterns of Black Nativism, 1830–1930.' *American Studies*, 23.1 (spring 1982), pp. 85–98.

Ignatiev, Noel. *How the Irish Became White*. New York: Routledge, 1995.

Jay, Gregory S. 'American Literature and the New History: The Example of Frederick Douglass.' In *Revisionary Interventions into the Americanist Canon*, ed. Donald Pease. Durham, NC: Duke University Press, 1994, pp. 211–42.

Jenkins, Lee. 'Beyond the Pale: Frederick Douglass in Cork.' *Irish Review*, 24 (1999), pp. 80–95.

———. '"The Black O Connell": Frederick Douglass and Ireland.' *Nineteenth Century Studies*, 13 (1999), pp. 22–46.

Johnson, J.W., ed. *The Book of American Negro Poetry*. Poe, NY: Harcourt, Brace & Worley, 1931.

Jones, Anne Goodwyn. 'Engendered in the South: Blood and Irony in Douglass and Jacobs.' In *Liberating Sojourn: Frederick Douglass and Transatlantic Reform*, ed. Alan J. Rice and Martin Crawford. Athens, GA, and London: University of Georgia Press, 1999, pp. 93–111.

Kaplan, Amy. 'Introduction: Left Alone with America.' In *Cultures of United States Imperialism*, ed. Amy Kaplan and Donald Pease. Durham, NC: Duke University Press, 1993.

———. 'Black and Blue on San Juan Hill.' In *Cultures of United States Imperialism*, ed. Amy Kaplan and Donald Pease. Durham, NC: Duke University Press, 1993, pp. 219–36.

———, and Donald Pease, eds. *Cultures of United States Imperialism*. Durham, NC: Duke University Press, 1993.

Kenny, Kevin. *Making Sense of the Molly Maguires*. Oxford: Oxford University Press, 1998.

Kersten, Holger. 'The Creative Potential of Dialect Writing in Later Nineteenth-Century America.' *Nineteenth Century Literature*, 55.1 (June 2000), pp. 92–117.

Lampe, Gregory P. *Frederick Douglass: Freedom's Voice, 1818–1845*. East Lansing, MI: Michigan State University Press, 1998.

Lawson, Bill E., and Frank M. Kirkland, eds. *Frederick Douglass, a Critical Reader*. Oxford: Blackwell, 1999.

Lee, Min, ed. *Larousse Dictionary of North American History*. New York and Edinburgh: Larousse, 1994.

Lefkovitz, Mary R., and Guy MacClean Rogers, eds. *Black Athena Revisited*. Chapel Hill, NC: University of North Carolina Press, 1996.

Leverenz, David. *Manhood and the American Renaissance*. London: Cornell University Press, 1989.

Levine, Robert S. *Martin Delaney, Frederick Douglass and the Politics of Representative Identity*. Chapel Hill, NC, and London: University of North Carolina Press, 1997.

——. 'Road to Africa: Frederick Douglass's Rome.' *African American Review*, 34.2 (2000), pp. 217–31.

——. '*Uncle Tom's Cabin* in Frederick Douglass's Paper: An Analysis of Reception.' *American Literature: A Journal of Literary History, Criticism, and Bibliography*, 64.1 (March 1992), pp. 71–93.

Lhamon, W. T. *Raising Cain: Blackface Performance from Jim Crow to Hip Hop*. Cambridge, MA: Harvard University Press, 1998.

Lloyd, David. *Anomalous States: Irish Writing and the Post Colonial Moment*. Dublin: Lilliput Press, 1993.

——. *Ireland after History*. Cork: Cork University Press, 1999.

Logan, Rayford F. *The Diplomatic Relations of the US with Haiti, 1776–1891*. Chapel Hill, NC: University of North Carolina Press, 1941.

Lorimer, Douglas A. *Colour, Class and the Victorians: English Attitudes to the Negro in the Mid-Nineteenth Century*. Leicester: Leicester University Press, 1978.

Lott, Eric. *Love and Theft: Blackface Minstrelsy and the American Working Class*. Oxford and New York: Oxford University Press, 1993.

MacDonald, Joyce Green. 'Acting Black: Othello, Burlesques, and the Performance of Blackness.' *Theatre Journal*, 46.2 (May 1994), pp. 231–49.

McClintock, Anne. *Imperial Leather: Race, Gender and Sexuality in the Colonial Contest*. New York and London, 1995.

McDowell, Deborah, and Arnold Rampersad, eds. *Slavery and the Literary Imagination*. Baltimore, MD: Johns Hopkins University Press, 1989.

McFeely, William S. *Frederick Douglass*. New York and London: Norton, 1991.

McKay, Nellie, and Henry Louis Gates Jr, eds. *The Norton Anthology of African American Literature*. New York and London: Norton, 1997.

Mahood, M.M. *The Colonial Encounter: A Reading of Six Novels*. London: Collins, 1977.

Marshall, Herbert, and Mildred Stock. *Ira Aldridge, the Negro Tragedian*. New York: Rockliff, 1958.

Martin, Jay, ed. *A Singer in the Dawn*. New York: Dodd, Mead & Co., 1975.

Martin, Waldo E., Jr. *The Mind of Frederick Douglass*. Chapel Hill, NC: University of North Carolina Press, 1984.

Matthiesson, F.O. *American Renaissance: Art and Expression in the Age of Emerson and Whitman*. London: Oxford University Press, 1968.

Meer, Sarah. 'Competing Representations: The Serenaders and the Ethnic Exhibition.' In *Liberating Sojourn: Frederick Douglass and Transatlantic Reform*, ed. Alan J. Rice and Martin Crawford. Athens, GA, and London: University of Georgia Press, 1999, pp. 141–65.

Michaels, Walter Benn, and Donald E. Pease, eds. *The American Renaissance Reconsidered*. Baltimore, MD, and London: Johns Hopkins University Press, 1985.

Miller, Perry. *Errand into the Wilderness*. New York: Harper, 1956.

——. *The New England Mind: The Seventeenth Century*. New York: Macmillan, 1939.

Mishkin, Tracy, ed. *Literary Influence and African-American Writers*. New York: Garland, 1996.

Montesinos, Maggie. *The Slumbering Volcano: American Slave Ship Revolts and the Production of Rebellious Masculinity*. Durham, NC: Duke University Press, 1992.

Moody, Richard. *America Takes the Stage: Romanticism in American Drama*. Bloomington, IN: Indiana University Press, 1955.

Morley, David, and Kuan-Hsing Chen, eds. *Stuart Hall: Critical Dialogues in Cultural Studies*. London and New York: Routledge, 1996.

Morrison, Toni. *Playing in the Dark: Whiteness and the Literary Imagination*. London: Picador, 1993.

Moses, Wilson Jeremiah. *Black Messiahs and Uncle Toms: Social and Religious Manipulations of a Religious Myth*. University Park, PA, and London: Pennsylvania State University Press, 1982.

——. *The Golden Age of Black Nationalism*. New York: Oxford University Press, 1978.

——. *The Wings of Ethiopia: Studies in African American Life and Letters*. Ames, IA: Iowa State University Press, 1990.

——. '"Writing Freely?" Frederick Douglass and the Constraints of Racialised Writing.' In *Frederick Douglass: New Literary and Historical Essays*, ed. Eric J. Sundquist. New York and Cambridge: Cambridge University Press, 1990, pp. 66–83.

Niemtzow, Annette. 'The Problem of Self in Autobiography: The Example of the Slave Narrative.' In *The Art of Slave Narrative*, ed. John Sekora and Darwin Turner. Chicago: Western Illinois University Press, 1982, pp. 96–109.

Nordoh, David J., ed. *Paul Lawrence Dunbar*. Boston: G.K. Hall, 1979.

O Callaghan, Seán. *To Hell or Barbados: The Ethnic Cleansing of Ireland*. Dingle: Brandon Books, 2001.

Ó Gráda, Cormac. *Ireland Before and After the Famine: Explorations in Economic History*. New York: Manchester University Press, 1993.

Oldham, Ellen M. 'Irish Support of the Abolitionist Movement.' *Boston Public Library Quarterly*, 10 (1958), pp. 173–87.

Olney, James. '"I was born": Slave Narratives, Their Status as Autobiography and as Literature.' In *The Slave's Narrative*, ed. Charles T. Davis and Henry Louis Gates Jr. Oxford and New York: Oxford University Press, 1982, pp. 148–74.

——. *Studies in Autobiography*. New York and Oxford: Oxford University Press, 1988.

——. 'The Founding Fathers: Frederick Douglass and Booker T. Washington.' In *Slavery and the Literary Imagination*, ed. Deborah McDowell and Arnold Rampersad. Baltimore, MD: Johns Hopkins University Press, 1989, pp. 1–24.

Paddon, Anna R., and Sally Turner. 'Douglass's Triumphant Days at the World's Columbian Exposition.' *Proteus: A Journal of Ideas*, 12.1 (spring 1995), pp. 43–47.

Pease, Donald E., ed. *Revisionary Interventions in the Americanist Canon*. Durham, NC: Duke University Press, 1994.

——, ed. *Visionary Compacts: The American Renaissance in Cultural Context*. Madison, WI: University of Wisconsin Press, 1987.

Pease, William H., and Jane H. Pease. 'Boston Garrisonians and the Program of Frederick Douglass.' *Canadian Journal of History*, 11 (September 1967), pp. 29–47.

Pettinger, Alasdair. 'Enduring Fortresses: A Review of *The Black Atlantic* by Paul Gilroy.' *Research in African Literatures*, 29.4 (winter 1998), pp. 142–48.

——. '"Send Back the Money": Douglass and the Free Church of Scotland.' In *Liberating Sojourn: Frederick Douglass and Transatlantic Reform*, ed. Alan J. Rice and Martin Crawford. Athens, GA, and London: University of Georgia Press, 1999, pp. 31–47.

Punter, David. *Gothic Pathologies: The Text, the Body and the Law*. Basingstoke: Macmillan; New York: St Martin's Press, 1998.

Quarles, Benjamin. *Frederick Douglass*. 1948. New York: n.p., 1964.

Raitton, Stephen. *Authorship and Audience: Literary Performance in the American Renaissance*. Princeton, NJ: Princeton University Press, 1991.

Rehin, George C. 'Blackface Street Minstrels in Victorian London and Its Resorts: Popular Culture and Its Racial Connotations as Revealed in Polite Opinion.' *Journal of Popular Culture*, 15 (summer 1981), pp. 19–38.

——. 'Harlequin Jim Crow: Continuity and Convergence in Blackface Clowning.' *Journal of Popular Culture*, 9.3 (1975), pp. 682–701.

Rewt, Polly T., ed. 'The African Diaspora and Its Origins.' *Research in African Literatures Special Edition*, 29.4 (winter 1998).

Reynolds, David S. *Beneath the American Renaissance: The Subversive Imaginary in the Age of Emerson and Melville*. New York: Knopf; Random House, 1988.

Reynolds, David S., and Debra J. Rosenthal, eds. *The Serpent and the Cup: Temperance in American Literature*. Amherst, MA: University of Massachusetts Press, 1997.

Reynolds, Harry. *Minstrel Memories: The Story of Burnt Cork Minstrelsy in Great Britain from 1836–1927*. London: Alston Rivers, 1928.

Riach, Douglas C. 'Blacks and Blackface on the Irish Stage, 1830–60.' *Journal of American Studies*, 7.3 (December 1973), pp. 231–41.

Rice, Alan. *Radical Narrative of the Black Atlantic*. London and New York: Continuum, 2003.

——. '"The dogs of Old England know that I am a man." Or Do They?' Paper given at the conference 'Frederick Douglass at Home and Abroad', Department of the Interior, Washington, DC, 13–16 September 1999.

——. '"Who's Eating Whom." The Discourse of Cannibalism in the Literature of the Black Atlantic from Equiano's *Travels* to Toni Morrison's *Beloved*.' *Research in African Literatures*, 29.4 (winter 1998), pp. 107–21.

Rice, Alan J., and Martin Crawford, eds. *Liberating Sojourn: Frederick Douglass and Transatlantic Reform*. Athens, GA, and London: University of Georgia Press, 1999.

——. 'Triumphant Exile: Douglass in Britain, 1847–1847.' In *Liberating Sojourn: Frederick Douglass and Transatlantic Reform*, ed. Alan J. Rice and Martin Craw-ford. Athens, GA, and London: University of Georgia Press, 1999, pp. 1–17.

Rice, C. Duncan. *The Scots Abolitionists, 1833–1861*. Baton Rouge, LA: Louisiana State University Press, 1981.

Rodgers, Nini. 'Ireland and the Black Atlantic in the Eighteenth Century.' *Irish Historical Studies*, 32 (2000), pp. 174–92.

——. 'Two Quakers and a Utilitarian: The Reaction of Three Irish Women Writers to the Problem of Slavery, 1789–1807.' *Proceedings of the Royal Irish Academy* 100C.4 (2000), pp. 137–57.

Roediger, David. *The Wages of Whiteness: Race and the Making of the American Working Class*. New York: Verso, 1986.

Said, Edward. *Orientalism*. New York: Vintage, 1979.

Scally, Robert James. *The End of Hidden Ireland: Rebellion, Famine and Emigration*. New York: Oxford University Press, 1995.

Schueller, Malini Johar. *US Orientalisms: Race, Nation and Gender in Literature, 1790–1890*. Ann Arbor, MI: University of Michigan Press, 1998.

Sekora, John. 'Black Message/White Envelope: Genre, Authenticity, and Authority in the Antebellum Slave Narrative.' *Callaloo*, 10 (summer 1987), pp. 482–515.

——. 'Is the Slave Narrative a Species of Autobiography?' In *Studies in Autobiography*, ed. James Olney. New York and Oxford: Oxford University Press, 1988, pp. 99–111.

——, and Darwin Turner, eds. *The Art of the Slave Narrative*. Chicago: Western Illinois University Press, 1982.

Sexton, Alexander. *The Rise and Fall of the White Republic: Politics and Mass Culture in Nineteenth Century America*. London: Verso, 1990.

Shalom, Jack. 'The Ira Aldridge Troupe: Early Black Minstrelsy in Philadelphia.' *Journal of Popular Culture*, 28.4 [1994], pp. 653–58.

Sharpe, Jenny. '"Something Akin to Freedom": The Case of Mary Prince.' *Differences: A Journal of Feminist Cultural Studies*, 8.1 (1996), pp. 31–56.

Shepperson, George. 'The Free Church and American Slavery.' *Scottish Historical Review*, 30 (1951), pp. 126–42.

Slotkin, Richard. *Gunfighter Nation: Regeneration through Violence; The Mythology of the American Frontier, 1600–1860*. Middletown, CT: Wesleyan University Press, 1973.

Smith, Valerie. *Self Discovery and Authority in Afro-American Narrative*. Cambridge, MA: Harvard University Press, 1987.

Spivak, Gayatri Chakravorty. 'Can the Subaltern Speak?' In *Marxism and the Interpretation of Culture*, ed. Cary Nelson and Larry Grossberg. Urbana, IL: University of Illinois Press, 1996, pp. 271–313.

——. 'How to Read a "Culturally Different" Book.' *Colonial Discourse/Postcolonial Theory*, ed. Francis Barker, Peter Hulme and Margaret Iversen. Manchester: Manchester University Press, 1994, pp. 126–50.

——. *Outside the Teaching Machine*. New York: Routledge, 1993.

Stauffer, J. *The Black Hearts of Men: Radical Abolitionism and the Abolition of Race*. Cambridge, MA: Harvard University Press, 2002.

Stephens, Michelle Ann. *Black Empire: The Masculine Global Imaginary of Caribbean Intellectuals in the United States, 1914–1962*. Durham, NC: Duke University Press, 2005.

Stepto, Robert B. *From behind the Veil: A Study of Afro-American Narrative*. Urbana, IL: University of Illinois Press, 1979.

——. '"I Rose and Found My Voice": Narration, Authentication and Authorial Control in Four Slave Narratives.' In *The Slave's Narrative*, ed. Charles T. Davis and Henry Louis Gates Jr. Oxford and New York: Oxford University Press, 1982, pp. 225–41.

——. 'Storytelling in Early Afro-American Fiction: Frederick Douglass's "The Heroic Slave".' *Georgia Review*, 36.2 (1982), pp. 355–68.

Stone, Albert E. *Autobiographical Occasions and Original Acts: Versions of American Identity from Henry Adams to Nate Shaw*. Philadelphia: University of Pennsylvania Press, 1982.

Sundquist, Eric J. 'Slavery, Revolution and the American Renaissance.' In *The American Renaissance Reconsidered*, ed. Walter Benn Michaels and Donald E. Pease. Baltimore, MD, and London: Johns Hopkins University Press, 1985, pp. 1–33.

——. *To Wake the Nations: Race in the Making of American Literature*. Cambridge, MA: Harvard University Press, 1993.

——, ed. *Frederick Douglass: New Literary and Historical Essays*. Cambridge: Cambridge University Press, 1993.

——, ed. *New Essays on Uncle Tom's Cabin*. Cambridge: Cambridge University Press, 1986.

Takaki, Ronald. *Iron Cages: Race and Culture in Nineteenth-Century American Culture*. New York: Knopf, 1986.

Tamarkin, Eliza. 'Black Anglophilia, or, the Sociability of Anti-slavery.' *American Literary History*, 14.3 (2002), pp. 444–78.

Toll, Richard C. *Blacking Up: The Minstrel Show in Nineteenth Century America*. Oxford: Oxford University Press, 1974.

Van Alstyne, R.W. *The Rising American Empire*. Chicago: Quadrangle, 1960.

Van Leer, David. 'Reading Slavery: The Anxiety of Ethnicity in Douglass's *Narrative.*' In *Frederick Douglass: New Literary and Historical Essays*, ed. Eric J. Sundquist. Cambridge: Cambridge University Press, 1993, pp. 118–40.

Vincent, David. *Bread, Knowledge and Freedom: A Study of Nineteenth-Century-Working-Class Autobiography*. London: Europa, 1981.

Walker, Franklin. *Irreverent Pilgrims: Melville, Browne and Mark Twain in the Holy Land*. Seattle, WA: University of Washington Press, 1974.

Walter, Krista. 'Trappings of Nationalism in Frederick Douglass's *The Heroic Slave.*' *African American Review*, 34.2 (2000), pp. 233–47.

Warren, Kenneth W. 'Frederick Douglass's *Life and Times*: Progressive Rhetoric and the Problem of Constituency.' In *Frederick Douglass: New Literary and Historical Essays*, ed. Eric J Sundquist. Cambridge: Cambridge University Press, 1990, pp. 253–70.

Wills, Claire. 'Language Politics, Narrative, Political Violence.' In 'Neocolonialism', ed. Robert Young. *Oxford Literary Review*, 13 (1991), pp. 21–59.

Yarborough, Richard. 'Race Violence and Manhood: The Masculine Ideal in Frederick Douglass's *The Heroic Slave.*' In *Frederick Douglass: New Literary and Historical Essays*, ed. Eric J. Sundquist. Cambridge: Cambridge University Press, 1990, pp. 166–88.

Zafar, Rafia. 'Franklinian Douglass: The Afro-American as Representative Man.' In *Frederick Douglass: New Literary and Historical Essays*, ed. Eric J. Sundquist. New York and Cambridge: Cambridge University Press, 1990, pp. 99–117.

Index